Religion and Identity in Europe

The Makings of Religious Enemies
in Antiquity and Today

Susanne William Rasmussen

Religion and Identity in Europe

The Makings of Religious Enemies in Antiquity and Today

University Press of Southern Denmark

© The author and University Press of Southern Denmark 2013
University of Southern Denmark Classical Studies vol. 24

Typeset and printed by Narayana Press
Cover Photo: Christian Sørensen

ISBN 978 87 7674 763 3

Printed with grantly support from:
Faculty of the Humanities, University of Southern Denmark
The Velux Foundation

University Press of Southern Denmark
Campusvej 55
DK-5230 Odense M
www.universitypress.dk

Distribution in the United States and Canada:
International Specialized Book Services
5804 NE Hassalo Street
Portland, OR 97213-3644 USA
www.isbs.com

Distribution in the United Kingdom:
Gazelle
White Cross Mills
Hightown
Lancaster
LA1 4 XS
U.K.
www.gazellebookservices.co.uk

Contents

Acknowledgements 7

Preface 9

Introduction 13
   The perspectives 16
   On constructing identity 19

Chapter 1
Cultural Flux and Fix – Perspectives on Religious Enemies in Antiquity 25
   Cult and cultural encounters – *religio* and *superstitio* 25
   Evocatio – summoning the patron deities of the enemy 27
   Tertullian 33
   Celsus 41
   Porphyry 46
   Augustine and Porphyry 51
   Religious pluralism and the regimen of God
   in the multicultural Roman Empire? 54

Chapter 2
Roman Portents and Christian Miracles –
Identity Formation and Rivalry 61
   Roman portents 61
   Religio-political procedure 65
   Emperors and omens 68
   Christians and miracles 70
   Miracles and conversion 73

Chapter 3
Religio-Political Reactions – Roman Patterns of Expulsion 83
   The Jews in Rome 83
   The Chrestus commotion 91
   Seneca and the Jews 93
   Nero's Christian scapegoats 98
   The Jewish uprising 101

Chapter 4

The Dialectics of Cultural Flux and Fix – Religious Romanization and The Making of Martyrs   105
   Martyrdom defined   108
   Pliny the Younger and Emperor Trajan   109
   Eusebius and the martyrs of Lyons   112
   The meditations of Marcus Aurelius   120

Chapter 5

Some Religio-Political Trends – Worship of The Emperor, The Sun, and The Saviour   131
   Augustus   131
   Emperor worship   135
   Elagabalus, god and emperor: the acculturation of the Syrian sun-god   138
   Emperor Aurelian and Sol Invictus   143
   The controversial conversion of Constantine   145

Chapter 6

God's Great Olive-Press – from Augustine to Huntington?   155
   Augustine and Manichaeism   155
   The Fall of Rome – and two opposing standpoints   159
   Benighted philosophers   163
   Universal values – the regimen of the West in a multicultural world?   167

Chapter 7

Cultural Flux and Fix – Perspectives on Religious Enemies in Contemporary Europe   171
   Globalization and religious pluralism   171
   Briefly, on a historical note   178
   Fixing identity in flux   180
   Rival definitions of reality   186
   European secularism   188
   Religion and identity in the United States   194
   Liberal democracies and the yawning abyss   197
   Religion, recognition, and competition   201
   Cosmos, conflict, and coexistence?   206

Conclusion   213

References   221

Illustrations   233

Index   235

Acknowledgements

First and foremost, I extend my heartfelt thanks to the Velux Foundation for providing the generous research grant that enabled me to write this book on religion, identity and the makings of religious enemies in Europe, in Antiquity and today. In the humanities it is indeed a great privilege – and in Denmark these days a rare one – to get the opportunity to conduct a lengthy, independent research project.

Also many thanks to the Faculty of Humanities at the University of Southern Denmark for co-financing the publication of this volume along with the Velux Foundation, and to artist Martin Bigum for allowing me to share one of his compelling paintings.

Further thanks are due to my colleagues Jens Erik Skydsgaard, Jesper Carlsen, Olav Hammer, and Tim Jensen for believing in the basic idea behind this project, and for lending their valuable professional support during its initial stages. I am also grateful to the following colleagues and friends, who were kind enough to read and constructively comment on the manuscript, in whole or in part: Mogens Herman Hansen, Anders Holm Rasmussen, Jørgen Podemann Sørensen, Marianne Aagaard Skovmand, Ittai Gradel, Carsten Lê Madsen, Me Christensen, and Thea Lund Christiansen. Naturally, however, any errors or omissions in this book remain mine and mine alone.

I also owe special thanks to Heidi Flegal, who unflinchingly translated the Danish manuscript into English with great diligence and a flair for taming my at times unruly sentences. This was no easy task, and she should certainly not be held responsible for any remaining obscurities or awkward turns of phrase.

Last but not least, I thank Christian and Vera for their enthusiasm, support, and patience throughout this project.

Copenhagen, August 2013   Susanne William Rasmussen

Preface

There is a huge difference between studying the religions and cultures of Antiquity and those of our own age. This is mainly because the sources on ancient history are terribly fragmented. What we do have available is a jumbled assortment of archaeological finds and scraps of text from various written sources and various periods, stretching across several centuries. On top of that, we often know little or nothing about the specific contexts in which the individual sources were produced. Small wonder that scholars of Antiquity can find it tempting to throw caution to the wind and engage in airy speculation. On the other hand, it is something of a relief to study people who are no longer among the living and therefore unable to participate in activities like filling out questionnaires about religion. Actually, the results of such questionnaire studies are often dubious, partly because it is difficult to quantify and measure religious sensibilities and involvement at all, and partly because both American and European research indicates that the respondents in such studies either exaggerate their degree of religious commitment (Americans) or understate it (Europeans). This issue is discussed in Chapter 7.

But regardless of whether people give misleading answers when questioned about their personal religious views, the globalization, culture contacts, and culture clashes that are taking place today are accompanied by an increasingly intense interest in, and assertion of, religions and religious views and identity. Many people have found this perplexing – not least those sociologists and historians of religion who have offered up a variety of flawed secularization theories in recent years. I agree that the time is ripe for decisive elements of these theories, and of the entire secularization paradigm, to be either revised or rejected, since we know that in nations that have been secularized religion has, indisputably, survived and is even seeing an upsurge in some places.

In short, we of the postmodern world can continue our efforts to democratize, rationalize, liberalize, individualize, secularize, integrate, and assimilate – until kingdom come. There is no indication whatsoever that this will cause religion to disappear, or to become a purely personal matter that lingers unobtrusively in the wings of the postmodern world's public stage.[1] There is a widespread sense of wonderment, among scholars and in the public and political debate at large, at the discovery that religion is an actual, active aspect of public life and not just a private concern. This wonderment shows, among many other things, that an anxious Europe remains immobilized in the quagmire of an antiquated secularization paradigm. However, if the basic premise is that religion ought to be banned from the public sphere, questions relating to culture contacts and religious conflicts simply cannot be studied, much less clarified. This certainly holds true for Antiquity, and for the current situation as well. Only by systematically and thoroughly analysing the sociological and identity-creating significance of religions, at a micro level and a macro level, can we hope to more profoundly understand or, dare I say, resolve the cultural and religious conflicts that exist in Europe today.

Unlike those who write books about the religions of Antiquity, the authors of works that analyse contemporary religion are expected to include in their preface, and as a matter of course, an account of their personal religious views. This spares readers the nuisance of guessing, and wondering. Let me simply say, however, that my own personal view on religion can be summed up very concisely by referring to William James, the scholar of religion who passed away long ago, and whose answer to the question of faith

---

[1] I am well aware of the problems associated with using the term "postmodern". I nevertheless choose to employ it here, chiefly in the meaning "postsecular", in recognition of the knowledge that – in direct opposition to the calculations done in "modern" secularization theories – religion actually makes itself felt in secular environments. In other words, modernity does not lead to the retreat of religion. Hence, in a postmodern present and future, religion and religious communities must be more systematically recognized and analysed as factors that not only play a role in people's private lives but also manifestly influence, and are influenced by, public life and the broader context in which people live and act. Cf. P. Berger, G. Davie & E. Fokas (2008) *Religious America, Secular Europe?*, Farnham; K. Eder (2002) "Europäische Säkularisierung – ein Sonderweg in die postsäkulare Gesellschaft?", *Berliner Journal für Soziologie*, Heft 3 (2002), pp. 331-343.

Fig. 1. *Europa and the Bull*. Mosaic from a Roman villa in Arles. Late second century CE – early third century CE. Now at the Musée de L'Arles Antique.

was this:[2] "What mankind at large most lacks is criticism and caution, not faith." Besides this, I would like to stress that I wholeheartedly embrace the Weberian ideal of "value-free" sociology and sociology of religion, which I sincerely hope the reader will find reflected in this work.

At any rate, although religious thinking is not one's own personal gateway to understanding the world, religions are important threads in the intricately woven fabric of human societies, based as they are on inherited cultural traditions, norms, values, and behaviours. That is why religion – directly and indirectly, and regardless of one's personal perceptions of religion as a positive or negative factor – is of fundamental significance to society at all levels, from the most detailed to the most general. What is more, various types of faith and religious identity constructions seem to be playing an ever more important role in our globalized world. Age-old controversies about

---

2   W. James (1956) *The Will to Believe: And Other Essays in Popular Philosophy*, New York NY, p. X.

the relationship between religion and politics, and about what place religion ought to hold in the private and public sphere, are once again at the top of our current agenda as a result of the cultural encounters ("acculturation") and religious conflicts arising in the wake of migration and globalization. Some refer to this phenomenon as the "resurrection" of religions in the postmodern world. I must say that I find the term somewhat grandiose, and also somewhat misguided. For one thing, religions as social internalization processes have always been at stake, and consequently Christianity has been a continuous source of normative guidance throughout European history. For another, if religious matters have seemed invisible in modern society, one very plausible reason for this is that scholarly acuity has been dulled by the narrow paradigm and the numerous secularization theories in circulation. In any event, the sudden upsurge of religions in many places around the world – also in Europe – is associated with an almost systematic stereotyping and constructing of religious enemies, accompanied in varying measure by fear, hate, threats, and violence.

Hence, the fundamental question that this book seeks to address from a modern-day point of view is very simple: When and how did the construction of religious enemy images in Europe actually begin? The answer to this question, which is far from simple, stretches back into Antiquity.

Introduction

"Why ponder? God commands."
Tertullian

The meeting between Roman culture and Christianity was a protracted affair: a dynamic cultural process that hopped, skipped, and lurched along for a period of three to four centuries. It is therefore striking that both the sources for and the history of research into this area reflect a certain lack of continuity in the Roman Empire during Late Antiquity. One moment the traditional Roman world seems to be upheld by age-old, unassailable norms and values, while the next moment these seem to have evaporated and been replaced by solid Christian values. Naturally, the reality of things would have been far more complex. One factor contributing to this snapshot-like understanding of events, which seems to depict a rapid and unproblematic shift, is the dominant position of the idealizing accounts provided by the Christian victors. The vast majority of portrayals we have of culture-contact events are written by Christians, and the non-Christian sources we do have are, alas, both sparse and problematic. Even so, there are certain features common to both source groups: Cultural encounters led to physical violence and verbal combat, to tangible conflicts and the construction of religious enemies. But they also led to coexistence and innovation, which we can detect in the converging, merging, and reinterpretation of different social and religious institutions and ideas. The meeting of Roman culture and Christianity – which, in reality, consisted of numerous contacts between Jewish, Christian, Greek, and Roman thinking and traditions – ended up producing a new motif that was, decidedly and decisively, new and unique in the great tapestry that was Europe.

    The aim of this book, which is structured around a series of analyses and case studies, is to examine how the construction of religious enemies came about in this crucial meeting of Roman and Christian religion and culture. What sociological factors were at work before and during the time we begin to find religious enemy images being constructed in the Roman Empire? How were the perceptions that Romans and Christians held of one another as religious enemies expressed in their attitudes and their interactions? Many different aspects relating to history, the history of religion, sociology, philosophy, and economy have played a role in the processes that saw Christianity prevail. The investigations in this book concentrate on two aspects: the conflicts arising from this culture contact; and the constructed religious enemies associated with these conflicts.

Chapter 1 begins by examining some of the central conflicts and fields of tension between Roman and Christian religion and culture, notably focusing on how clashes and the construction of enemies are intimately intertwined with the construction of identity, not just at a macro level, but at a micro level as well. This has a bearing on vital issues such as intrafamilial kinship, cultic affiliation and community, and the embedding of religion in imperial power. It also has a bearing on various rituals and ideas that relate not only to diverging perceptions of religion in the narrowest sense, but also to fundamental social norms, values, and institutions throughout Roman history. Pursuing this line of investigation, Chapter 2 sheds light on one of the most important religio-political institutions in traditional Roman culture – public portents – and discusses this institution in relation to a defining feature in early Christian faith – miracles. In Roman history we see that the shift from Republic to Empire also caused a shift in the nature of Rome's public portents. With the rise of imperial power, the importance of public portents came to concentrate less on the collective well-being of society and more on the legitimization of the individual emperor's status and power. In the present context, this change in the role of public portents and the subsequent Christian miracle rivalry on Roman soil are considered to be important sociological and religio-historical factors in the process by which Christianity gained a firm foothold in the religious landscape.

Chapter 3 discusses a number of selected and partially unresolved religio-political issues concerning how the Romans handled Jews, Christians, and internal Christ-related disputes going on in Rome. Continuing along these lines, Chapter 4 examines the periodic Roman persecution of Christians seen in relation to the religious Romanization and Christian violation of Roman cult and culture. This chapter also contains an analysis of Christian martyrdom as a central element, both in the institutionalization of Christianity and in its staging of itself, in that martyrdom structured and defined Christian teaching and identity in a new and dramatic way.

Chapter 5 elaborates on several issues, including the acculturation and religio-political use of the sun-god Sol Invictus, who despite his name was ultimately vanquished by the cult of Christ. Furthermore, this chapter deals with certain consequences of the idolization and worship of the Roman emperors, representing one of the key conflicts in this particular culture contact: the controversy about the cult of the Roman emperors and the Christians' refusal to participate in it. However, the curious about-face of Emperor Constantine the Great in favour of Christianity contributed immensely to the control and the consolidation of the Christian Church as a powerful organization. Constantine became the catalyst in the process that redefined the motley crew of Christian believers, which developed from a suspect and subversive *superstitio* into an esteemed, top-down-controlled, and formidable *religio*. Nevertheless, non-Christian Roman religion and culture long maintained their own tenacious toehold, as witnessed in the writings of the church father St Augustine of Hippo and others. Chapter 6 therefore looks in greater detail at selected passages from Augustine's works, which showcase the meticulous construction of religious enemies as part of a relentless attempt to eradicate pagan, meaning non-Christian, religion and philosophy. From an Augustinian point of view, the fall of the Roman Empire in 410 CE could be regarded as a manifestation of how the regimen of the Christian Almighty God, and universal Christian values, were destined to conquer multi-religious paganism.

It is striking that, implicitly or explicitly, similar views and questions about the regimen of God, and especially about the validity of universal ideas and values, are a prominent feature in contemporary multicultural Europe, with its agendas and discussions about so-called clashes of civilizations, EU expansions, the role of religions in liberal democracies, integration, freedom of religion, freedom of speech, the use of religious symbols, exotic apparel, and so on. In today's disharmonious cultural encounters we can also identify the systematic construction of religious enemies. Chapter 7 brings this angle to the table as it compares the culture contacts and religious enemies of the ancient Roman world with some of the religious conflicts and enemy images in contemporary Europe.

The perspectives

Although there are essential and obvious differences between life in Antiquity and life in modern-day Europe, the two have certain significant features in common: Life is lived in a multicultural world that is characterized by a high degree of religious pluralism, various processes of globalization, intensified identity constructions, and religious conflicts. When analysed as culture-contact processes, the Romanization of the past and the globalization of the present put the norms and actions of the involved parties into stark relief. And upon closer examination, our own globalized, enlightened Age of Information does not seem to offer any better understanding of "the other" than Antiquity did. In any event – and quite importantly in this context – just like the Romanization processes that took place in Antiquity, the globalization processes taking place today lead to an increased focus and increased pressure on religion and identity, both at an individual and a collective level. Also, presumably the individuals, groups, and nations of the future will increasingly assert their own socio-religious identities in the struggle for recognition, and in order to stake out a position of their own in a globalized world. Furthermore, certain striking and conflicting tendencies seen in ancient Romanization can be compared with observations of contemporary globalization: the tendencies to encompass both "global flow" and "cultural closure" (which I refer to as cultural "flux" and "fix" and explain later). The flux of past Romanization and modern globalization seem(ed) to increase the urge to fix upon (religious) identity in order to set oneself apart and find a secure foothold on the world's unpredictable multicultural terrain.

This book examines more closely how such social and religious mechanisms can unfold and exert a negative influence, and how cultural and religio-political tensions are expressed as images of religious enemies and acted out in Europe past and present. Because it focuses precisely on the stuff that cultural conflicts are made of, on the differences and the constructed enemies, there are bound to be a whole array of religio-historical aspects that regrettably cannot be discussed here. One aspect lies in the Christian messages of showing charity and loving one's fellow man, which are not drawn into the chapters that deal with the antique perspectives. Another aspect lies in the book's contemporary perspectives focusing specifically on the cultural heritage of *Europe* – that is, on the enemy images produced by Europe's ethnic, Christian majorities – while refraining from including a corresponding treatment of Islamic enemy images produced by Muslim minorities living in Europe.

When discussing perspectives in and between the past and present, I urge the reader to remember that the antique texts naturally deal with the questions and problems of Antiquity – not with those of today. The ancient sources must therefore, above all and to the greatest possible extent, be analysed on Antiquity's own terms. The analyses in this volume seek to fathom the meanings, intentions, and effects of the texts, and also to clarify what they express about the culture contact and religious conflicts as experienced at that time. This said, the approach taken does not render the classical texts "irrelevant" to the pressing questions of our time. On the contrary. In many cases these sources can promote understanding, not only by bringing to our attention the workings of more or less parallel social and religious mechanisms and issues in the past and present, but also by honing our ability to identify cultural variations in social, religious, philosophical, moral, and political classifications, ideas, and patterns of behaviour. This combined diachronic and synchronic way of viewing the topics at hand may well give us reason to indulge in what the Romans referred to as *ruminatio*. To chew our mental cud as we contemplate the prevailing dilemmas and questions that spring from Europe's cultural history: our own religions and cultures and those of others; universal values and religious relativism; hope and fear; co-existence and clashes; marginalization and the fight for recognition; identity construction and religious freedom. An all but indigestible diet. But perhaps a stint of historical and sociological ruminating is just what it takes to promote the cultural self-insight and open-mindedness that seems to be in such short supply these days in postmodern Europe?

***

Everyone agrees – by and large – that the foundation of European history builds on a Christian legacy. Some people, on the other hand, find it far less relevant to continue studying the non-Christian, Graeco-Roman past. Quite apart from the fact that knowledge about Antiquity is highly valuable in and of itself, our pagan background embodies a variety of dimensions that are useful to examine and compare with modern cultural circumstances. The pre-Christian and non-Christian portion of our European past discloses a wide range of views and values to which, admittedly, most people no longer subscribe, but which, precisely for that reason, can remind us of questions that we have long since ceased to ask. Or of questions to which we more or less automatically respond with implicitly Christian and/or (neo)evolutionist and/or (neo)liberalist assumptions and concepts.

Culture contacts and religious disputes involve different types of discussions and conflicts which, from a sociological point of view, are especially concerned with identity and social recognition. As will become apparent, this was also true in the religious debates of ancient Rome and the bickering between pagans and Christians about the worship of gods/God, miracle makers, brothel visits, gladiator spectacles, food orgies, binge drinking, luxury, vanity, and a profusion of other topics, from the oldest deities to the newest hairstyles. Likewise, this is true in today's European religious debates and their bickering about clashing civilizations, immigration, integration, social values and virtues, democracy, freedom of speech, the eating of pork, the oppression of women, sexual morals, and numerous other issues, ranging from the visibility of Christian crosses in classrooms and judges' apparel in courtrooms and to the use of Muslim headscarves, burqas, and niqabs in public spaces.

Those debating in Antiquity – just as those who debate today – were grappling with theoretical and religio-philosophical questions and with practical issues that arise from culture contacts. Questions such as: How can one live as a Christian minority in a multicultural world which – seen through Christian eyes – is entirely depraved? Then, as now, the ongoing discussions and the various viewpoints, attacks, and defences reveal a great deal about the links between religion and identity. About cultural insecurity and anxiety. About how the construction of religious enemies creates identity and a sense of community, both among the constructors and among those around whom the enemy image is constructed. In other words, a combined diachronic and synchronic analysis of culture contacts and constructed religious enemies can help us, for instance, to reflect upon what it actually means to have freedom of religion in a given society. When is religion violated? And when is the freedom of religion violated? How are minorities pressured into assimilation to comply with normative representations of what it means to be, say, Roman or Danish, Christian or Muslim? How do various normative representations devalue the culture of "the other", and how do they undermine the freedom to choose differently, to challenge, or to criticize?

On constructing identity

Generally, and also throughout this book, the concept of "identity" is frequently referred to in connection with the construction of enemies. However, both in scientific and non-scientific contexts it is often unclear just what the concept covers. This lack of precision arises because the identity concept springs from the relationship between individual and society and can therefore be viewed in many very different ways, across a wide field spanning from individual and social psychology, across sociology and philosophy, and over to anthropology. To be quite brief, there is no absolute or even approximated consensus as to a single definition of the term "identity". What the various scientific disciplines can agree upon, however, is that the concept of identity has to do with the question: "Who am I?", and with the things that differentiate oneself from actual or imagined others. Roughly speaking, specific attempts to define "identity" tend to gravitate towards, and actually cluster around, one of two opposing poles. Either identity is primarily regarded as an innate core or inborn individuality, or identity is primarily regarded as an expression of the individual person's own story, which, to a certain extent, is a work in progress that can be continuously constructed through interaction with other individuals. Although identity at a micro level is, of course, influenced by each individual's potential for developing certain personality traits, the investigations in this book will take a sociological approach where the main emphasis is that identity – like religion – is shaped and evolves in constant interaction between each individual person and the world around them.[3]

One question that keeps us bogged down in definitions is whether identity

---

3   Here I follow the sociological approach to religion that is represented, for example, in J.A. Beckford (2003) *Social Theory & Religion*, Cambridge. Cf. the chapter entitled "Religion: a social constructionist approach", pp. 11-29.

(or identities) should generally be characterized by stability or by flexibility. Studies of identity, particularly more recent ones, indicate that individuals in the postmodern world can often experiment with a wide range of different identities.[4] It must be stressed, however, that the ancient world offered nowhere near the same degree of flexibility or opportunity to experiment with identity construction.

In Antiquity, "identity" and "recognition" did not exist and were not discussed as concepts, as they are today. It goes without saying that this was not because the people living in Antiquity were devoid of what we call identities, or that identity was not dependent upon acknowledgment and recognition. It was presumably because the identity constructions of Antiquity were based, first and foremost, on very rigid social categories and a firmly stratified structure that everyone took for granted. Since the modern concept of "identity" simply has no semantic expression in the languages of Antiquity, one might be tempted to claim that the concept cannot properly be applied to the ancient world. Nevertheless, I find the concept of identity quite useful to help display and clarify various social mechanisms and patterns of attitudes and actions that we can discern in the ancient sources – even though all we can grasp at through the veils of time are scattered fragments, hints, and shadows. Furthermore, although during Antiquity there was no discourse that directly debated the concept of "identity", both non-Christian and Christian sources still took a keen interest in finding out "who they were" in relation to other cultures. What did it mean to be a Roman, or a Christian, or a Roman who was also a Christian? Clearly, the answers to such questions – then as now – were highly dependent upon social recognition. In Antiquity religion was one of the pivotal elements of such recognition, whether from a Roman or a Christian point of view.

---

4   Cf. S. Stryker & P.J. Burke (2000) "The Past, Present, and Future of an Identity Theory", *Social Psychology Quarterly* (vol. 63; 2000), pp. 284-297; B.E. Jensen (1999) "History and the Politics of Identity. Reflections on a Contested and Intricate Issue", *Historiedidaktikk i Norden 7. Bruk og misbruk af historien*, Trondheim, pp. 43-67; K.J. Gergen (1991) *The Saturated Self. Dilemmas of Identity in Contemporary Life*, New York NY; K.J. Gergen (2001) *Social Construction in Context*, London; U. Beck & E. Beck-Gernsheim (2002) *Individualization. Institutionalized Individualism and its Social and Political Consequences*, London; C.R. Jørgensen (2008) *Identitet. Psykologiske og kulturanalytiske perspektiver*, Copenhagen.

So recognition as an incontrovertible human need and a social necessity is nothing new, even though one does occasionally get that impression when looking into modern research on these issues.

What *is* new, and what has varied down through history, are the conditions under which people seek – or struggle – to attain recognition.[5] Yet when discussing what we, today, denote as "recognition", it is important to underscore that recognition in Antiquity was extensively built into, and anchored within, extremely rigid social categories that few people (if any) would ever call into question. As Charles Taylor has pointed out, the modern preoccupation with identity and recognition, and the questing discussions about the underlying concepts, are extensively produced by the demise of old social hierarchies.[6] On the other hand, cultures, nations, and individuals in a globalized world that is continuously being (re)shaped by cultural and religious interests and conflicts will increasingly become preoccupied with their own identity and status within the new *global* hierarchy.

When employing the concept of "identity" at a macro level, the research behind this book means a society's or a group's construction and assertion of a common frame of reference and a shared self-perception. This internalized collective identity relates to distinct classifications, norms, values, behaviours, institutions, and so on that are perceived as fundamental characteristics differentiating a particular society or group from other societies or groups.[7]

---

5   C. Taylor (1994) "The Politics of Recognition" in A. Gutmann (ed.) *Multiculturalism: Examining the Politics of Recognition*, Princeton NJ; A. Honneth (2003) "Die Pointe der Anerkennung: Eine Entgegnung auf die Entgegnung" in N. Fraser & A. Honneth (eds) *Umverteilung oder Anerkennung? Eine politisch-philosophische Kontroverse*, Frankfurt am Main; A. Honneth (2004) "Recognition and Justice: Outline of a Plural Theory of Justice", *Acta Sociologica* 47 (4) (2004), pp. 351-364; A. Honneth (2011) *Das Recht der Freiheit. Grundriss einer demokratischen Sittlichkeit*, Berlin; Z. Bauman (2001) "The Great War of Recognition", *Theory, Culture & Society*, 18 (2-3; 2001), pp. 137-150.
6   C. Taylor (1994); cf. P. Berger (1983) "On the Obsolescence of the Concept of Honour" in S. Hauerwas & A.C. MacIntyre (eds) *Revisions: Changing Perspectives in Moral Pilosophy*, Notre Dame IN, pp. 172-181.
7   Cf. G.H. Mead (1934) *Mind, Self, and Society*, Chicago IL; P. Berger (1963) *An Invitation to Sociology. A Humanistic Approach*, New York NY; P. Berger & T. Luckmann (1966) *The Social Construction of Reality. A Treatise in the Sociology of Knowledge*, New York NY; P. Gleason (1983) "Identifying Identity. A Semantic History", *The Journal*

Collective identity has to do with aspects such as how citizens in Europe, based on their own institutions, traditions, world-views, and religious ideas, wish to perceive themselves and others in their encounters with cultural and religious dissimilarity. Also, and not least, collective identity involves the individual countries' different political cultures and their handling of internal and foreign affairs, including discussions and decisions regarding social welfare reforms, value-based politics, immigration, religious symbols, and active engagement in warfare. In such matters of societal significance, religion and contentious religious issues will unavoidably affect the political processes and the interpretations of fundamental constitutional principles. Consequently, in the modern democracies of a globalized world – secularization processes notwithstanding – religions and religious conflicts are playing an ever more prominent role.

In Antiquity, what we refer to today as "collective identity" was, more than anything else, a question of the interaction between inherited religious and political traditions. This was true first of the Roman Republic's and later of the Roman Empire's particular religio-political institutions, issues of conferring Roman citizenship and the rights that went along with it, and various viewpoints and activities relating to domestic and foreign policy. Indisputably, religion and politics in Antiquity were two sides of the same prestigious and powerful coin. That is why the terms "religio-politics" and "religio-political" are frequently used throughout this work. Collective identity in ancient Rome was highly dependent upon participation in cultic activities that revolved around the Roman gods and the health, happiness, and safety of the emperor, the aim being to ensure the welfare of the empire and maintain cultural continuity.

Revisiting the definition of identity, it is fair to say that religious enemy images are generally constructed on the basis of more or less stereotypical, rigid, prejudiced, and distorted ideas of cultural contradictions, heresy,

---

of American History (69; 1983), pp. 910-931; V. Burr (1995) *Social Constructionism*, London; R. Jenkins (1996) *Social Identity*, London; S. Hall & P. du Gay (1996) *Questions of Cultural Identity*, London; Beckford (2003); S.W. Rasmussen (2008) "Priests, Politics and Problems in Identity Construction in Ancient Rome" in A.H. Rasmussen & S.W. Rasmussen, *Religion and Society. Rituals, Resources and Identity in the Ancient Graeco-Roman World*, Rome, pp. 259-265.

and religious fallacies.[8] In order to delimit one's own identity, the element that is foreign or heretical (that is, "the other") is sometimes simply culled out and set apart as an enemy against whom one can unite. And in today's Europe the enemy consists of people who are disparaged, marginalized, and attacked solely or primarily because of their religion. Yet interestingly, in parts of the present European self-perception, to quite a great extent religious enemies and their construction is something that primarily belongs to a remote past, not to a civilized present. This reasoning relies on the idea that religious enmity and constructed enemies have been overcome thanks to the Enlightenment, to secularization processes, and to the solidification of a European concept of tolerance.[9] But the question is whether this (immensely simplified) reasoning as currently preached and practiced in Europe would not be more appropriately classified as a collective self-deception?

In this context, the conclusions of a recent research enquiry published by the German think-tank Friedrich-Ebert-Stiftung give food for thought. This enquiry from 2011 finds that *in general*, European countries demonstrate a considerable – and worrying – hostility towards Muslims living in Europe. On average, about half of ethnic Europeans think there are too many Muslims living in their country. The enquiry also suggests that the precise proportion of the Danish population holding this view is 43%, while 45% of Danes believe that Muslims cause trouble and think that Muslim headscarves ought to be prohibited by law.[10] Contemporary xenophobia is

---

8   The analyses in this investigation do not make any pronouncements about the actual make-up of the individual constructed religious enemies. What they do is to focus solely on their religious, social, and political significance and functions in Antiquity and in the present.

9   On the concept of tolerance, see Derrida's treatment of the concept's inadequacy and foundation in Christianity in J. Derrida (2003) *Philosophy in a time of terror. Dialogues with Jürgen Habermas and Jacques Derrida*, Chicago IL; cf. J. Habermas (2009) "How to answer the Ethical Question: Derrida and Religion" in *Europe. The Faltering Project*, Cambridge, pp.17-36.

10 The results from the Friedrich-Ebert-Stiftung enquiry have been collected in an anthology (2011) available at http://library.fes.de/pdf-files/do/08338.pdf. The percentages for Denmark are taken from a study done at the Department of Political Science and Government at Aarhus University, which is not yet accessible to the public. Cf. "Living together: Combining diversity and freedom in 21st-century Europe", report of the Group of Eminent Persons of the Council of Europe, published May 2011. Members of the

directly linked to religion: Whereas today's social norms render it more or less unacceptable to offer actual racist commentary, evidently there are no norms that prevent Europeans from making derogatory and biased statements about Islam as a religion, or about Muslims as adherents of this religion. Put differently, the enquiry from Germany indicates that intolerance towards Muslims is widely considered to be socially acceptable.

Such findings must undoubtedly be considered in connection with today's globalized and rapidly shifting world and its ever-more permeable boundaries, which seem to be promoting identity-related insecurity, anxieties, and conflicts.[11] Globalization is not only about cultural flows. It also entails constant efforts towards cultural closure and fixing at multiple levels. This raises important questions about who is creating new boundaries, why they are doing so, and against whom. In this perspective, globalization seems to make it ever more pressing to consider the questions of who we are, and who our enemies are. As it turns out, apparently religion – implicitly or explicitly – is of decisive importance to the answers we come up with. Just like our modern multicultural world, the world of Antiquity fostered a whole host of cultural encounters and religious movements, of which Christianity was just one among many. Taking a broader view of the antique religious landscape it is therefore thought-provoking that – at least as far as we know – the cult of Christ was the only cult that regarded all others as rivals.

Group: J. Fischer, E. Bonino, T.G. Ash, M. Hirsch, D. Hübner, A. Kadioglu, S. Licht, V. Lukin and J. Solana.

[11] Cf. D. Moïsi (2009) *The Geopolitics of Emotion. How Cultures of Fear, Humiliation and Hope are Reshaping the World*, London.

Chapter 1

Cultural Flux and Fix – Perspectives on Religious Enemies in Antiquity

Cult and cultural encounters – *religio* and *superstitio*

One of the several meanings of the Latin word *religio* is worship, or "cultivation of the gods" (*cultus deorum*),[12] which in Roman religion covered a wide variety of deities, including some that were of non-Roman origin. This is hardly surprising, given that Rome was multicultural as far back as we can trace it. Whether the Romans were peacefully trading goods with other peoples or stealing women from neighbouring tribes to avoid dying off, or even fighting full-scale wars and creating a far-flung empire, they were engaged in various types of cultural encounters. The interesting thing from our point of view is that during the pre-Christian period, the various conflictual culture contacts were mainly related to Rome's internal and external political and military issues rather than to religion. In other words, numerous images of constructed enemies were in circulation throughout the Roman world, but Rome was not fighting her enemies because of their gods, or even opposing the gods of her enemies at all. Quite the opposite. It often happened that prior to military campaigns the Romans would appeal to the enemy's patron deities, imploring them to change sides. Consequently, Rome's traditionally polytheistic religion has often been described as quite open-minded in this respect. Nevertheless it is also clear that the carriers of Roman religion had no problem putting their

---

12 Cf. Cicero's definition in *De Natura Deorum* 2.8: ... *religione id est cultu deorum*. For a general overview of Roman religion and culture, see, for instance, M. Beard, J. North, & S. Price (1998) *Religions of Rome*, vols I–II, Cambridge; J.B. Rives (2007) *Religion in the Roman Empire*, Oxford; J. North & S. Price (eds) (2011) *The Religious History of the Roman Empire. Pagans, Jews and Christians*, Oxford.

foot down to mark partial or complete opposition to adverse influences from foreign religions.

The complex concept of *religio* has been defined here as "cultivation of the gods", but this definition contained an implicit understanding that the gods were worshipped in the correct and appropriate manner, in compliance with the inherited and annexed religious traditions. This would include religious celebrations written into the Roman calendar and also rituals prescribed as expiations of official public portents (see Chapter 2), as well as the religio-political procedures, interpretations, and written records of the various officials and priests. The ideas and perceptions undergirding *religio* were by no means dogmatic (like the Christian teachings), but were built around a variety of legends and mythical explanations of the rituals.

Whereas *religio* was concerned with applying the appropriate rituals and ideas in dealings within the sacral sphere, the Roman concept of *superstitio* denoted a variety of flawed rituals and religious misconceptions. Consequently, *religio* and *superstitio* stand out as two seminal concepts in Roman culture. The powerful Roman elite, whose members held all the religious and political offices, could apply these concepts to debate, regulate, consolidate, or eradicate various types of rituals and attitudes in Roman society. One example is Cicero's description of Roman public portents in his work *De Divinatione* (*On Divination*) as being both a religious science (*scientia*) and *religio*, as opposed to foreign divination, which he classifies as *superstitio*.[13] The Roman historian Livy also gives various accounts of *superstitio*. For the year 213 BCE, for instance, he describes how foreign rituals and private diviners were increasingly gaining ground in Rome as a result of violent unrest during the Second Punic War (219-201 BCE).[14] The city's women in particular, Livy tells us, were easily moved and showed a strong propensity for *superstitio*, subsequently neglecting the Roman rituals. The ensuing attempt by Roman officials to confiscate the foreign ritual objects and remove the crowd from the Forum nearly ended in physical violence. This episode later resulted in a Senate decision declaring that in sacred and public places, no one was permitted to make sacrifices according to rituals that were new or foreign. What is more, anyone who possessed books con-

---

13 Cicero, *Div.* 2.76.
14 Livy 25.1.6-12.

taining prophecies, prayers, or ritual prescriptions had to hand them over to the praetor of the city before 1 April.

It is typical of Livy's examples that *superstitio* is perceived as a threat against Roman *religio*, against the ancestral customs (*mos maiorum*), and against the state (*res publica*). He presents these episodes as particular events that would occasionally arise in relation to crises in Roman society, such as plague, drought, or the horrors of war. Yet although these descriptions demonstrate a clear focus on countering the various types of *superstitio* that came from outside Rome, they rarely indicate or allude to any construction of concrete religious enemies. In fact, all in all the literature and the archaeological sources bear witness to the contrary: Even as they fought from time to time against foreign *superstitio*, when involved in actual cultural encounters the Romans largely tended to include or absorb foreign religious elements into Roman culture. They would include foreign gods and rituals, reshape them, Romanize them, and incorporate them into official Roman religion.

Evocatio – summoning the patron deities of the enemy

One example of this inclusive (and highly pragmatic) Roman approach is a ritual called *evocatio*, (literally a "summoning away"). In this ritual the Roman general, seeking to win over the enemy's patron deity before launching an attack on enemy territory, makes a promise (*votum*) intended to cause the deity to side with the Romans. The earliest example of *evocatio* that we know of took place in 396 BCE, when Rome conquered the Etruscan city of Veii.[15] Before attacking the city, the Roman general addressed Uni, the patron goddess of Veii, encouraging her to accompany the Romans back to their capital city – once they had achieved victory, of course – and promising that she would be given a temple that was worthy of her elevated position. This story, also handed down by Livy, further describes how, after the city fell, a select group of Roman soldiers entered the temple of Uni to carry off her statue. When one of the soldiers, appropriately awe-struck – or perhaps,

---

15   Livy 5.21.1-7.

as Livy puts it, youthfully high-spirited – asked the goddess whether she would accompany the victors to Rome, the statue nodded in acquiescence. According to Livy's account the goddess then allowed herself to be transported to Rome without incident. Here, under the name of Juno Regina, the goddess was given a temple on the Aventine, and this new temple was consecrated by the same general who had summoned her away to side with the Romans. Through such religio-political manoeuvring foreign territories could be conquered in accordance with the divine powers, and foreign gods and cultures could be subsumed into Roman religion and culture.

An inscription discovered in the city of Isaura Vetus in Asia Minor proves that the principle behind the *evocatio* ritual continued into the Late Republic.[16] The text mentions the Romans conquering the city (in 75 BCE) and the performance of the Roman general's *votum*. Originally the inscription was presumably part of the temple that the general had ordered to be consecrated to the city's patron deity and erected on site. This implies that in the Late Republic, a temple built to honour the patron deity of a vanquished people was no longer erected in Rome itself, but was built within the relevant Roman provincial territory, and so the ritual of *evocatio* was adapted to reflect Rome's spectacular military expansion. In step with the Empire's conquests, the focus of the ritual is transferred from the city of Rome itself to the newly acquired provinces, which would demarcate and consolidate the expansion of the Roman Empire and the scope of Roman religio-political power and identity. This type of religious flexibility and incorporation underscore the dynamics of the Romanization processes and the close links between Roman society, Roman expansion, and the assertion of Roman identity.

The Romanization of the provinces, and the role of religion in this process, is still hotly debated among the scholars. One issue is whether Romanization consisted of relatively uncomplicated religious and cultural encounters, or whether it actually involved major conflicts between the Roman authorities and the many different peoples and local elites. Where such questions are

---

16　*L'année épigraphique* (1977), p. 816. Cf. A.S. Hall (1973) "New Light on the Capture of Isaura Vetus by P. Servilius Vatia", *Akten des VI Int. Kongresses für Griechische und Lateinische Epigraphik* (*Vestigia* 17), Munich, pp. 568-571; J. Le Gall (1976), "Evocatio", *Mélanges J. Heurgon* I, 519-524, Rome; Beard, North & Price (1998) vol. 1, pp. 132-134.

concerned, however, it is practically impossible to give any general answers, because the circumstances seem to have varied greatly, depending on the time, the place, and the nature of each particular problem. Nevertheless, as far as Christianity is concerned the following chapters illustrate the level of rivalry, violence, and passion that could be associated with acculturation and the processes of Romanization. The most intense manifestations are found in Chapter 4, which deals with Christian persecution and martyrdom, and Chapter 5, which treats the crucial role that worship of the Emperor played in Romanizing the Empire.

Modern scholarship on religion in the Roman Empire has often emphasized that the Roman authorities only intervened in foreign cult if it disturbed the peace and order.[17] While this is undoubtedly a characteristic Roman feature, obviously it is not the entire story. From a sociological point of view it was not just a question of the Christ cult's members disturbing the peace in and outside Rome with their new and eccentric religious ideas and behaviours.[18] Given that the followers of this cult would acknowledge Jesus Christ and none other as the sole divine power, and that they refused to sacrifice to the Roman deities and make offerings for the health and well-being of the Emperor, in the eyes of the Romans they were undermining the very foundations of Roman culture, hewing away at the cornerstones of the city itself and at the distant fortifications of its far-flung Empire. Seen in this perspective, the traditional polytheistic religion established crucial links between Rome's past, present, and future and was therefore a decisive element in the construction of a collective Roman identity.

It would go far beyond the scope of this book to venture into treating the many scholarly discussions of the concept of "monotheism". Suffice it to say that whereas Roman religion was essentially inclusive, Christianity as a monotheistic religion was exclusive, in the sense that it tended to exclude all other religions.[19] In this context, however, the core problem is not so

---

17   See, for instance, Rives (2007) p. 200.
18   On the use of the term "cult of Christ" throughout this book, cf. Paul's letter to the Corinthians (*1 Cor.* 1:1-3), in which Paul speaks of his readers as "all that in every place call upon the name of Jesus Christ our Lord. Cf. *1 Cor.* 13; *Acts* 2:38.
19   Cf. J. Assmann (2006) *Monotheismus und die Sprache der Gewalt*, Vienna; J. Assmann (2010) *The Price of Monotheism*, Stanford. On the pluralism of religious life in Imperial Rome, see, for instance, Beard, North & Price (1998) pp. 245-312; Rives (2007); S. Price

much the question of monotheism versus polytheism, but rather the new and rigid distinction between the True God and false gods. The issue here is not the number of gods, but the firm belief that alongside the One True God there are only false gods, whom it is forbidden to worship. Exclusion is the decisive point in this matter. Christianity recognized no other gods than the Christian Almighty God, and Christian writers consistently relegated all non-Christian deities to the realm of demons, which by definition must be routed. Roman religion had to be opposed as a despicable false religion, an aberration whose practitioners must be treated as infidels and enemies. This division of humanity into two camps is formulated quite clearly in many of the Christian sources: On one side stood the servants of Christ, and on the other the devil-worshippers, whose Roman culture was often described as morally bankrupt and deeply depraved.

Here it must be stressed, however, that there are variations in the Christian sources' views on Graeco-Roman culture. But the various versions of both Judaism and Christianity still retained ideas of an omnipotent God who was radically different from the traditional Roman deities. A God who made new demands on his followers, introducing concepts like proselytizing, religious truth, piety, humility, and obedience in faith as well as in conduct.[20] One very significant element was that the very concept of faith played a central role in Christianity – contrary to Roman religion, where the decisive element had nothing to do with faith, but rather with correctly performing the various cult rituals. Traditional Roman religion was not primarily preoccupied with what each individual Roman was supposed to think and believe in religious terms. But it was keenly concerned with their practical execution of ritual acts and activities. It was of the utmost importance, for instance, that offerings were made without any mistakes or disruptions. The Greek writer Plutarch speaks of the Romans' religious diligence, which obliges them to repeat their sacrificial rituals if even the slightest slip-up occurs. Say one of

---

(2011) "Homogeneity and Diversity in the Religions of Rome" in North & Price (2011) pp. 253-275; J. North (2011) "Pagans, Polytheists, and the Pendulum" in North & Price (2011) pp. 479-502.

20 On the commission to make all nations disciples of Christ, see, for instance, *Mat.* 28:18-20. On Jesus as the way and the truth, see *John* 14:6. On Christian obedience and humility, see *Phil.* 1:27-30; 2:1-16.

the horses drawing a wagon in the procession stops, or one of the drivers thoughtlessly grips the reins with his left hand. In that case the Romans will interrupt the procession and begin again. In fact, Plutarch states that a sacrifice has been known to be repeated 30 times because the participants were constantly suspected of some oversight, or some inaccuracy in the ritual procedure.[21] Ritual expertise and meticulous ritual performance were definitely crucial elements in Roman *religio*.

The traditional communal cult, consisting of state-organized public rituals and sacrifices to the Roman pantheon of deities, were related to society's overall welfare and generally left personal interests aside. The so-called Mysteries and Oriental cults, on the other hand, more specifically targeted the individual, offering the prospect of personal initiation and/or salvation, for instance from illness or misfortune.[22] These cults contained elements such as "suffering" in various forms, and release from this suffering. Sometimes myths about the suffering, dying, and resurrected god guaranteed the sufferers that earthly happiness would return, or convinced them that happiness awaited in a world beyond this one. The promise of salvation was originally very closely linked with ritual prescripts such as secret initiation rituals, requirements to ritual cleansing, sexual abstinence, fasting, or the prohibition of wine, meat, or other foodstuffs. In this aspect, the cult of Christ and its promise of salvation stood out from these other cults. According to the Christ cult, misfortune and perdition were not caused by ritual mistakes, but by lacking or misguided faith. Also, unlike other cults in Graeco-Roman religion Christianity relied on dogmas and sacred scriptures to instruct followers how to differentiate between the one and only true faith and false beliefs. In traditional Graeco-Roman religion the text was embedded in ritual and subordinated to it, and the rituals served to keep up a cosmic order otherwise threatened with collapse. In Christianity, however, the text held the cardinal importance and ritual was reduced to

---

21   Plutarch, *Parallel Lives*, *Coriolanus* 25. Cf. J. North (2008) "Action and Ritual in Roman Historians; or how Horatius held the door-post" in A.H. Rasmussen & S.W. Rasmussen (2008) pp. 23-42; J.Podemann Sørensen (2008) "A Theory of Ritual" in A.H. Rasmussen & S.W. Rasmussen (2008) pp. 13-22.

22   Concerning fundamental problems in relation to the two terms "Mysteries" and "Oriental Cults", see G.S. Gasparro (2011) "Mysteries and Oriental Cults: A Problem in the History of Religions" in North & Price (2011) pp. 276-324.

a supplementary role. The world owed its continuing existence and order, not to the performance of rituals, but to the dogmas and sacred scriptures and the will of God. Only the one true (Christian) faith could lead to redemption and deliverance.

It was precisely this Christian fixation on the concept of faith that reinforced religious rivalry and produced the constructed enemy images to which it gave rise. The basis of this rivalry was the monotheistic view of the Christ cult, along with its sharply delineated dualistic ideas and the introduction of the Last Judgement. On that day of ultimate reckoning, everything evil will be condemned, symbolized by the downfall of Satan himself into the eternal fires. And along with him will be destroyed all those who do not actively fight on God's side in the battle against all things evil – such as Roman infidels and Christians who have fallen by the wayside. Needless to say, these ideas expressed a distinct and harsh religious polarity: between God and Satan, good and evil, light and darkness, truth and lies, salvation and perdition, and so forth. Similarly, people were consistently and categorically divided into two camps: the redeemed and the damned.

We find the conflicts between the redeemed and the damned reflected very strongly in the type of Christian writings known as "apologetics", although admittedly there are several very different definitions of this concept.[23] The apologetic texts of the Christian church fathers are also extremely varied, depending on who wrote them, when they were written, and in what historical and geographical context. Even so, they do share certain common features. Above all, such texts appeal to the Roman authorities and other readers with arguments that refute allegations made against Christianity. They also attempt to clarify questions about how Christianity relates to Jewish and Graeco-Roman culture; questions assumed to be interesting for non-Christians and Christians alike, and most particularly for doubting believers and potential converts to Christianity. Apologetic writers also attack and ridicule Roman religion and philosophy, saying that the proponents of Roman religion are actually supporters of superstition and enemies of the truth. Finally, such writings seek to resolve various internal Christian

---

23   On the issue of apologetics as an actual genre, see M. Edwards, M. Goodman & S. Price (eds) (1999) *Apologetics in the Roman Empire*, Oxford.

controversies while at the same time illustrating the author's personal views and piety.

Tertullian

One of the early Christian sources that probes into these questions is the Carthaginian church father Tertullian (circa 160-222 CE). His *Apologeticum* (*Apology*, circa 197 CE) eminently embodies that particular hard-line approach that blends a defence of the Christian faith as a universal truth with attacks on pagans as enemies of Christian teaching.[24] Other of Tertullian's writings also deliver a poignant defence of Christianity mixed with scathing criticism of Roman religion and culture. Several of his works consequently offer valuable insights into the problems that the Christians perceived as typical of the meetings between the Roman Empire and the Christian communities.

In his introduction to the *Apologeticum*, Tertullian explicitly addresses the Roman authorities and officials who treated cases brought against Christians. However, both the style and the contents of this work suggest that it was intended for a wider audience consisting of non-Christians and Christians. Tertullian lists and rebuts accusations against the Christians for crimes including infanticide, cannibalism, sex orgies, and incest – then promptly makes these same allegations against the Romans.[25] He also mentions their religio-political accusations against the Christians, explaining why Christians

---

24 Cf. H.R. Drobner (2007) *The Fathers of the Church*, Peabody MA, transl. S.S. Schatzmann from *Lehrbuch der Patrologie* (1994); C. Becker (1954) *Tertullians Apologeticum. Werden und Leistung*, Munich; T.D. Barnes (1971) *Tertullian. A Historical and Literary Study*, Oxford; R. Klein (1968) *Tertullian und das römische Reich*, Heidelberg; M. Fiedrowicz (2000) *Apologie im frühen Christentum. Die Kontroverse um den christlichen Wahrheitsanspruch in den ersten Jahrhunderten*, Paderborn. A large number of generally recognized reviews and treatments of the Christian church fathers emphasize and analyse the apologetic style and content of the texts under discussion, rather than examining their hostile attacks on the traditional Graeco-Roman world. This is true of older and newer works alike, the latter group including Drobner's treatment, which summarizes the aim of the church fathers' writings solely in light of their defensive function and their explanations and justifications of Christianity, cf. Drobner (2007) p. 73.
25 Tertullian, *Apologeticum* 7-9.

do not wish to worship or cultivate the Roman deities or make sacrifices for the Emperor. He makes fun of Roman rituals and derides Rome's deities, depicting them as demons that are ridiculous and dangerous.[26] He dwells on the sexual aspects of the Roman myths and rituals describing, for instance, how in the pagan world people fornicate between the altars in the temples and sacrifice rotting flesh.[27] Tertullian also argues against making the Christians serve as scapegoats for bad omens and catastrophes that have taken place during Rome's history:[28]

> If the Tiber rises to the walls, if the Nile does not rise to the fields, if the sky is rainless, if there is an earthquake, a famine, a plague, immediately the cry arises, "The Christians to the lion!"

He then goes on to list the numerous accidents and catastrophes chronicled *before* the coming of Christ, concluding that it must be the Romans' own paganism that has caused all the calamities:[29]

> You therefore are dangerous to human affairs, you are to blame for public misfortunes, drawing them always upon us, since you despise God and worship statues.

Tertullian thus interprets all of Rome's troubles as God's punishment brought down upon the Romans – while praising Christian chastity, goodness, and faith in the One True God as the diametrical opposite to the depraved Roman world. The financial constructions of the Christian movement are also mentioned, with emphasis on the principle of free will: Although the Christian congregations do have a kind of treasury, contributions from individuals are voluntary. Christian donations (unlike those of the pagans) are not used for drinking bouts or food orgies, Tertullian explains, but to pay for living costs and funerals for paupers, orphans, old

---

26 Tertullian, *Apol.* 10-36.
27 Tertullian, *Apol.* 15.7; 14.1.
28 Tertullian, *Apol.* 40.1-9.
29 Tertullian, *Apol.* 41.1.

slaves, and others in need, stressing the Christian community of property:[30] "And so we, who are united in heart and soul, have no hesitation about sharing a thing. Among us all things are common – except wives," he points out, comparing this with the Roman world, where husbands (he claims) "most patiently" lend their wives to friends and acquaintances.

Tertullian is deeply distressed by the rising number of divorces in his day and age, and in his letters *Ad uxorem* (*To My Wife*) he deals with the dilemma arising from culture contacts that result in mixed marriages. A Christian woman who is married to an unbeliever, he underscores, will inevitably find herself at odds with the heathen world. She will be confronted with the rowdiness of drinking in public houses, the world of the theatre, the celebrations of pagan gods, the stench of incense, and the ritual decoration of private homes, which remind the disdainful Tertullian of newly opened brothels. Everything around her will be foreign, hostile, and damned, he concludes.[31] In another work on women, *De Cultu Feminarum* (*On the Apparel of Women*), Tertullian further details appropriate guidelines for the norms and comportment of a Christian woman: She must be chaste, must not present herself as enticing or challenging, and must not adorn herself with jewellery and cosmetics, which are despicable expressions of sinful vanity. The *Apologeticum* further treats the inappropriate behaviour of the Roman women and Rome's crumbling morals, providing descriptions of how women drink wine, embellish themselves excessively, and generally conduct and present themselves in a way that makes it impossible to tell the difference between wives and prostitutes.[32]

Tertullian praises a marriage between two Christians as the ideal social and religious counterpart to the excesses of the Roman lifestyle, emphasizing the strength of the things they have in common: The spouses can pray together, fast together, and share the singing of psalms and a variety of other activities. He further discusses whether a Christian woman ought to remarry if her husband dies. This was a generally accepted practice in the

---

30 Tertullian, *Apol.* 39.6; 39.11.
31 Tertullian, *Ad Uxorem* 6.
32 Tertullian, *Apol.* 6.3-6. Cf. G. Clark (2004) *Christianity and Roman Society*, Cambridge; A. Cameron (2011a) "Early Christianity and the Discourse of Female Desire" in North & Price (2011) pp. 505-530.

traditional Roman world, and although it was also permitted among Christians, Tertullian advises his own wife against remarrying if he dies before her. He finds justification for this in the story of Adam and Eve, concluding simply and with apparently indisputable logic: one rib, one woman.[33]

The writings of this church father contain a caustic criticism of Roman culture. At the same time they also bear witness to criticisms that non-Christians levelled at the Christians, berating them for distancing themselves from life as it was lived in society at large, for example, and for not contributing to the good of society as a whole. Tertullian, meanwhile, rejected such criticism utterly. Because Christians also have a life that must be lived, naturally they too need meat markets, shops, baths, and workshops, he argues: although Christians are not allowed to participate in pagan rituals and celebrations, they do buy food and other necessities just like everyone else. He rather haughtily concludes that the only sort of people in Roman society who can complain about not profiting from Christians are pimps and ruffians, assassins and poisoners, soothsayers and astrologers, and others of that ilk.[34]

Tertullian emphasizes in his *Apologeticum* that he intends to explain the organization of the Christians in order to quell rumours and shed light on the Christian community. He describes the Christian meetings, which feature prayers and readings from the sacred scriptures and detail the significance of admonitions and punishments in the name of God.[35] At Christian gatherings decisions are made about excommunication from the congregation, where the person who has transgressed can be "banished from the communion of prayer and assembly and all holy fellowship."[36] He also describes the course of the Christian *agape* meal (the "meal of love"): No one lies down at table until an introductory prayer has been said, and the meal is followed by the washing of hands, lighting of candles, reading from the Scripture, song, and a closing prayer. Tertullian describes the meal itself as very humble compared with the eating and drinking that goes in the pagan cults. And it is worth bearing in mind that occasionally the Romans themselves also

---

33   Tertullian, *Ad Uxorem* 2.
34   Tertullian, *Apol.* 42.1-6; 43.1-2.
35   Tertullian, *Apol.* 39.
36   Tertullian, *Apol.* 39.4.

pointed out the typical Roman vices such as vanity and hedonism, not least in connection with religious festivals, when gluttony was even more in evidence than usual. As Seneca the Younger (circa 1-65 CE) wrote of his contemporaries:[37]

> *Vomunt, ut edant, edunt ut vomant.* (They vomit that they may eat, and they eat that they may vomit.)

Tertullian also attacks the shows and pantomimes of the Roman world, which dramatize religious and historical narratives and myths on stage. In a piece entitled *De Spectaculis* (*On the Shows*) he vividly describes what these public spectacles bring with them: commotion, fights, aggravation, and a total lack of self-control, and Tertullian states that: "Just as there is a lust for money, a lust for dignity, for greed, for impurity, for vainglory, so there is a lust for pleasure. The shows are a sort of pleasure."[38] All in all it becomes quite clear that we are dealing with a Christian who has a heathen past, and indeed one who has a profound insight into the sinful culture he now condemns. We do not know precisely when Tertullian converted to Christianity, but clearly the "before" and the "after" of his conversion are an important element in the accounts provided by him and by other Christian writers. This is evident, for instance, when Tertullian, treating the Christian ideas of the Last Judgment – the day on which the dead are resurrected and adjudged according to their merits and sins – refers to his own pagan past:[39]

> We too once laughed at this: we sprang from your ranks. Christians are made Christians, and not born such.

The pagans undoubtedly found the Christian concept of the Last Judgment incredibly amusing. In addition, Tertullian's comment that a person is not born a Christian but becomes a Christian actually expresses a sociological fact that is of obvious importance. But over and above all this, the decisive

---

37 Seneca the Younger, *Ad Helviam* 10.3.
38 Tertullian, *De Spectaculis* 14.
39 Tertullian, *Apol.* 18.4, cf. 15.5.

Fig. 2. Relief from the first century CE, found at Ariccia, south of Rome, and now in the Palazzo Altemps in Rome. The relief illustrates the celebration of religious rites, probably in connection with the Egyptian cult of Isis. Its motifs reflect not only the religious diversity of ancient Rome, but also some of the merrier aspects of pagan religion, which the Christian church fathers would thunder against for 300 years or so.

problem in relation to this meeting of cultures is that – in the eyes of a Roman – all the things in the Roman world that Tertullian and other Christian writers vilify, classifying them as superstitious nonsense and depravity, relate to a multitude of very important institutions: inherited traditions, modes of thinking, and ways of life; religious celebrations, ceremonies, and processions; races at the circus; comedies, tragedies, and pantomimes at the theatre; gladiator fights at the amphitheatre; triumphal processions in the streets; and much more. All of these institutions and traditions hold great social, legal, military, and political significance. Moreover, they are all solidly anchored in two cornerstones of Roman culture: *cultus deorum* (worship of the deities) and *mos maiorum* (customs of the ancestors).

In his criticism of Roman culture, Tertullian also argues polemically against the various philosophical schools, poking fun at their countless disagreements, doubts, and unresolved issues relating to the nature of God, the universe, and the soul. He also claims that the philosophers have stolen

Fig. 3. Detail from the Ariccia relief.

some of their ideas from Christianity, and have distorted or misconstrued the true Christian doctrine.[40] Continuing along these lines, he sets to work refuting the contemporary perception that Christianity is only one of many philosophical schools of thought, wondering at the strange contradiction that, if this is genuinely the case, then why on Earth does Roman society honour the philosophers with statues and financial support while condemning the Christians to be thrown to the wild beasts for sport?[41] He concludes with a comparison concerning age and reasoning, asserting that Christianity is the elder culture, and superior. In doing this he does concede that the origins of Christian teaching go back only to the time of Tiberius, but he then proceeds to emphasize that the books of the Pentateuch form the foundation of Judaism and of Christianity, and that these texts are far older than any of the pagan gods, temples, oracles, rituals, poets, or philosophers. Reaching a similar conclusion in a text he wrote against heretics, he asserts

---

40 Tertullian, *Apol.* 46.10-48. In another work of his about the soul, *De testimonio animae*, Tertullian likewise criticizes the Greek philosophers' erudite discussions about the soul.
41 Tertullian, *Apol.* 46.4.

that in relation to Christianity, Greek philosophy and its various offshoots are absolutely superfluous:[42]

> What then hath Athens in common with Jerusalem? What hath the Academy in common with the Church? What have heretics in common with Christians? ... We have no need of speculative inquiry after we have known Christ Jesus.

As the true alternative to Roman gods and Greek philosophers, he presents the Christian doctrine's promise of religious salvation: deliverance from all evil and the power of demons; the prospect of genuine communion with the one and only God; resurrection from the dead; and eternal life.

All in all, Tertullian's writings plainly show how religious conflicts and the construction of religious enemies not only relate to disagreements on religion in the narrowest sense, but touch upon numerous other cultural focal points. To quite a large extent, defending the Christian faith and criticizing the pagans, not to mention constructing religious enemies (in both camps), revolves around the issues of social recognition, cultural continuity, and the establishment of a collective identity. The religious conflict puts the two cultures' identities to the test, pitting them against one another. And the culture contact throws the involved identities into perspective, making apparent the degree to which almost all aspects of society are thoroughly steeped in religion. That is why Tertullian and other disgusted Christian writers who construct religious enemies are striking at the very foundation of Roman culture and identity.

This makes it all the easier to understand why this foundation is vigorously defended by Graeco-Roman philosophers such as Celsus (second century CE) and Porphyry (third century CE), who likewise construct religious enemies around the Christians and vehemently criticize Christianity. Up until the second half of the second century CE, we have very few concrete testimonials of the early encounters between traditional Roman and Christian religion and culture as seen through non-Christian eyes. What is more, the works of the non-Christian critics are almost exclusively known by the

---

42 Tertullian, *De Praescriptione Haereticorum* (*On the "Prescription" of Heretics*) 7.

treatment they received in Christian works, which in fragmented fashion quote these criticisms with a view to defending Christianity. Obviously this causes a number of problems in assessing the sources: the anti-Christian texts were quoted selectively and paraphrased tendentiously, and these problems are still being discussed by modern scholarship. In spite of all this, these philosophers remain significant sources from our point of view, which endeavours to investigate the cultural encounter. Based on the philosophers' criticism of Christianity it is possible, at least to some extent, to reconstruct their views not only of Christianity but also of the traditional world to which they themselves belonged.

Celsus

According to the Greek philosopher Celsus, the strongest reason for rejecting the new Christian religion was precisely that it was undermining the traditional norms and values of the Roman world. Celsus wrote a work in Greek *On the True Doctrine*, which harshly attacked Christianity while defending traditional religion and philosophy. This text was presumably written around 170 CE, although the precise date is still hotly debated. The existence of this work is known only because it was treated by the Christian apologist Origen, who wrote his *Contra Celsum* (*Against Celsus*) around 240 CE to refute Celsus and his criticism of Christianity.[43] The target group that Origen sets out to reach is a mix of non-Christians and Christians in doubt, and as the author states in his preface in *Contra Celsum*: It is not written for the true Christians, but for those who have either not yet become acquainted with the faith in Jesus Christ, or those whom the apostle [Paul]

---

43 Cf. *Celsus. On the True Doctrine. A Discourse Against the Christians*. Translated with a general introduction by R.J. Hoffmann (1987), Oxford; *Origen: Contra Celsum*. Translated with an introduction and notes by H. Chadwick (1980), Cambridge (3); *Origen Werke*, published by P. Koetschau (1899), *Die Griechischen Christlichen Schriftsteller der ersten drei Jahrhunderte*, Leipzig; Porphyry: *"Gegen die Christen". 15 Bücher. Zeugnisse, Fragmente und Referate*, published by A. Von Harnack (1916), Berlin; cf. M. Fiedrowich (2001) *Apologie im frühen Christentum. Die Kontroverse um den christlichen Wahrheitsanspruch in den ersten Jahrhunderten*, Paderborn; Edwards, Goodman & Price (1999).

calls "weak in faith".[44] Evidently, Origen imagines that both these groups might be influenced by the critical speculations that Celsus puts forward, by his attack on Christianity as the true doctrine, and by his defence of traditional Roman religion and culture. The quoted excerpts from the Celsus text have a somewhat Platonic orientation, but the details of his philosophical affiliations are still under discussion. However, the mere fact that Celsus is difficult to place in relation to the schools of philosophical thought do not make him a bad source. Perhaps quite the reverse, since his objectives do not seem to be dictated by some narrow interpretation or personal stake in any particular religious or philosophical idea.

Celsus primarily criticizes Christianity's rejection of the continuity of Roman culture, meaning the political, religious, and philosophical traditions of the Roman Empire. He considers the Christians' exclusive view as a consequence of their perceptions that they are chosen, and that they can be saved from the world by God and by the incarnation of God's son. But according to Celsus, these ideas are based on a flawed understanding of the nature of God. For if God descends to walk among men, he must undergo a change from that which is good, beautiful, and blissful to that which is despicable, evil, and unhappy. And as Celsus puts it, God does not undergo that kind of change. Only a mortal being undergoes changes, whereas an immortal being is and remains immutable.[45] Celsus is outraged at the Christian idea that God created mankind in His image, and that He became a man himself, and that He even went so far as to rise from the dead. The philosopher finds it absurd that Christians should imagine that on Judgment Day the dead will be resurrected in flesh and blood, and that the sinners will roast over hot coals. Additionally he finds Christianity to be completely devoid of philosophical insights, and with no requirement at all for actual, logical argumentation. Celsus is not only critical towards Christianity. He is also, quite simply, baffled. And the fact that Christians specifically refute philosophy and claim that faith alone will suffice only confirms his assumption that Christianity is no match for philosophy.

Origen counters this in his *Contra Celsum* by arguing that Christianity is actually the highest wisdom, and that Jesus was a sage who, like Socrates,

---

44   Origen, *Contra Celsum* praef. 6.
45   Origen, *Contra Celsum* 4.14.

preferred to die for his cause rather than betray it.[46] (The issue of Socrates as a sort of pre-Christian martyr is discussed in Chapter 4.) But for Celsus the Christian faith is by no means capable of recognizing truth, and he claims that any sound thinking that does occur in the Christian doctrine has been filched from Greek philosophy, and from Plato in particular.[47] In short, the good things in Christianity are not new, and the new things are not good.

As Celsus sees it, the reason why Christianity gained a certain following in the world was that the cult of Christ enticed people into supporting it by means of deceitful stories and miracle-mongering – as the discussion of miracles in Chapter 2 will treat in some depth. Celsus describes Christ as a confidence trickster, a charlatan, and a street-corner miracle-maker who attracted and exploited those naive enough to believe his messages. According to the author's explanation, that is also why the Christ cult recruits its followers among social outcasts, simpletons, uneducated people, slaves, tradesmen, and hysterical womenfolk. He attacks the numerous tall tales in Christianity: man's being shaped by God's hands, God's blowing on man to give him breath, woman's being created from man's rib, and a serpent's having spoken out against the dictates of God. Celsus finds these statements to be absolute rubbish, adding that only a weak God would not have the power to prevent the very human beings He has created from sinning.[48] As the devout believer he is, Origen defends the story of Creation by declaring that it should be regarded as an allegory: Applying the allegorical principle of interpretation means that the Christian message has a chance of reaching people in all layers of society. As Origen sees it, the stories in the Bible possess a simplicity that makes them accessible to those with an uncomplicated mind, even while offering hidden philosophical truths that appeal to the more scholarly mind.[49]

As concerns the origins of Christianity, Celsus the philosopher continues to wonder about the actual basis of the Christ cult. The thing is, to a Roman the cult of Christ seems to be strangely ahistorical, and to have a

---

46 Origen, *Contra Celsum* 2.17.
47 Origen, *Contra Celsum* 1.68; 5.59; 6.60; 6.63; 5.14; 2.33; 2.54; 7.45.
48 Origen, *Contra Celsum* 4.36.
49 Origen, *Contra Celsum* 4.38.

very odd relationship with Judaism.[50] This particular relationship, between Christianity and Judaism, seems to be quite a sore spot, and one that critics of Christianity are eager to prod at whenever the opportunity presents itself. Celsus regarded Jesus as nothing more than an upstart who broke with the old Jewish laws and traditions. The philosopher accuses the Christ cult of distancing itself from Judaism without being capable of replacing it as a religious foundation. Origen responds to this part of the criticism by stating, among other things, that the Jews did not understand the wisdom they had possessed, which is why they killed the prophets and Jesus Christ.[51] Origen goes on to describe Jesus as the oldest of all beings, in that he is depicted as a form of personified wisdom that is older than Moses, even though it was not until after that time that Jesus Christ became a human being in the flesh. The Christian author thereby rebuts not only the accusations that Jesus is a recent invention, but also the claim that Christianity demonstrates disdain for erudition and a lack of philosophical insight: His response to the criticisms from Celsus consists in representing Christianity as the oldest and highest wisdom and the only true philosophy.[52] The discussion about the relationship between Christianity and Judaism reveals diverging views on religion and on cultural history.[53] According to Celsus, the Jews had distinct rules, laws, and customs, just like any other culture. Origen counters this relative point of view with an absolute position based on the Christian idea of the universal reign of God, granting that the Christians have broken with Jewish custom, but arguing that this is only because Jesus has given them a better divine and universal law.

As will have become apparent, it is primarily the absolute and exclusive features in Christianity that Celsus sees as undermining factors. He emphasizes that different cultures organize their affairs differently, have different types of government, and therefore act differently – also in religious matters. It is precisely this mode of thinking (which in modern terms could be called a moderate, culture-relative method of understanding "the other") that represents the views that are incompatible with Christianity and which

---

50   Origen, *Contra Celsum* 2.4.
51   Origen, *Contra Celsum* 5.42.
52   Origen, *Contra Celsum* 2.4; 5.37.
53   Origen, *Contra Celsum* 5.25-40.

therefore provoke adamant protests from Christian writers. Celsus criticizes the Christians not only for having religious ideas that undermine existing customs and institutions, but also for their tendency to isolate themselves – which effectively means moving religious ideas and activities from the public to the private sphere.

Celsus does more than just criticize, however. He also appeals directly to the Christians, urging them to give up their exclusivity of faith and instead recognize the existence of a divine order consisting of a number of deities that vary depending on location and culture, but which are subordinate to the supreme deity. Celsus similarly advises the Christians to show deference and loyalty to the divine nature of the Roman Emperor's power. The philosopher's appeal to the Christians demonstrates that there is much more at stake in his criticism than flashing his own rhetorical prowess in ridiculing peculiar details of Christian religious practice. It reflects a pragmatic way of thinking when tackling a real-life religio-political conflict arising from a specific culture contact situation in the Roman world.

Part of modern scholarship (like certain Christian writers in Antiquity) have rejected Celsus as a reliable source, accusing him of standing for arbitrary polemical argumentation against Christianity, and of being misinformed, imprecise, unfair, and inconsequential as a philosopher.[54] Whether one finds these accusations justifiable or not, it is beyond discussion that his work embodies a number of objections, arguments, and thoughts that were expressed and were influential in the Roman world of the second century CE. We are therefore obliged to conclude that however prejudiced, imprecise, and unfair his representations and views may appear, he cannot be rejected as a source of information. Whatever else one may think of Celsus, his criticism highlights two important features. The first is the dialectic process linked to the culture contact and the religious conflict at hand: Writers in both camps studied each other, argued against each other, and mutually affected

---

54 For more on this question, see T.D. Barnes (1973) "Porphyry Against the Christians: Date and Attribution of Fragments", *JTS* 24 (1973), pp. 424-442; U. von Wilamowitz-Moellendorf (1900) "Ein Bruchstück aus der Schrift des Porphyrius gegen die Christen" in ZNW 1 (1900) p. 101ff; J. O'Meara (1959) *Porphyry's Philosophy from Oracles in Augustine*, Paris; R.L. Fox (1986) *Pagans and Christians*, London, p. 586; Edwards, Goodman & Price (1999); R.L. Wilken (2003) *The Christians as the Romans Saw Them*, New Haven NJ (2nd rev. ed.); Clark (2004).

each other. In other words, these exchanges are an important indication of an acculturation process and a dynamic confrontation of religions. The second feature highlighted here is the frequent use that both camps make of stereotypes and constructed religious enemies in their strategies of verbal combat – strategies used not only to attack but also to defend.

Porphyry

> "The most learned of philosophers, though the most bitter foe of the Christians."

This is how Augustine described the Greek philosopher Porphyry (circa 233-305 CE) who dispatched one of the most remarkable and influential attacks on Christianity during that period.[55] The significance and staying power of Porphyry's criticism is unmistakable. For one thing, Christian writers were still campaigning against his work well into the fifth century. For another, Emperor Theodosius II decided as late as 448 to order the burning of Porphyry's work *Against the Christians*. It is fair to say that for a very long time Porphyry was considered one of Christianity's most dangerous opponents. Some even claim that in the context of modern theological scholarship, the critical questions posed by Porphyry the philosopher still hold a certain relevance.[56]

We know slightly more about Porphyry than we do about Celsus – which is still not much. Porphyry left his native city of Tyre for Athens, where he studied philosophy extensively before travelling to Rome in 263. Here he joined the circle around the neo-Platonic philosopher Plotinus (205-270), whose posthumous writings he later had published. Regrettably, most of Porphyry's own work has been lost, and the only fragments that we know of from his criticism of Christianity have been preserved by way of Eusebius,

---

55 Augustine, *De Civitate Dei contra Paganos* (*The City of God against the Pagans*)19.22.
56 Adolf von Harnack labelled Porphyry's work *Against the Christians* as "perhaps the most extensive and thoroughgoing treatise that has ever been written against Christianity. ... Even today Porphyry remains unanswered." A. von Harnack (1908) *The Mission and Expansion of Christianity in the First Three Centuries*, London, I, p. 505.

Augustine, and other Christian writers. Porphyry's assault on Christianity and his defence of Graeco-Roman religion and philosophy was mainly embodied in the 15-volume work *Against the Christians*, but also expressed in his *Philosophy from Oracles*. Although Porphyry was apparently strongly influenced by Plotinus, his writings take a harder line than his mentor's, his style characterized by vicious attacks on Christianity and impassioned defences for traditional religion.

It must be remembered, however, that although the Christian apologetic writers allude to and quote Porphyry, clearly bearing witness to a fierce criticism of Christianity, modern scholarship still disagrees on precisely how much and which points of the criticism can rightly be attributed to him. Some scholars are convinced that about half of the preserved fragments of the work *Against the Christians* have been taken from a completely different text, or written by a completely different person,[57] contending that no decisive evidence exists to demonstrate that these fragments actually originated with Porphyry.[58] Yet despite the problematic issues and uncertainties in examining these sources, it is still possible to form an impression of the criticism and the pressing contemporary questions and dilemmas that the church fathers grappled with in Antiquity. Whether the relevant fragments were written by Porphyry or not, we still have in hand significant testimony setting out ideas and arguments that were part of the religious conflict unfolding in the Roman Empire in the third century CE. And bear in mind that these were critical arguments that Christian writers still felt obliged to address and attempt to refute in the fourth and fifth centuries.

Apart from the occasional positive statements, the gist of Porphyry's arguments is that both the Old Testament and parts of the New Testament – as well as the whole evangelical proposition of Jesus Christ being the son of God – are absurd, intellectually dubious, and riddled with unreasonable claims, internal contradictions, and historical falsifications. Most notably,

---

57 The suggested alternative source is the treatise *Apocriticus* by Macarius Magnes. Cf. R. J. Hoffmann (1994) *Porphyry's Against the Christians. The Literary Remains*. Edited and translated by R.J. Hoffmann, Amherst NY, pp. 18-23.

58 Cf. Barnes (1973) pp. 424-442. Cf. Harnack (1916); Wilamowitz-Moellendorf (1900) p. 101ff; O'Meara (1959); Fox (1986) p. 586; Wilken (1974) pp. 117-123; Hoffmann (1994).

Porphyry refuses to accept the fundamental premise of Christianity: that salvation takes place by means of a historical revelation. That is why he wishes to sow doubt as to the credibility of this revelation by pointing out illogical and self-contradictory elements in the gospels about Jesus Christ.[59] Porphyry seems to be very much at home in the Christian scriptures, which he subjects to a meticulous and highly critical examination regarding their contents and sources. When compared with the criticisms presented by Celsus, who was somewhat earlier, Porphyry seems to have had more Christian apologetic works available to him for use in furthering his arguments and making a more detailed critique. In other words, critically examining the sources and taking a historical view of the material are important elements for Porphyry. He refutes the claim that one can base one's views in this matter on faith alone, which is what the Christian doctrine encourages its faithful followers to do. And as for the credibility of the sources, he simply and clearly asks for reliable documentation.[60] Porphyry's conclusion seems clear: Christianity must be rejected as a movement that threatens traditional culture and is religiously, socially, and morally destabilizing.

Porphyry's rejection of Christianity is intimately linked with a defence of the traditional cultures – which, however, he also attempts to place within a new philosophical framework. This is evident in his *Philosophy from Oracles*, in which his aim is to unite traditional oracular cults with the religious thinking of the philosophers. For this is also a pivotal aspect of Porphyry's thought: that not just one but several different existing cultures might contain elements of truth, given that the supreme being had created various societies and was therefore worshipped, "cultivated", in different ways and in different manifestations according to the different cultures.[61] In doing this, Porphyry builds the idea of religious diversity into a monotheistically oriented scaffolding. This reflects two essential religious and social realities in the Roman world of that age. First, the existence of a large number of different religious and philosophical cults and groupings, and second, the existence of a trend of inclusive and generally monotheistic thought that could potentially bring the various movements closer together.

---

59   Hoffmann (1994) pp. 32-36; 39-52.
60   Porphyry, *Adv. Christ.* Frg. 12ff; 30ff in Harnack (1916); Hoffmann (1994) pp. 77-93.
61   Augustine, *De Civ. Dei* 10.32.

One of the more significant Christian contributions in the debate against Porphyry was written by the bishop and church historian Eusebius of Caesarea (circa 260-340 CE), whose 25-volume work *Against Porphyry* was a response to Porphyry's *Against the Christians*. Obviously keen to respond to Porphyry's criticism, Eusebius was well aware of the renowned Greek philosopher's reputation and his position as a representative of well-argued criticism, which was founded in his solid knowledge of Christian scripture, works, and apologetic writings.[62] In addition to the question of religious diversity and monotheism, Porphyry also raises the question of how Christianity is related to Judaism and traditional Graeco-Roman culture. Here it is quite interesting to follow the way Eusebius, a seasoned polemicist, responds. One reaction is his claim that Plato's thinking is not anchored in traditional Greek ideas, but is rather associated with Jewish thinking which, chronologically speaking, predates it. So for Eusebius, Platonism is substantially true – not because it contains Greek wisdom, but because it contains Jewish wisdom that has been handed down as Greek wisdom.[63] Such an interpretation must have been rather far-fetched from a philosophical perspective, but Christians must also certainly have considered it a highly controversial point of view.

One of Eusebius's major apologetic works contains a lengthy passage that has been attributed to Porphyry.[64] In this context Eusebius underscores that he wishes to allow the heathen authors to speak for themselves, and that he therefore quotes a series of passages relating to Phoenician, Egyptian, and Greek religion. One is the relevant passage attributed to Porphyry, which says, among much else:[65]

> How can men fail to be in every way impious and atheistical, who have apostatized from those ancestral gods by whom every nation and every state is sustained? Or what good can they reasonably hope for, who have set themselves at enmity and at war against their preservers,

---

62 On the assumption that Porphyry built upon and argued against Origen, whose significance as an apologist was absolutely decisive to Eusebius, see the contribution M. Frede (1999) "Eusebius' Apologetic Writings" in Edwards, Goodman & Price (1999) p. 232.
63 Eusebius, *Praeparatio Evangelica* 11.8.1.; cf. Frede (1999) pp. 247-248.
64 See Wilamowitz-Moellendorf (1900) p. 101ff. and Harnack (1916).
65 Eusebius, *Preparatio evangelica* 1.2.1-4; cf.1.1.

and have thrust away their benefactors? For what else are they doing than fighting against the gods? And what forgiveness shall they be thought to deserve, who have turned away from those who from the earliest time, among all Greeks and Barbarians, both in cities and in the country, are recognized as gods with all kinds of sacrifices, and initiations, and mysteries by all alike, kings, law-givers and philosophers, and have chosen all that is impious and atheistical among the doctrines of men? ... They have not adhered to the God who is honoured among the Jews according to their customary rites, but cut out for themselves a new kind of track in a pathless desert, that keeps neither the ways of the Greeks nor those of the Jews.

Eusebius's aim in reproducing these questions was, presumably, to describe the horrible heathen world that the Christians were obliged to confront, and preferably would conquer. A fight against the multitude of false gods, rituals, and religious ideas that infested the world around them. To Eusebius, this quote from Porphyry illustrated the Hydra-like qualities of the polytheistic world the Christians were facing. On the other hand, in Porphyry's opinion the old religious traditions and general religious diversity constitute a strong foundation from a cultural and a cultic point of view. This foundation consisted of a wide-ranging catalogue of deities and cults, and they all shared a common frame of religious reference that encompassed the whole gamut of religious thinking and practice found among human societies – not only in the Greek sphere of influence, but amongst all peoples. It was a foundation that throughout the ages had supported the existence of urban citizens and rural folk, philosophers and kings. A foundation that was the guarantor of religious and cultural continuity. In this perspective, the passage cited above illustrates Porphyry's perception of how serious a threat Christianity, with its ever-growing number of adherents, posed against the religious pluralism of the traditional world.

Augustine and Porphyry

Obviously, Porphyry's view stands in stark contrast to the Christian way of thinking, which is that one and *only* one path can lead to God and to salvation. It becomes abundantly clear that this is a significant point of dispute in the religious conflict – and in the dialogue – throughout Late Antiquity when we look at the treatment that Porphyry is accorded by the church father Augustine (354-430 CE).

After originally converting to neo-Platonic Christianity, Augustine later shifted his position, and over time he also came to look critically upon neo-Platonism (a subject treated in greater detail in Chapter 6). And Porphyry is one of those whose work must bear the brunt of the attacks in Augustine's literary discourse. In his *De Civitate Dei contra Paganos* (*City of God against the Pagans*), which represents one of the high points in the apologetic tradition in Latin, the church father is particularly diligent in his response to Porphyry's criticism and arguments. Looking, for instance, at book 10.32 in this work (*De Civitate Dei* for short), we find the theme to be Porphyry's notion that various religious movements offer different paths to God. And the chapter heading quickly establishes its style and content:

> Of the universal way of the soul's deliverance, which Porphyry did not find because he did not rightly seek it, and which the grace of Christ has alone thrown open.

Augustine refers to the conclusion of the first book in Porphyry's work on the return of the soul to God (*De Regressu Animae*), contending that Porphyry writes here that:[66]

> no system of doctrine which furnishes the universal way for delivering the soul has as yet been received, either from the truest philosophy, or from the ideas and practices of the Indians, or from the reasoning of the Chaldæans, or from any source whatever, and that no historical reading had made him acquainted with that way, he manifestly

---

66 Augustine, *De Civ. Dei* 10.32.

> acknowledges that there is such a way, but that as yet he [Porphyry] was not acquainted with it.

If we are to believe Augustine in this matter, then Porphyry has no doubt that such a way does exist since "he [Porphyry] does not say that there is no such way". Porphyry, a man of no mediocre abilities, does not question that such a way exists, as Augustine puts it, continuing:[67]

> And no wonder; for Porphyry lived in an age when this universal way of the soul's deliverance—in other words, the Christian religion – was exposed to the persecutions of idolaters and demon-worshippers, and earthly rulers, that the number of martyrs or witnesses for the truth might be completed and consecrated, and that by them proof might be given that we must endure all bodily sufferings in the cause of the holy faith, and for the commendation of the truth. Porphyry, being a witness of these persecutions, concluded that this way was destined to a speedy extinction, and that it, therefore, was not the universal way of the soul's deliverance, …

In this instance we find Augustine reducing Porphyry's criticism so it seems to rely solely on the conclusion that because Rome's emperors persecuted Christians, the Christian doctrine could hardly represent a tenable pathway to the redemption of the soul. (The significance that Christian martyrdom held for the acculturation we are investigating here is discussed at length in Chapter 4.) In addition, Augustine takes the opportunity to interpret the course of history, the prosecution of Christians and the Christian martyrs as God's underscoring of the victory of the one universal path to Him, and of salvation obtained through suffering. At the end of Augustine's book 10, the author sums up God's will and all that is predicted and promised in the scriptures of the universal way:[68]

---

67   Here Augustine is alluding to the persecution of Christians that took place during Porphyry's lifetime under the reigns of Emperor Decius (249-251), Emperor Valerian (257-260), and Emperor Diocletian (284-305).
68   Augustine, *De Civ. Dei* 10.32.

> For the incarnation of Christ, and all those important marvels that were accomplished in Him, and done in His name; the repentance of men and the conversion of their wills to God; the remission of sins, the grace of righteousness, the faith of the pious, and the multitudes in all parts of the world who believe in the true divinity; the overthrow of idolatry and demon worship, and the testing of the faithful by trials; the purification of those who persevered, and their deliverance from all evil; the day of judgment, the resurrection of the dead, the eternal damnation of the community of the ungodly, and the eternal kingdom of the most glorious city of God, ever-blessed in the enjoyment of the vision of God – these things were predicted and promised in the Scriptures of this way;

Although in Augustine's discourse Porphyry does not draw the monotheistic aspect of the Christian religion into doubt, his accommodating religious diversity within a monotheistic scaffolding is in contravention of Christian doctrine. Religious diversity is, in itself, the very cornerstone in traditional Graeco-Roman religion that Christianity fought so hard to undermine, and which apparently in Augustine's day still remained a serious problem for the Church. That is why it was so essential for Augustine and other Christian writers of the fourth and fifth centuries to state their positions and to continue to speak out against the views of a prominent third-century philosopher like Porphyry. And that is precisely why, in his *De Civitate Dei*, Augustine must continue to build on the constructed image of a religious enemy that revolves around two distinct yet related pivotal elements: firstly, a systematic denigration and branding of all Graeco-Roman cults as *superstitio*; and secondly, systematic attacks on significant representatives of Graeco-Roman philosophy, including neo-Platonism (mainly as represented by Plotinus and Porphyry) and Stoicism (notably demonstrated by Cicero and Seneca). Augustine's construction of religious enemy images is also part and parcel of the wider focus on the themes of sin and repentance, and suffering and salvation, which we shall be revisiting in Chapters 4 and 6.

Religious pluralism and the regimen of God in the multicultural Roman Empire?

Overall we must conclude that although here we are dealing with an extremely fragmented and highly problematic body of sources, it is still possible to trace elements and obvious trends throughout an ongoing religious debate in Late Antiquity. And the debate we see reflects a dynamic and conflictual interaction between two different religions, two different views of the past and the present, and very different expectations to the future. The mutually fuelled religious conflict and construction of religious enemies on both sides reveal decisive differences, not only with respect to monotheism and polytheism, but also with respect to the concept of truth, the links between religion and (moral) philosophy, social and religious innovation and organization, and the perception of history. One of the greatest religious innovations – and one that must have been difficult to digest for a philosopher such as Porphyry – was very probably the incarnation. The concept of God becoming human, and living and acting as a human being among others, and suffering death on the cross, must have been a rather peculiar new idea to any philosophically minded Greek or Roman. The Christian doctrines of incarnation and resurrection insisted that divinity and humanity, immortality and mortality, were not incompatible, and furthermore this innovation was not introduced as a new kind of mythical explanation but as a historical fact. Also, as mentioned earlier the notions of creation, the authoritative commandments, and the concept of divine mercy were new religious elements that caused a significant amount of wonder, bafflement, and outrage amongst contemporary non-Christians. The Christians asserted that mankind was bound by sin and subjected to the judgment of God, but at the same time they preached that through faith and repentance a person could be freed, redeemed, and obtain God's forgiveness. This was a religious message that was very new indeed. Another new message was that the end of the world was a part of God's master plan. Not to mention the Christian concept of faith, which was a decisively new idea when seen in a traditional Roman context. But faith alone was not adequate for the philosophical critics of Christianity. The existence of deities was certainly generally accepted in the Graeco-Roman world, but the various stories about them – the myths – were in many cases perceived as the products of poets and writers. This did not imply, however, that the stories were considered to be without importance. The point is that these stories about Greek and Roman gods were by no means regarded as embodying any exclusive or historical truth, unlike what the Christians claimed their various narratives did. In doing this the Christians present their religion and the establishment of the Christian community as a singularly momentous and absolutely decisive turning point in history. And the fact that this view is often – implicitly or explicitly – perpetuated in modern thinking is, of course, associated with the fact that Christianity actually won.

As demonstrated, however, the conflicts we are investigating were not merely about having an animated exchange of clever religious arguments. These exchanges are definitely very serious discussions that certainly use irony and sarcasm very liberally, but which also touch upon topics large and small and shed light on tensions and dilemmas in the contact between cultures. These are issues such as history versus myth, religious and cultural differences, social recognition and exclusion, religious pluralism and cultural continuity, relative versus absolute standpoints, the practice of a critical approach to religious texts, and discussions of presenting tradition and age as valid arguments for credibility. Other issues include the organization of societies, bonds of kinship and cultic community; the relationship between religion and politics, human and divine laws, the Regimen of God, and worship of the emperor, *religio* and *superstitio*; and relationship between Judaism and Christianity, and between Graeco-Roman philosophy and the Christian doctrine. From a sociological perspective focusing on the construction of religious enemies, it is absolutely critical that the new community of Christianity was based upon a purely religious foundation in a way that conflicted with the traditional Graeco-Roman perception of family relations and kinship. As the Gospel of Matthew emphasizes, the person who cannot be an enemy of his own housemates and his own parents cannot be a follower of Jesus Christ:[69]

---

69 *Mat.* 10:34-38. Cf. Max Weber (1920) *Die Wirtschaftsethik der Weltreligionen. Vergleichende religionssoziologische Versuche. Gesammelte Aufsätze zur Religionssoziologie*, Bd. I, Tübingen 1920, pp. 237-275.

> Think not that I am come to send peace on earth: I came not to send peace, but a sword. For I am come to set a man at variance against his father, and the daughter against her mother, and the daughter-in-law against her mother-in-law. And a man's foes shall be they of his own household. He that loveth father or mother more than me is not worthy of me; and he that loveth son or daughter more than me is not worthy of me.

Thus, by severing the bonds of kinship, Christianity created a new social and religious community and a new congregation based solely on religiousness, which was not bound by (but was, rather, opposed to) the non-Christian world's traditional norms, values, and practices. This new and quite remarkable religious mindset and its overthrow of the traditional social organization was undoubtedly one of many important reasons for the Christians' systematic construction of religious enemies on the one hand, and for the Romans' occasionally very violent counter-reactions on the other. In this perspective, the Roman counter-reactions were expressions of religio-political manifestations and intentions of fixing the influx of a new, foreign, and culturally undermining movement – an aspect that will be further developed as we move along.

At the time when Celsus was writing down his thoughts on Christianity, the actual knowledge people had about Christianity (in its various forms) was fairly limited, at least in certain respects. Nevertheless, the objective of his criticism of Christianity, and later of Porphyry's criticism, was to present an erudite, philosophically oriented discussion of a relatively new religious movement. They discussed the movement's rituals and ideas and its religious organization and methods of recruitment. They discussed the Christian Scriptures, which at that point were circulating in the Roman world, and also the historical and philosophical content of its doctrines, as well as its weaknesses, internal contradictions, and consequences.

The Christian writers, on their part, defended their religion and their organization in the Roman world that surrounded them, which they perceived as degenerate. And staunchly insisting upon the Christian doctrine as the universal truth, they demonstrated in their apologetic treatises that, as a matter of principle, religious pluralism in a multicultural world was simply not to be tolerated. These writings pursued the same line of thinking, with a simplified division of the world into true believers, who must be defended, and pagan enemies, who must be converted.

The aim of the philosophers was to launch verbal attacks at a Christian religion that was regarded as a threat to the foundation and the identity of the Roman Empire. In several different respects, the philosophers' criticisms seem to be dictated by a desire to protect and preserve the traditional religious and political institutions, norms, and values of the Graeco-Roman world. When seen from this angle, their critical approach probably has more to do with fearing the demise of the existing traditional cultures than it has to do with whether this or that Christian idea seems to be more or less absurd.

Questions of religious, moral, and cultural superiority become an important theme in the religious conflict. Both camps operate with a superordinate framework of reference, which they appear to share – yet their discussions reveal how within this framework the parties differ on key points, each perceiving the other as an inferior enemy. Both camps construct images of religious enemies. The philosophers construct an image depicting the Christians as superstitious fanatics who are destroying the traditional social order and imperial power, thereby obstructing religio-political stability and cultural continuity. The Christians depict the Romans as a superstitious and depraved polytheistic culture that obstructs the dogmas of the new Christian religion, the universal historical idea of the regimen of God all over the world.

In short, the clear, unambiguous religious norms, values, and alleged truth of Christianity and its affirmed religious authority appear as a sharply delineated alternative, a sort of inverse mirror-image, of the non-dogmatic religious pluralism of the multicultural Roman Empire.

In recent scholarship there have been certain (evolutionistic) tendencies to minimize the distance between traditional Graeco-Roman religion and the new cults of the Imperial period, including the cult of Christ.[70] These tendencies have especially stressed the so-called late pagan monotheism and

---

70   On "pagan monotheism" see, for instance, P. Athanassiadi & M. Frede (eds) (1999) *Pagan Monotheism in Late Antiquity*, Oxford. For some excellent reflections on this subject, see J. North (2011) "Pagans, Polytheists, and the Pendulum" in North & Price (2011) pp. 479-502. Cf. A. Cameron (2011b) *The Last Pagans of Rome*, Oxford, pp. 14-32.

the circumstance that pagans and Christians were, after all, living in the same world and therefore in many ways had shared frames of reference and so on. Nevertheless, as emphasized here and in the following chapters, the construction of religious enemies is a striking consequence of the formation and the clashes of identities. The conflictual interaction reflects seminal differences in norms, values, attitudes, and behaviour between the carriers of traditional religions on the one hand, and the proponents of the new cult of Christ on the other. In this context it is important to note that the cult of Christ demanded conversion: A radical turning towards the new religion resulting from an equally radical break and denial of the old religion. The Christian brand of monotheism was very exclusive, regarding all other cults as rivals, while most of the pagan supporters of monotheistic thinking did not fight against polytheistic practices, but continued to support the worship of the traditional gods.

***

Despite both parties using stereotyping, which is quite common in connection with the construction of enemies, their constructions are somewhat different. The enemy image the philosophers construct of Christians appears to be the more flexible of the two, given that the philosophical message is embedded in religious pluralism and a culture-bound, relative perspective: Different cultures venerate the divine in various ways. At the same time the official Roman religion is supposed to secure the welfare of the Empire and bind together the Empire itself in an overall Roman identity. In other words, if only the Christians, as a parallel to their Christ cult, would sacrifice to the Roman deities and for the Emperor (as all other followers of local cults did, throughout the vast Roman Empire), then the religious conflict would have been resolved. What made the Christians an especially problematic deviant religion was their total rejection of Roman customs, of Roman rituals, and thereby of Roman welfare and identity.

The construction of a Christian identity is, to a considerable degree, described as a liberation from the ruling social order and the usual cultural approach to the world. And the fact that here we are dealing with a group identity under pressure is evident in the way the community of like-minded (Christians) is praised in strongly idealizing terms as the opposite of the utterly demonic world that surrounds them. The enemy image that the Christian writers construct appears to be more static and immutable in the sense that the problem can only be resolved by total conversion of the pagans to Christianity, the only true doctrine. This circumstance indeed created discordant attitudes and interaction between Christians and non-Christians, but it probably also played a role in keeping the Christian movement intact during its initial period of contact with Roman culture. It brought about a crystal-clear mental, religious, and social segregation into "us" and "them", which permeates both the self-perception of the Christians and the non-Christians' perception of the Christian community. The Christian enemy image reflects a multi-faceted demonization process. For the Christian apologists, one thing is beyond doubt: Man has a soul that lives on after death and is doomed to live on in either eternal bliss or eternal torment. The factors determining where a person's soul ends up are one's faith in God and one's behaviour while living a life that may or may not be in accordance with the instructions laid down by God.

Further to the question of personal salvation or damnation, it is of paramount importance that both the construction of religious enemies and the recruiting of new followers to the cult of Christ are founded on two of the most influential psychological mechanisms in the human life and mind: hope and fear. Man's hopes in life and fear of death; the issue of there potentially being a life after death; and if so, the hope of salvation. "Where there is no fear, in like manner there is no amendment [and] repentance is vain," Tertullian asserts.[71] So it is that fear effectively constitutes a precondition for salvation, and from a Christian point of view this makes fear a positive motivational factor. This stands in stark contrast to, say, a position such as that expressed in the writer Lucian's account of Alexander of Abonoteichus. This story claims that the religious institution of oracles and divination exists only by virtue of the two greatest tyrants in the lives

---

71 Tertullian, *De Paenitentia* 2; *De Spectaculis* 29-30.

of humankind: hope and fear.[72] Chapter 7 explores how these and other psychological and emotional factors not only controlled the lives of private individuals in Antiquity, but also play a dominant role in our postmodern world's culture conflicts and construction of religious enemies.

---

72 Lucian, *Alexander* 8. The debate about Lucian's text and its questions of fiction and/or historical realities concerning Alexander of Abonoteichus and the Glucon oracle is still going on. See, for instance, A. Bendlin (2011) "On the Uses and Disadvatages of Divination. Oracles and their Literary Representations in the Time of the Second Sophistic" in North & Price (2011) pp. 226-241.

Chapter 2

Roman Portents and Christian Miracles – Identity Formation and Rivalry

The main concern of this chapter is to shed light on two matters: Roman divination – one of the most important and most enduring religious institutions in traditional Roman culture – and Christian miracles – a cornerstone cemented into the ancient foundations of the Christian faith. The system constructed around interpreting pagan portents demonstrates the vital roles that this facet of religion played in society and also makes clear the intimate links between Roman religion and politics in Antiquity. And precisely because of its fundamental significance in building Roman culture, the pagan institution of divination became a favourite target in the scathing attacks launched by numerous Christian writers. That is why this chapter also focuses on the wondrous deeds reported and the miracle rivalry that took place in connection with the propagation of Christianity.

From a sociological perspective, miracle rivalry is considered to have been an important element in the construction of new Christian identities, and in legitimizing, consolidating, and spreading the new cult of Christ. In more ways than one Christians built up a new world, and significant building blocks in this process of construction and identity formation were miracle rivalry and the religious enemy images associated with it.

Roman portents

Divination was a pervasive activity in Rome's history, practised from its initial founding and during the regal period, throughout the Republican era, and well into the Roman Empire. The institution of public portents was absolutely elemental to the structure of Roman society, as reflected in

Cicero's assertion that Rome took no action in war or peace without first having observed omens based on birds or entrails.[73] As a Roman institution, public portents served various functions and carried significant weight in religious, social, military, and political affairs (guiding foreign as well as domestic policy decisions). Divination served as the quintessential guarantor of cultural continuity, so it is hardly surprising that Christian sources speak with such vehemence against this institution, labelling the belief in pagan portents as sad, bizarre, obscene superstition.

In practical terms the Roman institution of divination, which was strongly influenced by Etruscan religion, fell into three main categories of portents: the observation of birds (*auspicia*); the reading of entrails (*exta*); and the occurrence of unusual phenomena called prodigies (*prodigia*).[74] Interpreting bird observations, most notably from ravens, vultures, and crows, and examining and interpreting signs in the entrails of sacrificial animals were fixed procedural elements in standard Roman religious practices. These procedural elements were a precondition for all major political activity in Rome. Public acts such as passing laws, organizing public gatherings, holding elections, assembling the Senate, and inaugurating temples could only take place if portents were taken – and had a positive outcome.

Favourable portents were good omens that indicated divine approval of the public acts one intended to carry out. According to Rome's historical-mythical oral tradition the physical founding of the city itself was based upon auspices, and portents also became a vital part of all military operations. Prior to every campaign portents were taken from *exta*, usually from sacrificial sheep or cattle. The ritually slaughtered animal's liver, heart, lungs, or spleen were scrutinized to divine the gods' opinion of the intended military operation. The scattered sources generally indicate that the diviners would primarily inspect the animal's liver, assessing its shape, colour, protrusions, and potential deformities. In this practice of extispicy,

---

73 Cicero, *Div.* 1.3.
74 See, for instance, V. Rosenberger (1998) *Gezähmte Götter. Das Prodigienwesen der römischen Republik*, Stuttgart; S.W. Rasmussen (2003) *Public Portents in Republican Rome*, *ARID* supplementum XXXIV, Rome; S.W. Rasmussen (2008) "Ritual and Identity: a Sociological perspective on the Expiation of Public Portents in Ancient Rome" in A.H. Rasmussen & S.W. Rasmussen (eds) (2008) *Religion and Society. Rituals, Resources and Identity in the Ancient Graeco-Roman World*, *ARID* supplementum XL, Rome, pp. 37-42.

Fig. 4. Relief depicting extispicy, the reading of entrails. This relief, from the early second century CE, bears witness to the crucial role of divination, which besides being thoroughly documented for the Roman Republic also continued well into the period of the Roman Empire. Probably originating from Trajan's Forum, this piece is now part of the Roman Art Collection at the Louvre.

findings were basically divided into favourable and unfavourable portents, respectively called *laeta exta* (literally "happy entrails") and *tristia exta* ("sad entrails"). Many of the sources refer to *caput iocineris* ("the head of the liver"), which was obviously of paramount importance when reading entrails. A lacking or deformed "head" on the sacrificial animal's liver was a terrible omen, whereas a liver with an overgrown or double "head" was very favourable indeed. The same applied if the gall bladder was found to be double.[75]

The third main category of portents was prodigies, a highly diverse group of extraordinary phenomena including earthquakes, solar eclipses, light-

---

75   Rasmussen (2003) pp. 117-148.

ning bolts and thunder, hermaphrodites, hermaphroditic lambs, two-headed calves, five-hoofed foals, mules that were able to reproduce, and all manner of other unusual occurrences. However, prodigies could also be phenomena that, seen from a modern perspective, were extremely unlikely, such as cows or oxen speaking or breathing fire, a cock turning into a hen, substances like blood, milk, mud, or stones raining from the sky, milk or blood bubbling up from the ground, honey or milk flowing from the altar of Jupiter, or statues of deities crying, bleeding, or sweating. Instances of wrongful human behaviour could also be classified as prodigies if the behaviour was contrary to Roman tradition. Examples might be a Vestal virgin of Rome breaking her vow of chastity, or a military commander ignoring bad omens whilst campaigning.[76]

The Romans interpreted most prodigies as unfavourable omens signalling that Rome's peace with the gods (*pax deorum*) had been disrupted. That is why the prodigies were expiated each year. Expiation rituals consisted, for instance, in carrying out certain types of sacrifices or processions, preparing meals for the gods, or erecting statues and temples. The sources also list various standard expiations triggered by the occurrence of particular prodigies, say the discovery of a hermaphrodite. According to Livy, such a person must be removed from Roman soil and drowned: The unfortunate hermaphrodite would be confined in a box, taken out to sea, and thrown overboard.[77] A remark found in the writings of Pliny the Elder does suggest, however, that Roman culture altered its perception of hermaphrodites over time. Whereas such individuals were originally considered prodigies, Pliny indicates that they later came to be regarded as a source of (carnal) pleasure.[78]

From a sociological point of view, all of these prodigies indicate different kinds of social disorder or societal imbalance. Their ritual expiation was therefore a means to re-establish social order and stability. In this fashion the Roman institution of public portents served to safeguard and perpetuate the norms and values that reigned in society, thereby ensuring cultic and cultural continuity.

---

76 For a tabular list of prodigies and expiations during the Roman Republic, see Rasmussen (2003) pp. 53-116.
77 Livy 27.37.5-7.
78 Pliny, *NH* VII.3.

Religio-political procedure

The sources enable us to draw a picture of a very specific religio-political procedure used in Republican Rome to handle the class of portents known as prodigies.[79] When a peculiar phenomenon had been observed, the event was reported to the Senate in Rome. Such phenomena could apparently be reported to a consul by anyone who saw them. The consuls would present their prodigy reports, after which the Senate could consult one or multiple priesthoods before deciding whether or not the phenomenon in question was a public *prodigium*, which would then require expiation. The Senate appears to have had three options when processing a prodigy report:

1. to refuse to recognize the bizarre phenomenon as a *prodigium*, referring for instance to the unreliability of the witness
2. to accept the phenomenon as being a *prodigium*, but to deny it status as a public prodigy with relevance for the state
3. to recognize the phenomenon as a public prodigy, meaning it was an unfavourable omen that consequently had to be dealt with through public expiation.

The fact that the Senate and the involved priesthoods thus defined, interpreted, and acted as mediums for communicating the will of the gods naturally demonstrates that they wielded a considerable amount of religio-political power. In other words, the Senate and the priesthoods – effectively the Roman elite – were in a position to establish what was, or was not, in accordance with the acceptable norms, values, and behaviours of Roman society.[80] Indeed, the sources clearly show that public portents and the fixed religio-political procedures that went along with them were a crucial fix point for Roman society as a whole. One thing that supports this assertion is that public portents seem to have been the first item on the Senate's agenda – implying that in the Roman world, discussing such matters took

---

79 Rasmussen (2003) pp. 35-52.
80 Prodigies could be interpreted by the two Roman priesthoods *decemviri sacris faciundis* and *pontifices*, and also by the Etruscan *haruspices*, cf. Rasmussen (2003) pp. 169-182.

precedence even over affairs of war and peace.[81] What is more, consuls were not permitted to leave Rome for their provinces until ritual atonement of the recognized public prodigies had been completed. In fact, the sources contain several examples of consuls having to delay their departure because of portents and their subsequent rituals of public expiation.[82] In this way portents played a role in legitimizing, institutionalizing, and regulating social and religious attitudes and behaviours.

Furthermore, the institution of public portents established religious links between the past, the present, and the future: The past lay in applying the ancestors' traditional knowledge to interpret the divine omens; the present lay in the here-and-now of making amends through expiation, thereby re-establishing social stability; and the future lay in the ritual expiatory acts' ability to appease the gods and thereby (hopefully) safeguard the balance, well-being, and continuity of society.

Research history in this field has sometimes tended to follow the Christian church fathers, who perceived the portents of the Roman world as bizarre and irrational *superstitio*.[83] Other scholars have regarded public portents as an institution that was primarily motivated by political plotting and power-brokering and was invented by the Roman elite to manoeuvre certain decisions through the political system.[84] Yet for one thing, the sources demonstrate with great clarity that divination was a firmly integrated institution in official Roman *religio*, and only in very few instances do the sources reject public portents as *superstitio*. Another thing is that we find relatively few examples of actual political manipulation carried through by means of public portents. Even though the potential for political exploitation was definitely and patently present, the concrete examples of deception and trickery are far from sufficient to explain the existence of a religio-political institution that functioned consistently, year in and year out, for many centuries.

---

81 Livy 24.11.1.
82 Livy 24.47.7; 27.11.1; 27; 23; 32.9.1.
83 See, for instance, F.B. Krauss (1930) *An Interpretation of the Omens, Portents, and Prodigies Recorded by Livy, Tacitus, and Suetonius*, Philadelphia PA, pp. 23-25; R.J. Goar (1972) *Cicero and the State Religion*, Amsterdam, pp. 57-74.
84 See, for instance, H.H. Scullard (1951) *Roman Politics 220-150 B.C.*, Oxford; U. Heibges (1969) "Religion and Rhetoric in Cicero's Speeches", *Latomus* 28;1969, p. 846; L.R. Taylor (1975) *Party Politics in the Age of Caesar*, Berkeley CA, pp. 87-90.

Over the years scholars of Antiquity have also thought long and hard about Roman beliefs, pondering whether Romans genuinely believed in such portents, be it auspices taken from interpreting avian behaviour, readings from examining animal entrails, or prodigies such a rains of blood, sweating statues, or talking cows. So: Did the Romans seriously think that a statue of a god would sweat with anxiety or anger, or did they know that such a statue could not have been bothered by fits of sweating, but simply had a surface where condensation happened to gather? There are two necessary objections to this question that must be raised: Firstly, any sort of modern scientific distinction between phenomena that are possible/impossible in terms of physics is utterly irrelevant in the Antique context currently under discussion. The crucial point is that the Senate actually treated such prodigy reports on things like perspiring deities and talking cows, and subsequently acted upon them. This shows that portents had a high priority among the political community and were of decisive importance to Roman society and history. Secondly, posing an either/or question like the one above is somewhat misleading when discussing the topic in terms of the sociology of religion. A society can most certainly be familiar with the causes of an unusual phenomenon, its actual scientific or astronomical explanation for instance, and yet at the same time in certain situations choose other explanations as *more* relevant and *more* important from a religious and societal point of view. A good example of this is solar eclipses, which could be perceived and recognized as portents in Antiquity despite the fact that the ancient civilizations were well aware of their "natural" explanation and even able to calculate when they would occur. Or consider the ability of beasts to behave oddly, for instance by producing intelligible speech and thus becoming a line of communication between gods and mortals. This was just one of many Roman religious beliefs. Provided the Senate recognized such a portent, the talking animal would be considered a concrete expression that the gods were displeased. According to the expiation guidelines followed by the priests, a speaking cow or ox was to be tended and guarded with particular diligence and would henceforth graze on public lands.[85]

---

85 For more on speaking cattle, see the prodigy table in Rasmussen (2003), items 7; 59; 77; 92; 93; 112; 123. See also Livy 35.21.5; 41.13.3; Obsequens 27; Pliny the Elder *Naturalis Historia* (*Natural History*) 8.183.

Emperors and omens

It is interesting that portents during the imperial era reflect the change in the way the Roman Empire was ruled after the fall of Republican Rome. Their significance shifted, from being a matter of collective public concern to being more narrowly focused on the individual emperor and his power – or lack of it.

In the year 69 CE the generals of Rome were virtually standing in line to succeed one another as Emperor. Civil war was a reality. Galba had had himself declared emperor but was murdered when Otho, previously one of his supporters, bribed the Praetorian Guard to shift their allegiance – to him. Otho, who was then hailed as emperor by the Praetorian Guard, committed suicide after he was subdued by Vitellius. And just a few months after Vitellius had been elevated to the imperial throne, he himself was assassinated. The ultimate victor in the civil war was Vespasian (emperor 69-79 CE), supreme commander in the war effort against the rebellious province of Judaea, who gained Senate recognition as Rome's new emperor on 22 December 69. The Senate's decision to officially confirm Vespasian's position of power has survived as an eminent inscription from the period, allocating to Vespasian all of the formal powers previously invested in the emperors Augustus, Tiberius, and Claudius. (The religio-political status of the Roman emperors is treated at some length in Chapter 5.)

Furthermore, in his biographical account of Vespasian's imperial reign, the Roman historian Suetonius describes how Vespasian, while in Alexandria, received the news of his victory in the civil war: Vespasian went to visit a temple of Serapis to consult the auspices as to the duration of his power, and there he had an unusual vision portending his victory. According to Suetonius, the new emperor also exhibited extraordinary healing powers:[86]

> Vespasian as yet lacked prestige and a certain divinity, so to speak, since he was an unexpected and still new-made emperor; but these also were given him. A man of the people who was blind, and an-

---

86   Suetonius, *Div. Vesp.* 7.

other who was lame, came to him together as he sat on the tribunal, begging for the help for their disorders which Serapis had promised in a dream; for the god declared that Vespasian would restore the eyes, if he would spit upon them, and give strength to the leg, if he would deign to touch it with his heel. Though he had hardly any faith that this could possibly succeed, and therefore shrank even from making the attempt, he was at last prevailed upon by his friends and tried both things in public before a large crowd; and with success.

This account from Suetonius illustrates how the portents of the Roman Empire could establish and/or consolidate the power, status, and prestige of particular individuals. In fact, it really does not take much of a mental leap to move from this type of pagan omens to Christian miracles. From a Christian perspective certain aspects of Roman divination turned out to be extremely enduring, stubbornly surviving as vestiges of Rome's heathen cultural heritage and causing great frustration among the fathers of the Christian church.

Although they were vehemently attacked, it gives food for thought that some of the pagan omens actually recur, albeit in revised form, in descriptions of certain Christian miracles. As early as 100 years before the birth of Christ, Roman religious tradition mentions omens from bleeding loaves of bread, talking cows, weeping statues, and the like. Christian miracles contain analogous accounts of Holy Communions where the Host bleeds, and where bread is transformed into flesh and wine into blood. As the following section shows, the various versions we have of early Christian miracles also include episodes with talking donkeys, lions, and dogs, and even a wooden cross that speaks. Such miracles are good examples of how the institutionalization of Christianity contained important elements of the paganism it ostensibly rejected.

Although pagan portents and Christian miracles, respectively, merit investigation within their own numerous and diverse contexts, generally speaking there can be no doubt as to their essential importance and functions. Portents and miracles alike served as religiously legitimizing and identity-generating institutions in the world of Antiquity. Not only did they provide a means of consolidating the prevailing social, political, and religious positions and ideas. They were also able to portend, legitimize, and consolidate new political and religious figures and cults. The traditional institution of Roman divination was most notably a powerful tool for linking the past, the present, and the future, and for ensuring social balance and cultural continuity. The Christian miracles, on the other hand, were primarily a powerful tool for legitimizing and manifesting an innovation: a new cult with a new god – the one and only God – and with a different system of beliefs and rituals, and new and different values and modes of behaviour.

Christians and miracles

An important and very basic element in Christian faith was the belief in miracles, which first and foremost included believing in the resurrection of Christ. In the words of the Christian apostle and missionary Paul of Tarsus:[87]

> Now if Christ be preached that he rose from the dead, how say some among you that there is no resurrection of the dead? But if there be no resurrection of the dead, then is Christ not risen: And if Christ be not risen, then is our preaching vain, and your faith is also vain. Yea, and we are found false witnesses of God; because we have testified of God that he raised up Christ: whom he raised not up, if so be that the dead rise not.

From a sociological point of view the Christian miracles were religiously quite effective: they legitimized new religious ideas and ways of behaving as well as a new religious identity.[88] Acts that aroused awe and wonder were convincing and won converts for the Christian ideas. Often these miracles illustrated the very cultural encounter, the clash, between Christianity and the pagan world because they encouraged people to reject pagan ways and

---

87 *1 Cor.* 15:12-15.
88 On relevant aspects of Christian identity in this context, see J. Lieu (2004) *Christian Identity in the Jewish and Graeco-Roman World*, Oxford; J. Lieu (2011) "Forging of Christian Identity and the *Letter to Diognetus*" in J. North & S. Price (eds) *The Religious History of the Roman Empire. Pagans, Jews and Christians*, Oxford, pp. 435-459.

embrace the Christian faith. Christian miracles where therefore portrayed not only as a sign, but also as an acid test for the one true faith. This is exemplified in one of the seminal Christian accounts from the first century about a miracle that occurred while the apostles Barnabas and Paul were visiting the Roman colony of Lystra in Asia Minor:[89]

> And there sat a certain man at Lystra, impotent in his feet, being a cripple from his mother's womb, who never had walked: The same heard Paul speak: who steadfastly beholding him, and perceiving that he had faith to be healed, said with a loud voice, "Stand upright on thy feet." And he leaped and walked. And when the people saw what Paul had done, they lifted up their voices, saying in the speech of Lycaonia, "The gods are come down to us in the likeness of men." And they called Barnabas, Jupiter; and Paul, Mercurius, because he was the chief speaker. Then the priest of Jupiter, which was before their city, brought oxen and garlands unto the gates, and would have done sacrifice with the people. Which when the apostles, Barnabas and Paul, heard of, they rent their clothes, and ran in among the people, crying out, and saying, "Sirs, why do ye these things? We also are men of like passions with you, and preach unto you that ye should turn from these vanities unto the living God, which made heaven, and earth, and the sea, and all things that are therein: Who in times past suffered all nations to walk in their own ways. Nevertheless he left not himself without witness, in that he did good, and gave us rain from heaven, and fruitful seasons, filling our hearts with food and gladness." And with these sayings scarce restrained they the people, that they had not done sacrifice unto them.

Here the miracle is a means to convert others, and to clarify and distinguish true faith from pagan beliefs. For the lame man in the story, the Christian miracle brings healing, personal salvation, and a new Christian identity. For Barnabas and Paul, the Christian miracle performed among heathens initially leads to a misinterpretation of their status, as they are

---

89 *Acts* 14:8-18.

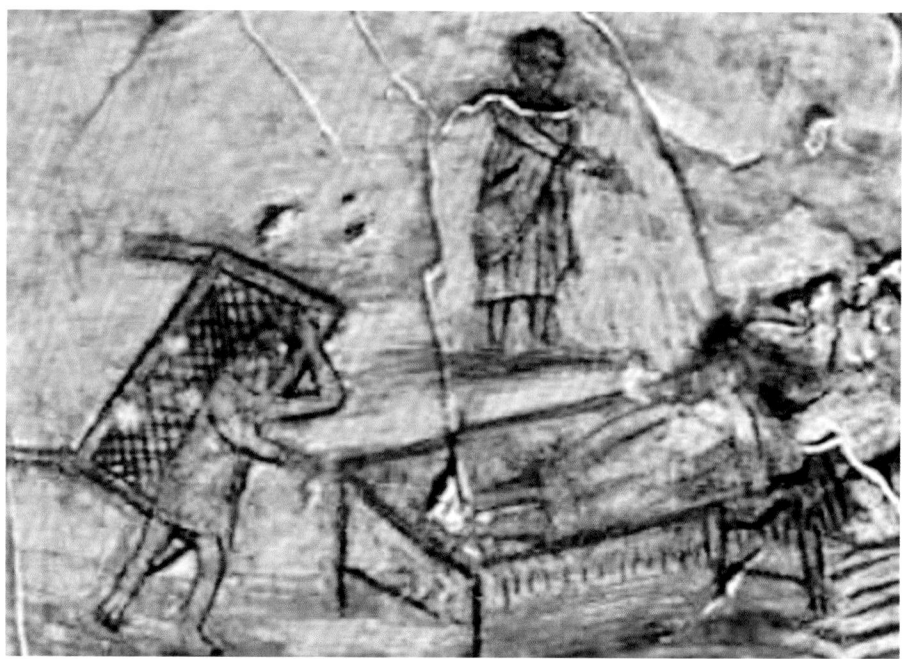

Fig. 5. *The Healing of the Paralytic*, c. 235 CE. Wall fresco from the baptistery at Dura-Europos (in Modern Syria), now part of the Dura-Europos Collection at the Yale University Gallery of Fine Art. This wall painting, portraying the miraculous healing of the paralytic, is one of the earliest known representations of Christ. On the right, the paralytic lies on his bed; in the centre stands Christ, who according to the Gospel of Matthew (9:6-8) is saying, "… that you may know that the Son of Man has power to forgive sins: rise up, take up your bed and walk"; and on the left, the man is seen walking away with his bed. Cf. Luke 5:18-25; Mark 2:3-12.

taken for deities. But the true interpretation is explained in the Scripture, and from a Christian perspective the miracle confirms the Christian view, demonstrating the difference between genuine faith and pagan beliefs. The miracle also simultaneously consolidates Paul's position as a pivotal figure in the propagation of the Christian doctrine. Furthermore, the prophesies and miracles of Jesus Christ bear witness to his religious identity as one sent by God, and as the worker of the wondrous deeds God sent him to Earth to perform.

Miracles and conversion

Miracles helped to recruit new followers for Christ and to reinforce the faith of those who were already believers. But because there were different versions of early Christianity, the various miracles were also interpreted in different ways. Even so, a shared feature was that miracles were regarded as extraordinary signs of God's almighty power over, and judgments passed upon, mortals and their fates. The early Christians saw miracles as manifestations that openly and publicly prove the Lord's existence, power, and control for all to witness; the immediate audience as well as those hearing or reading the accounts of miraculous events. And Christian miracles could serve either to reward or to punish humankind.

This made the combination of miracle rivalry and missionary work an essential element in the promulgation of the Christian doctrine. Important sources that support this include Paul's letters and narratives in The New Testament book of *Acts*, which recount the apostles' extensive travels and strategies to spread the word of Jesus Christ. Among numerous other events, *Acts* describes Paul's stay in Ephesus and the related miracles, rivalry, and conflicts between Christians and Jews, along with the conversion of Jews and Greeks to Christianity. The claim here is that within two years the whole population of the province of Asia became familiar with the word of the Lord Jesus.[90]

Naturally, from a historical point of view this claim seems a trifle over-confident. It does, however, reflect the bold ambitions of the new religion's mission strategy.[91] The Bible text describes miracles and rivalry that

---

90 *Acts* 19:8-10. Cf. G.W. Clarke (1996) "The origin and spread of Christianity" in *The Cambridge Ancient History*, 2nd ed. vol. X, pp. 848-872, Cambridge; M. Humphries (2006) *Early Christianity*, London.

91 In his letter to the Romans, Paul describes his missionary work as follows (*Rom.* 15:18-21): "For I will not dare to speak of any of those things which Christ hath not wrought by me, to make the Gentiles obedient, by word and deed, through mighty signs and wonders, by the power of the Spirit of God; so that from Jerusalem, and round about unto Illyricum, I have fully preached the gospel of Christ. Yea, so have I strived to preach the gospel, not where Christ was named, lest I should build upon another man's foundation: But as it is written, To whom he was not spoken of, they shall see: and they that have not heard shall understand."

amply illustrate the distinction between pagan and believer, the fear and awe of God's omnipotence, and the conversions to which this gave rise:[92]

> And God wrought special miracles by the hands of Paul: So that from his body were brought unto the sick handkerchiefs or aprons, and the diseases departed from them, and the evil spirits went out of them. Then certain of the vagabond Jews, exorcists, took upon them to call over them which had evil spirits the name of the Lord Jesus, saying, "We adjure you by Jesus whom Paul preacheth." And there were seven sons of one Sceva, a Jew, and chief of the priests, which did so. And the evil spirit answered and said, "Jesus I know, and Paul I know; but who are ye?" And the man in whom the evil spirit was leaped on them, and overcame them, and prevailed against them, so that they fled out of that house naked and wounded. And this was known to all the Jews and Greeks also dwelling at Ephesus; and fear fell on them all, and the name of the Lord Jesus was magnified. And many that believed came, and confessed, and shewed their deeds. Many of them also which used curious arts brought their books together, and burned them before all men: and they counted the price of them, and found it fifty thousand pieces of silver. So mightily grew the word of God and prevailed. After these things were ended, Paul purposed in the spirit, when he had passed through Macedonia and Achaia, to go to Jerusalem, saying, "After I have been there, I must also see Rome."

Modern scholarship is sometimes sceptical of the miracles described in the various Christian narratives[93] – in much the same way as historians are sceptical of the pagan portents of Antiquity. In our current discussion of religious and sociological aspects, however, any questions of factuality and credibility in a strictly scientific or historical sense are of negligible importance. What is important here is, first, the religious and social significance attributed to these miracles as demonstrated in the narratives. A second important aspect is the way in which the narratives themselves categorize and reveal the distinctions, conflicts, and rivalry between "true" and "false"

---

92   *Acts* 19:11-21.
93   Cf. Humphries (2006) pp. 120-125.

miracles (that is, between *religio* and *superstitio*). Thirdly, the narratives explicitly and decisively exhibit the links between "true" miracles and the consequent conversion of non-believers to Christianity.

Modern scholars are likewise sceptical of the claims made in these narratives of extensive mass-conversions to the Christian faith. In the context of source criticism it is certainly not unreasonable to harbour misgivings when confronting Christian writers' own descriptions of the successful dissemination of the teachings they consider to be the one true doctrine of faith. However, here it is important to bear in mind that the borders in the religious landscape of the Roman Empire were very fluid, and so it is not unthinkable that quite a large number of non-Christians – for instance in connection with the miraculous workings of the Christians in Ephesus – were ecstatically transported by the thrill of the moment, and/or by fear, and so could very well have praised the Lord en masse, as described in *Acts*. By the same token it is equally possible that the next day, or the next week, some of these converts to Christianity had, for all intents and purposes, largely returned to their domestic cults.

Many Christian texts deal with prophecies and miracles, and descriptions of such events are particularly bountiful in the *apocrypha*, the extra-canonical texts that were not included in the Bible. One such text, known as *The Gospel of the Saviour*, includes passages that depict the crucifixion of Jesus in a version of the event that contradicts the versions in the canonical gospels. In a fragment of *The Gospel of the Saviour*, Jesus himself precisely predicts his own impending death and addresses the cross on which he is to be crucified. He consoles the cross, telling it not to weep or be afraid but to know its Lord, who will ascend upon it, and he promises that the cross will share in his wealth.[94]

Another apocryphal text, *The Gospel of Peter*, recounts the ultimate miracle: the resurrection of Jesus Christ. A notable feature in this gospel is the words Jesus is reported to have spoken on the cross: "My power, O power, you have forsaken me!" His death on the cross is followed by omens. The Sun disappears so that the Jews think night has fallen, and when they remove the nails from the victim's hands the whole earth shakes, terrifying

---

94 Cf. H.C. Kee (1983) *Miracle in the Early Christian World*, London.

the people.⁹⁵ The Jews, realizing that they have brought a great evil upon themselves, seal the tomb of Jesus and set guards about it to prevent anyone from stealing the body. That night the soldiers see two men descend from heaven. The stone at the mouth of the tomb rolls away of its own accord, and both men enter. Jesus is later seen leaving the sepulchre where he was entombed, supported by the two men and followed by the cross itself, which also comes walking out. "And they heard a voice out of the heavens crying, 'Have you preached to those who sleep?' and from the cross there was heard the answer, 'Yes.' "⁹⁶ In a theological interpretation of these apocryphal events, the cross can be seen as a communicative link to those waiting in kingdom of the dead. This interpretation accords the speaking cross a vital role in the act of Christian salvation mediated by the crucifixion of Jesus.

A variety of miraculous deeds are also portrayed in the apocryphal texts concerning the acts of the apostles, which presumably date from the second or third centuries, and which were probably inspired by the *Acts* of the New Testament. Several of these texts also display features known from pagan portents, such as talking animals or a hail storm from a clear sky. The apocryphal *Acts of Thomas*, for instance, tell of a wild donkey that speaks, addressing a crowd and beseeching the people to believe in Jesus Christ and his disciples.⁹⁷ In *The Acts of Paul*, the protagonist is condemned to be thrown to the wild beasts. However, instead of being devoured he is saved by a violent storm of hail that pelts down out of the blue, killing many spectators and all of the wild animals except a single lion – which happens to be capable of speaking with humans. Paul speaks to the lion and says: "And how were you captured?" The lion replies, speaking with its own voice, "Just as you were, Paul." Many of the terrified spectators who survive the hail storm are converted to Christianity by this miraculous sequence of events, and both Paul and the lion leave the arena unharmed.⁹⁸

---

95 The apocryphal *Gospel of Peter* 5:15-20; 6:21-24. See J.K. Elliott (1993) *The Apocryphal New Testament. A Collection of Apocryphal Christian Literature in an English Translation based on M.R. James*, Oxford. For such omens in the canonical texts, see the New Testament, *The Gospel of Matthew* 27:45 and 51; *The Gospel of Mark* 15:33 and 38; *The Gospel of Luke* 23:44-45.
96 *The Gospel of Peter* 9-10.
97 *The Acts of Thomas* 78-79.
98 *The Acts of Paul* 7.

The culture contact's relentless miracle rivalry in the name of spreading the gospel and winning new followers is demonstrated very clearly in the apocryphal *Acts of John*, which include an account of his visit to the temple of Artemis in Ephesus to recruit new followers of Christ. John speaks to the pagan worshippers of Artemis:

> How many miraculous deeds did you see me perform, how many cures! And still you are hardened in the heart and cannot see clearly. What now, men of Ephesus? I have ventured now to come up to this idol's temple, to convince you that you are wholly without God and dead to human reasoning. Behold, here I stand. You all assert that Artemis is powerful. Pray to her, that I alone die! Or if you cannot accomplish this, I alone will call upon my God to kill you all because of your unbelief.[99]

According to the apocryphal text, the Ephesians become petrified with fright after witnessing the miracles of John. Then, while he is speaking, the altar and the representations of the goddess suddenly tumble down, half of the temple collapses, and as the main beam drops from the roof it strikes the priest of Artemis, killing him with a single blow. This episode ostensibly causes many of the pagans gathered there to convert, as they shout out loud:[100]

> "There is only one God, that of John, only one God who has compassion for us; for you alone are God; now we have become converted, since we saw your miraculous deeds. Have mercy upon us, God, according to your will, and deliver us from our great error." And some of them lay on their faces and cried; others bent their knees and prayed; others rent their garments and lamented; still others tried to escape.

Here the clash of religions is depicted through an apostle of Christ and a priest of Artemis locked in a contest so fierce that not only the knees of the pagans but the very columns of the temple tremble and buckle. This is a

---

99   *The Acts of John* 39.
100 *The Acts of John* 42.

miracle meant to forewarn the pagans and to expose the Artemis cult's defeat and the Christian God's power and control even over the fate of non-believers. Note that speaking to the heathens in Ephesus, John employs a highly adversarial, threatening approach to make them convert to his faith:[101]

> You drunkard and brawler, realize that you lose your senses by serving a vile, filthy passion! You who have pleasure in gold and ivory and precious stones, do you see the things you love when the night has set in? You who indulge in soft raiment and depart this life, will these help you in the place you go to? Let the murderer know that the merited punishment is double in the time after he goes from here! In like manner the poisoner, sorcerer, robber, defrauder, sodomite, thief, and all who belong to that band, accompanied by your works you shall go into the fire that never shall be quenched, to utter darkness, to the pit of torture, and to external damnation. Therefore, men of Ephesus, repent; understand also that kings, rulers, tyrants, boasters, warmongers depart naked from this world, to suffer pain in everlasting torment …

Miraculous healing is also a highly efficient method of converting heathens, as evidenced in descriptions of the religious collisions between Christians and pagans. The travelling missionary and apostle Andrew, for example, (known from the four canonical gospels as a brother of Peter) was particularly renowned for his power to cure all manner of diseases and exorcise demons. The apocryphal *Acts of Andrew* describe his arrival at Patras, where he converted the Roman proconsul's wife. Andrew is thrown into prison, but undaunted he continues to preach from his cell. The proconsul's reaction is swift: He accuses Andrew of being a nuisance and an enemy who has poisoned the mind of the proconsul's wife and ensnared her into believing

---

101 *The Acts of John* 35-36. A far less dramatic and far more entertaining miracle, recounted in the apocryphal *Acts of John* 60-61, takes place at an inn, where John is trying to sleep but is disturbed by bedbugs. He orders them to disappear and to stay away from the servants of the Lord. The vermin obey him, and the next morning John, his mood greatly improved, says to them: "'Since you have been wise to heed my warning, go back to your place!' When he had spoken and had risen from the bed, the bugs hastened from outside the door to the bed, ran up the legs into the joints and disappeared."

in the god of the Christians.[102] At his command, Andrew is flogged and crucified. Andrew, however, smiles and laughs, and for three days and three nights he speaks from the cross to the multitude of people gathered round. The rebellious crowd demands his release, but this only moves Andrew to lament their laxity and love of the flesh – and indeed, Andrew looks forward to being liberated from his earthly life. When the proconsul decides to release him from the cross, Andrew heaps his own share of rebuke on him, labelling the proconsul as an enemy, a fraud, a flatterer, a braggart, a shameless devil, a harasser, and a murderer. The narrative culminates as Andrew's successful mission for Christianity ends with his death as a martyr: Still on the cross, and still volubly exulting the Lord even with his last breath, Andrew finally gives up the ghost.[103]

The *Acts of Peter* take us into the midst of a veritable and very concrete miracle war in Rome between a certain Simon Magus and the apostle Peter. Simon Magus is described as an enemy and a destroyer of the cult of Christ, branded as the messenger of Satan, a bewitcher, and a sorcerer with the ability to fly.[104] It is said of Simon that he:[105]

> addressed the people and said with a shrill voice, "On the following day about the seventh hour you shall see me fly over the gate of the city in the same form in which I now speak to you."

When the people actually did see Simon fly the next day, their esteem for him grew considerably. To make matters worse, the cult of Christ actually began to lose followers because of Simon's airborne antics. But Peter rose to the challenge, travelling to Rome to champion the Christian cause. When Peter was denied access to Simon Magus he addressed the crowd, telling them:[106]

> "You are about to see a great and wonderful sign." And Peter saw a big dog, tied by a big chain, and he went and loosened him. The dog,

---

102 *The Acts of Andrew* 51.
103 *The Acts of Andrew* 62-63.
104 *The Acts of Peter* 7-29.
105 *The Acts of Peter* 4. Cf. the New Testament's book of *Acts*, 8:9-24.
106 *The Acts of Peter* 9.

being loosed, became endowed with a human voice and said to Peter, "What will you have me do, servant of the ineffable living God?" to which Peter said, "Go inside and tell Simon in the presence of the people, "Peter sends word to you to come outside. For on your account I have come to Rome, you wicked man and destroyer of simple souls."

The dog ran into the house, and lifting up its front paws it shouted out Peter's message, loud and clear. The apostle obtained even more converts to Christianity by snatching a smoked fish hanging in a window (and therefore quite obviously dead) and tossing the fish into a pool, where it miraculously began swimming about.[107] Wondrous deeds of this sort certainly did win new believers for the Christian faith, and in *The Acts of Peter* the holy man is victorious in the battle against Simon. According to the apocryphal account, Peter was able not only to stop followers from leaving the Christ cult, but also to re-establish peace and order amongst the Christian congregation in Rome.

As these examples show, miracle rivalry was a struggle for religious identity and recognition, and a fight to win over new believers. This rivalry was basically about establishing who represented the "genuine" miracles and the true *religio*, and who was simply touting suspicious, false sorcery and magic, which was classified as *superstitio*. In all probability, this religious rivalry was of decisive importance to the spread of the various versions of early Christianity, for instance as reflected in the apocryphal texts. It is true that modern theological scholarship sometimes asserts that these written sources are unreliable, precisely because they contain so many strange and intriguing miracles.[108] Nevertheless, from a sociological perspective the apocryphal texts cannot be dismissed offhand simply because they do not enjoy official status as part of the canon of the Christian Church. One miracle can hardly be considered as more (or less) strange, colourful, intriguing, genuine, and/or (un)reliable than any other – whether the account of the miraculous event

---

107 *The Acts of Peter* 13.
108 An exampe is Drobner's remark that the apocryphal texts were not canonized "partly because they are overgrown with legends and abstruse miracle accounts and, on the whole, therefore do not demonstrate the same reliability as the canonical books." Drobner (2007) p. 14.

itself is, or is not, part of an apocryphal source. Hence, any inclination to reject apocryphal miracles and consign them to a special category reserved for particularly spurious miracle-peddling and monstrously mistaken popular superstition bears a distinct resemblance, although in modern guise, to the miracle rivalry of the ancients. In strictly sociological terms, the present context obliges us to treat canonized and apocryphal miracles on an equal footing, and therefore to give them equal credence as expressions of the variety of religious ideas associated with the Christ cult. It is most notably the attempts in the early research history to point to an "original" and "normative" core within early Christianity that seem pointless – bearing in mind that the different religious groupings within Judaism and Christianity by no means were clearly defined or homogeneous entities.[109]

***

To summarize, the examples presented here reflect important features and functions of miracles: They can be used to convince unbelievers, and they can also be used to warn, threaten, and punish in order to promote the conversion of non-believers to Christianity. Miracles that warn and punish are especially illustrative of the Christian construction of religious enemy images, as they concentrate on the Almighty God's control over non-believers and those who go up against God. Such miracles underscore God's power over the fate of all human beings, Christian and non-Christian. To all those who see, hear, and read about the marvellous events, miracles appear to express various types of divine intervention. These formidable manifestations confirm and warn all who witness them that the Lord supports the cult of Christ and ultimately possesses the power to intervene in human lives and worldly events.

The various apocryphal texts distinctly depict the apostles as missionaries and miracle-workers who recruit new followers through their wondrous deeds. At the same time, the New Testament book of *Acts* and similar texts among the apocrypha are strongly reminiscent of martyrdom narratives,

---

109 Cf. A.H. Becker & A.Y. Reed (eds) (2003) *The Ways that Never Parted: Jews and Christians in Late Antiquity and the Early Middle Ages*, Tübingen; S. Price (2011) "Homogeneity and Diversity in the Religions of Rome" in North & Price (2011), pp. 253-275.

describing how the Christian mission, in particular, causes the missionaries to make powerful enemies in situations where early Christianity meets established Roman culture. As the sources demonstrate, however, the missionary apostles veritably long for the persecution and death sentences resulting from their Christian mission on Earth: to preach to non-believers, causing them to repent and be saved. The accounts of apostolic suffering carry a triumphant tone, rejoicing as the martyrs are released from their earthly burdens and mortal flesh. And the Christian premise that justifies martyrdom is the notion that Truth cannot be found in the earthly realm. This key aspect of the encounter between Roman religion and Christianity is discussed in Chapter 4 – following the investigation in Chapter 3 of several basic issues that defined early interaction between Rome on the one hand and Jews and Christians on the other.

Chapter 3

Religio-Political Reactions – Roman Patterns of Expulsion

The Jews in Rome

To facilitate a broader understanding of the early stages of acculturation and religious conflict in ancient Rome, this chapter homes in on a few selected (and in some respects still unresolved) questions concerning the Romans' views on, and treatment of, Jews and Christians.

From about 200 CE and in the centuries that followed, Rome – a rapidly growing metropolis and an increasingly important seat of power – attracted a wide variety of people from foreign lands and cultures, including Jews. Their numbers remain unknown. While the sources, few and fragmented, tell us very little, modern scholars venture to guess that the size of the Jewish minority in Rome was somewhere between 20,000 and 60,000 around the end of the Roman Republic.[110] Like many Greeks, Spaniards, Gauls, Africans, and Syrians, the Jews also came to Rome as slaves, skilled craftsmen, and merchants, and some even achieved Roman citizenship. Based on the literary and epigraphic material it is fair to estimate that during the imperial era, Rome had 11 or so synagogues. Although no archaeological traces of those buildings exist today, remains have been found during excavations in Ostia of a synagogue, the earliest phases of which date back to the first century

---

110 Cf. H. Solin (1983) "Juden und Syrer im westlichen Teil der römischen Welt. Eine ethnisch-demographische Studie mit besonderer Berücksichtigung der sprachlichen Zustände", *ANRW* II.29.2, pp. 587-789; M. Stern (1984) *Greek and Latin Authors on Jews and Judaism*, 3 vols, 1974-1984, Jerusalem; D. Noy (2000) *Foreigners at Rome: Citizens and Strangers*, London; E. Gruen (2002) *Diaspora. Jews amidst Greeks and Romans*, London, pp. 15-53; M. Goodman (1997) *The Roman World. 44 BC – AD 180*, London; M. Goodman (2007) *Rome & Jerusalem. The Clash of Ancient Civilizations*, London.

BCE.[111] Furthermore, archaeological excavations just beyond the outskirts of ancient Rome include seven Jewish catacombs dated to the late second (to early third) century CE onwards.[112]

Rome was one of the first major cities that Christianity reached during its earliest dissemination. However, it is not possible to give any exhaustive picture of the Christians and the conditions under which they lived in Rome, neither during the first, second, or third centuries. Regrettably, the limited number of surviving sources are simply too spread out in space and time, and too insubstantial. Christians did verifiably settle in Rome during the 50s CE, but we do not know how quickly they grew in number.[113] Modern scholarship estimates that around the third century CE the Christian community in Rome numbered somewhere between 10,000 and 30,000 – possibly even as many as 50,000.[114] But the very early Roman Christians met in small groups in private homes, and excavations of the city have revealed no certain traces of Christian (cult) structures in Rome before the time of Constantine the Great. Their private religious meetings undoubtedly served as fertile ground for the native Romans' seeds of suspicion, enmity, and gossip that the sources imply. As mentioned earlier, opponents of Christianity claimed that the Christian community consisted solely of ignorant slaves, foolish womenfolk, poor widows, social outcasts, and the deprived and destitute.

The image of Christianity as a religion that particularly attracted people who were poor or suffering has often been repeated in the research, and undoubtedly to a certain extent this reflects reality. Nevertheless, this image is probably also a result of Christian ideals, and of the self-understanding that pervades some of the sources. This makes it difficult to form a reliable impression of the social width and breadth of Christianity. In fact, certain

---

111 Cf. Beard, North & Price (1998) vol. II, pp.107-108; CIL VI.9821; L.M. White (1990) *Building God's House in the Roman World. Architectural Adaptation among Pagans, Jews and Christians*, London.
112 Cf. L.V. Rutgers (1995) *The Jews in Late Antique Rome*, Leiden; Beard, North & Price (1998) vol. 1, p. 270.
113 Paul wrote a letter to the Christians at Rome around 55 CE.
114 Eusebius, *Historia Ecclesiastica* (*Ecclesiastical History*) VI.43.11. Transl. from A.C. McGiffert (1890) *Nicene and Post-Nicene Fathers*, Second Series, vol. 1, P. Schaff & H. Wace (1890), Buffalo NY. Revised and edited by Kevin Knight (2009). Cf. Beard, North & Price (1998) vol. 1, p. 267.

sources actually indicate that Christians were recruited from virtually every level of the social hierarchy. Inscriptions found on sarcophagi, for instance, bear witness to the Christian beliefs harboured by even very prominent and wealthy men and women, although initially one can imagine that the Roman elite was more sparingly represented among the followers of Christ.[115]

Quite a few of the Christian sources from Antiquity convey the view that compared with Christianity, Judaism constitutes an erroneous and/or inferior interpretation of the relationship between God and human beings.[116] Jesus was a Jew, and Paul was a Jew as well as a Roman citizen, and many of the religious perceptions in the two religions seem to spring from one and the same tradition. However, this by no means simplifies the investigation of, or the relationship between, Judaism and Christianity. On the contrary. Both Jesus and Paul based their thinking, time and again, on the Jewish scriptures, which the Christians referred to as the Old Testament, but even in Jesus's day Judaism was no unified, clear-cut religion. The designation "Jew" was more of an umbrella term covering a multiplicity of groupings, each with its own interpretation of the Jewish Bible, and each claiming to have a monopoly on the proper interpretation. This sort of effort to monopolize in matters of personal faith was by no means characteristic of traditional Roman religion. Not only do we find evidence of the relatively unproblematic coexistence of a hotchpotch of gods and cults on the Roman religion scene. We also find that there was no particular focus on beliefs themselves, but rather a strong focus on ritual know-how; on the correct performance of rituals and participation in the official Roman state and imperial cult.

Another important religious issue that differentiated Judaism (and Christianity) from traditional Roman religion was the intermingling of religion, morals, and laws. The Jewish moral code was anchored in divine instruction and in ancient laws handed down as the word of God.[117] In this context it is interesting that the Roman historian Tacitus emphasizes in his *Historiae*

---

115 Cf. P. Lampe (2003) *From Paul to Valentinus: Christians at Rome in the First Two Centuries*, Minneapolis MN; Beard, North & Price (1998) vol. I, pp. 295-296; vol. II, pp. 334-335.
116 Cf. Goodman (2007); M. Humphries (2006) *Early Christianity*, London, pp. 97-141.
117 Cf. Goodman (2007) pp. 278-285.

how, in order to ensure his future dominion over the people of Israel, Moses introduced entirely new rituals, which were the opposite of what one sees practised by all other peoples:[118]

> To establish his position over the race for the future, Moses introduced novel rites, quite different from those of the rest of the human race. In them everything we hold sacred is profane, and conversely they permit what for us is taboo.

Similarly, the Roman satirist Juvenal calls attention to the absurdity in the Jews' practice of learning to recite Jewish law by heart while completely lacking respect for Roman law. According to Juvenal, they live and abide solely by the laws handed down by Moses:[119]

> Accustomed to despise Roman laws, they learn, follow and observe Jewish law, whatever Moses handed down in his arcane volume: for example, that one should show the way only to a fellow believer, and with people in search of drinking water that one should assist only the circumcised. But it is the father who was at fault; for him every seventh day was given up to laziness, and kept apart from all the concerns of life.

Each and every aspect of Jewish moral doctrine hinged upon religion. Jewish law was also anchored in religion, in that it was regarded as being handed down directly from God to Moses. Roman law, on the other hand, was traditionally perceived as resulting from political decisions, which were made by various assemblies and in later times also by the emperor. Still, this does not mean that Rome's deities played no role in the legal domain. As explained in Chapter 2, divine approval or disapproval in the shape of various types of portents was of fundamental significance to Roman policy-making, including the passing of laws.

---

118 Tacitus, *Historiae* (*Histories*) 5.4. Translation taken from Beard, North & Price (1998) vol. II, p. 273.
119 Juvenal, *Saturae* (*Satires*). 14.102 –106. Translation taken from Beard, North & Price (1998) p. 275.

In general, the non-Christian writers of Antiquity do not seem particularly preoccupied by the presence of Jews in and around Rome, and indeed, the sources only mention them briefly. This also holds true for the earliest references to Jews, where Valerius Maximus states that Jews and Chaldeans were expelled from Rome in 139 BCE.[120] Although the reasons for this expulsion remain unclear, the decision was part of a pattern discernible in Roman religio-politics, one element of which was occasionally banishing various groups of strangers, such as Greek philosophers, Chaldean astronomers, magicians, Jews, and followers of the Isis cult. What is noteworthy about the expulsion in 139 BCE is that the Chaldean astrologers were kicked out of Rome at the same time the Jews were. In other words, the matter was broader than the identity of certain people as Jewish, and was probably more specifically motivated by the Roman authorities' wish to make an example. Seen in this perspective, the bout of expulsion is a demarcation in the face of groups of foreigners in Rome, carried out because of religious ideas and rituals that were classified in a Roman context as *superstitio*. In short, it would have been a religio-political demonstration of power to curb the propagation of *superstitio* in Rome.

According to the historian Tacitus, in the year 19 CE the Roman Senate discussed whether the city ought to prohibit Egyptian and Jewish cults. The resulting senatorial decree ordered that 4000 individuals incriminated by this type of *superstitio* were to be deported to Sardinia. Moreover, the remaining followers of these cults would be banished from Italian soil if they had not given up their pagan rituals by a stipulated date.[121] A similar though not identical account is found in Suetonius's biography of Emperor Tiberius.[122] According to his biographer, Tiberius curtailed foreign cults, Egyptian and Jewish in particular, even going so far as to force devotees to burn their ceremonial robes and other cultic paraphernalia. The emperor also used military service as an excuse to station young Jewish men in provinces with an unhealthy climate, and he drove the rest of their people out of Rome with threats of life-long slavery if they did not comply. Suetonius further

---

120 Valerius Maximus 1.3.3.
121 Tacitus, *Annales* (*Annals*) 2.85.
122 Suetonius, *Tiberius* 36; cf. Cassius Dio, *Historia Romana* (*Roman History*) 57.18.5a.

states that Tiberius also expelled the astrologers, but later pardoned them because they promised to stop practicing their arts.

These two text passages and their information have been the object of extensive scrutiny and led to numerous interpretations in scholarly discussions about Roman attitudes to, and Rome's treatment of, the Jews at Rome.[123] One topic of discussion is whether the limitations described above should be regarded as a new imperial approach to Jewish religion *in particular*.[124] Here one must not overlook the fact that the Senate's decision and both passages in the text refer not only to the cult of the Jews, but also to that of the Egyptians, in addition to which Suetonius also speaks of a group of foreign astrologers in Rome. Thus, the sanctions in question apply to no fewer than three groups with foreign religions. This suggests that here (as in the above-mentioned instance from 139 BCE) the Senate sought to carry out a general manoeuvre against practitioners and propagators of foreign *superstitio*. Manoeuvres of this sort can therefore be interpreted as more or less heavy-handed demonstrations to achieve temporary "cultural closure" (which I refer to elsewhere as "fix"). These demonstrations were initiated by the Roman rulers with a view to manifesting the significance of traditional Roman *religio* as a move to counter the foreign *superstitio* that accompanied the massive culture inflow ("flux") so characteristic of Rome during this period. Seen in this perspective, the object of the Senate's discussions and decrees was to consolidate Roman religion, which they then did by means of an institutionalized – though only occasionally employed – pattern of religio-political expulsion. It was therefore hardly a step in establishing some strikingly new or permanent religious enemy image, the construction of which specifically targeted the Jews as a people. Presumably the case as it stood in 19 CE – and similar cases – are, above all, a matter of exerting religio-political control and asserting the predominance of traditional Roman religion and identity in a world that was strongly characterized by numerous processes of migration, acculturation, and Romanization – effectively the "globalization" of that age.

Cicero, writing in 59 BCE, also refers to the Jews' religious notions as

---

123 Cf. Gruen (2002) pp. 15-53.
124 Cf. H.D. Slingerland (1997) *Claudian Policymaking and the Early Imperial Repression of Judaism at Rome*, Atlanta GA.

"barbaric *superstitio*",[125] additionally pointing out that the Jews in Rome have a strong sense of community, and that if necessary they are willing to demonstrate to promote their cause. We can therefore reasonably deduce that even though the Roman authorities periodically banished Jews (and other groups), and even though many Romans looked askance at Jewish beliefs and customs, the Jews were still included in Roman society in such a way that they overtly showed a willingness, and were given or took the opportunity, to exert pressure on the Roman society in which they lived.[126] So when Cicero rants against the Jews and their *superstitio*, this should hardly be interpreted as expressing a particular constructed enemy image that existed at that time. Rather, it should be viewed as an element employed by Cicero, astute lawyer and legendary orator that he was, as part of his professional strategy and fierce rhetoric – the same sort of rhetoric that Cicero equally (or even more vociferously) used against other peoples in the case he was arguing at the time, and in later, similar cases.[127]

A remark found in the writings of Suetonius further demonstrates that the Jews were a group of foreigners who were comparatively well integrated in Roman society. Describing the people's grief in connection with the funeral of Julius Caesar in 44 BCE, the historian mentions that large numbers of non-Romans also joined in the mourning:[128]

> At the height of the public grief a throng of foreigners went about lamenting each after the fashion of his country, above all the Jews, who even flocked to the place for several successive nights.

Still, the beliefs and customs of Judaism clearly filled the Romans with wonder, resentment, and mirth. One source that states this very plainly is

---

125 Cicero, *Pro Flacco* 67.
126 Cicero, *Pro Flacco* 67 and 69; cf. Gruen (2002) pp. 19-22.
127 Cf. Gruen's rejection of Cicero as a representative of Roman anti-Semitism, Gruen (2002) p. 20: "Much ink has been spilled over the attitude of Cicero towards Jews. Does he represent a virulent form of anti-semitism, an example of Roman hostility to that religion and its practitioners? ... Cicero's rhetorical outbursts did not restrict themselves to the Jews, even in this speech – let alone elsewhere in his vituperative repertoire. The needs of the moment dictated the level of vitriol."
128 Suetonius, *Divus Julius* 84.

Tacitus, whose commentary construes the Jewish sabbath as slothfulness, pure and simple:[129]

> They say that they decided to rest on the seventh day because that marked the end of their toils; then the lures of sloth led them to give over the seventh year too to inactivity.

The sources show similar views on the Jewish practice of ritual circumcision, which the Romans apparently found a source repulsion, astonishment, and hilarity. Petronius writes of a well-educated Jewish slave who has only two faults: He is circumcised – and he snores.[130] The poet Horace and satirists such as Juvenal and Martial also lampoon Jewish ritual circumcision, which is occasionally linked to an excess of lust. Regarding the Jews' inclinations in sexual matters, Tacitus further states:[131]

> They eat apart, they sleep separately, and though they are a most lascivious people they abstain from intercourse with foreign women; but among themselves nothing is illicit. They established the practice of circumcision to show that they are different from others.

In connection with ritual circumcision it is also noteworthy that during the reign of Emperor Antonius Pius, in the second century CE, by imperial order Jews were only permitted to have their own sons circumcised. If a Jew had any other boy or man circumcised, slaves included, then he could be sentenced to the same punishment as was meted out for castration.[132] This Roman stance seems to carry quite a powerful message: In the Roman cultural sphere Jews were allowed to follow their own customs and traditions, but must not spread them to non-Jews.

Finally, the Romans found it curious and comical that the Jews abstained

---

129 Tacitus, *Historiae* 5.4. Translation taken from Beard, North & Price (1998) vol. II, p. 274.
130 Petronius, *Sat.* 68; cf. 102.
131 Tacitus, *Historiae* 5.5. Translation taken from Beard, North & Price (1998) vol. II, p. 274. Cf. Goodman (2007) pp. 308-309.
132 Justinian, *Digesta* 48.8.11.

from eating pork, which they themselves considered a delicacy. The reason the Jews did not eat pig meat, Petronius deduced, must be that their god was a swine.[133]

The Chrestus commotion

The biographer Suetonius wrote of Emperor Claudius that:[134]

> Since the Jews constantly made disturbances at the instigation of Chrestus, he expelled them from Rome.

This small sentence about the ongoing commotion associated with "Chrestus" in Antique Rome has led to considerably more and longer sentences on the issue than the original remark, in ancient and modern scholarship. The opinions of theologians, historians of religion and of ancient history, and classical philologists vary widely as to whether the "Chrestus" spoken of in the above passage was, indeed, Jesus Christ of Nazareth. They also differ as to the nature of the "disturbances" that the sentence mentions. Apparently Chrestus was a fairly common name, and Suetonius gives no context references, so one guess is as good as another. But precisely because no details are given as to which Chrestus is at issue, it is reasonable to assume that the sentence alludes to someone who – at least in Suetonius's day – was widely and generally known, namely "Jesus Christ".[135] The *tumultus* alluded to in the Latin biography probably took place in the year 49 CE, at a time when the person in question, upon whom the figure of Jesus Christ is presumably based, had already been executed. However, the wording of the Latin sentence hardly necessitates the physical presence of the Chrestus that is mentioned, or his involvement in the "tumult". (I venture to adhere to this

---

133 Petronius, *Anthologia Latina*, frg. 696.
134 Suetonius, *Claudius* 25.4: *Iudaeos impulsore Chresto assidue tumultuantis Roma expulit*. Cf. H. Botermann (1996) *Das Judenedikt des Kaisers Claudius. Hermes*, vol. 71; Slingerland (1997); Gruen (2002) pp. 38-41.
135 Cf. Botermann (1996) pp. 95-102.

view even though as a point of philology this question remains disputed to this day.)[136]

So although we do not know the reason for this Chrestus commotion, nor the scope or severity of the turbulent events, it is a well-known fact that sometimes only a handful of people have to be present for religious clashes to arise. Even before Jesus died, he and "His word" were interpreted in many different ways. A situation in which diverging perceptions of the figure Jesus Christ gave rise to discussions and heated arguments (possibly with an element of religious mission) internally among "Jews" and/or "Christians" in Rome is quite a plausible scenario, and even a predictable one, in light of the many groupings that existed. Unfortunately, the issue remains unresolved, mainly due to the paucity of sources. It is impossible to paint any unambiguous picture when discussing questions relating to Jewish and early Christian groups and their disagreements, for instance regarding the role and status of Jesus and of the "salvation" he was believed to bring; the perception of his "rising from the dead", and so on and so forth. Just pause to consider the different perception models of the relationship between Judaism and Christianity expressed in the gospels of Matthew and John, and also in the epistles of Paul, which vary depending on differences in the social contexts implied.[137]

What is truly significant in the context of the early commotion about Chrestus in Rome is how confidently we can claim that the Jews' lacking recognition of Jesus as the Messiah (*Christus*) was a source of significant internal tension and rivalry, and that this lacking recognition must have constituted a threat against the identity formation of new Christian movements. Keep in mind that initially this identity construction was probably quite fragile, partly because it was just emerging and partly because the groups in question constituted a religious minority that was thinking decidedly new and different thoughts in a world ruled by Rome.

---

136 The words *impulsore Chresto* are perceived very differently in the scholarship. The interpretation that the "Christ" in question did not need to be physically present, but was merely an object (a deity) that caused disagreements and disturbances among cult members, is based upon other similar uses of the word *impulsor*, for instance in Plautus, *Aulularia* (*The Pot of Gold*) 737: *Deus impulsor mihi fuit*. For further examples, see Botermann (1996) p. 101. For the opposite view, see, for instance, Gruen (2002) p. 39.

137 Cf. Lieu (2011) pp. 435-459.

Whatever the actual facts at the time, evidently Claudius, who was Rome's emperor in 49 CE, felt that the calamities had to be stopped and the trouble-makers deported. Very probably their deportation should primarily be seen as yet another example of the pattern mentioned earlier, which had to do with expelling groups of foreigners in order to limit foreign *superstitio* and consolidate Roman *religio*. Regardless of the backdrop for the commotion about Chrestus, and regardless of the emperor's motives, certainly there was also a strong signal behind the message that Claudius sent, demonstrating the religio-political might of the imperial office.

Seneca and the Jews

Amongst a multitude of other topics, Augustine's work *De Civitate Dei*, which will be treated in greater depth in Chapter 6, relates and interprets what Seneca purportedly said about Jews. Referring to Seneca's *De Superstitione*, Augustine writes:[138]

> Along with other superstitions of the civil theology Seneca also censures the sacred institutions of the Jews, especially the sabbath. He declares that their practice is inexpedient, because by introducing one day of rest in every seven they lose in idleness almost a seventh of their life, and by failing to act in times of urgency they often suffer loss. As for the Christians, however, who were even then most hostile to the Jews, he does not mention them either favourably or unfavourably, not wishing to praise them in defiance of the custom of his country, or to attack them, which would perhaps have been against his own way of thinking. But when speaking of the Jews he says: "Meanwhile the customs of this accursed race have gained such influence that they are now received throughout all the world. The vanquished have given laws to their victors."

---

138 Augustine, *De Civ. Dei* 6.11. Given that Seneca died in 65 CE, his work *De Superstitione* must have been written prior to the Jewish uprising against the Romans (66-70 CE).

Augustine includes this passage on Seneca under the heading "What Seneca thought of the Jews", and interpreting the quote from Seneca's work in Augustine's text has caused much gnashing of teeth in modern research.[139] One of the questions baffling scholars is: Why would Seneca level such a vicious attack against the Jews? The details are unclear, but the word that Seneca (as rendered by Augustine) applied to the Jewish people – namely *sceleratissima* – is ominously unambiguous, as the meanings of this superlative are: the most disgusting/despicable/ungodly/accursed. That is why the Augustine text is sometimes used to broadly substantiate the claim that Seneca (and by extension the Romans) harboured particularly strong anti-Semitic sentiments. This conclusion can only be reached by means of the broadest sort of generalization – which could well be attributable more to the antipathies of Augustine than to those of Seneca.

In this connection it must be emphasized that even though Augustine states that he is directly citing Seneca's *De Superstitione*, the work itself has not survived. That is to say, we have no way of knowing whether Augustine (or the source he used) is actually providing a correct rendition of Seneca's original text and quoting him verbatim. But even if we do assume that the quote is correct, there are two things we must bear in mind. Firstly, we must not forget Seneca's original objective: The entire work dealt with *superstitio*, which would obviously limit reader expectations of finding descriptions of any positive characteristics in the Jews, or in other practitioners of *superstitio*. Secondly, it is still not inconceivable that in this passage discussing Seneca's views Augustine is depicting his predecessor's opinions using an extremely coarse brush. He may very well have wished to exaggerate Seneca's negative attitude towards Jews in order to create an appropriate backdrop for his own readers' understanding of the very different and much prettier picture of Seneca's potential attitude towards the Christians – again an attitude to which Augustine himself refers in *De Civitate Dei*.

So Augustine's portrayal of the situation is based on Seneca's statements concerning a specific religious custom, the Jewish sabbath. Seneca clearly disapproves of this custom and perceives it as unwarranted idleness. Against this backdrop Seneca's remarks that Jewish customs have spread everywhere,

---

139 Cf. Gruen (2002) p. 44; Goodman (2007) pp. 390-391.

and that the "vanquished have given laws to their victors" express both annoyance and irony. Still, this remark is probably above all an expression of (his) frustration that Jewish customs, which Seneca regards as an ethnically founded brand of *superstitio*, have perceivably spread beyond their ethnic boundaries. This is an example of how, in processes of cultural flux and acculturation, individual customs like the sabbath can spread without the cultural phenomenon itself (in this case Judaism as a religion) necessarily spreading to the same degree. And this is precisely the case with observing the sabbath as a day of rest. Over time this practice spread to the entire Roman Empire, one reason being that the Jews held important positions in the trade and merchant guilds, and another being that the Jewish sabbath later transmuted into the Christian practice of setting aside Sunday as a day of worship.

This particular Jewish tradition certainly caused widespread incredulity and outrage in many regions of the Roman world. It is not surprising, then, that according to Seneca (and to Cicero, and to numerous other Roman and Greek writers) the Jewish religion was unequivocally perceived as foreign *superstitio*. Nor is it any wonder that the Jewish brand of monotheism and Jewish customs, notably including circumcision, the sabbath, and unusual taboos, gave rise to annoyance, wonder, and ridicule. Based on the sources themselves, however, we cannot justify concluding that this would necessarily have led to some sort of particularly Roman antipathy against the Jews. Moreover, it must be emphasized here that in many cities of the Roman Empire we have found literary and archaeological evidence demonstrating that Judaean immigrant groups adopted and adapted to local cultural practices and interacted with their Roman or Greek neighbours.[140]

The above quote from Seneca is the only place in the surviving sources where this author is said to mention the Jews directly, and according to Augustine he does not mention the Christians at all. However, in consid-

---

140 P.A. Harland (2011) "Acculturation and Identity in the Diaspora. A Jewish Family and 'Pagan' Guilds at Hierapolis" in North & Price (2011) pp. 385-418. Cf. J. Lieu, J. North & T. Rajak (eds) (1992) *The Jews among Pagans and Christians in the Roman Empire*, London; J. Lieu (1996) *Image and Reality. The Jews in the World of the Christians in the Second Century*, Edinburgh; P.A. Harland (2009) *Dynamics of Identity in the World of the Early Christians: Associations, Judeans, and Cultural Minorities*, London.

ering Augustine's speculation that this is because Seneca showed restraint in praising the Christians out of respect for Roman tradition, or because criticizing the Christians would go against Seneca's own convictions, this reasoning probably says more about Augustine and his own literary strategy than it does about Seneca. In fact, we cannot rule out the possibility that Seneca's lack of references to the Christians is simply a matter of the author's not distinguishing in any significant way between Jews and Christians in a work that has the aim of describing superstition; for he may well have seen them as two groups that were basically wading around in the same squalid swamp of *superstitio*.

This leads us directly into another critical minefield of scholarship and research into early Christianity: the question of when the followers of Jesus Christ began to identify themselves as "Christians" in the sense that as a religious group (or groups) they began to perceive themselves as distinct and different from other brands of Judaism.[141] Adjacent to this is the question of when and how extensively the world around them, and most particularly the Romans, began to identify these Christians as a group or organization that was noticeably different from other brands of Judaism.

Concerning the first question of when the Christians split off from other Jewish factions, looking solely at the use of the term *christiani* is not necessarily adequate when arguing the case for a clear formal or organizational division. The reason is that this term can simply be perceived as a cover term for "the Christian Jews", meaning the Jews who presumed that Jesus was *Christus*, the Messiah. Based on the views of the later writer and church father Augustine there were, of course, two completely distinct groups rooted in the same religious tradition, only one of which (namely the Christian) possessed the true version of this religious tradition. And therefore Augustine's passage dealing with Seneca unmistakably emphasizes the existence of animosity very early on between Jews and Christians. This notwithstanding, the organizational and identity-related divisions in Antiquity between Jewish and Christian groups was a complex process with many and varied social and religious aspects. So enforcing the focus on constructed enemy images, it should be underscored that from a later Christian point of view, the Ro-

---

141 See, for instance, J.D.G. Dunn (1999) (ed.) *Jews and Christians. The Parting of the Ways A.D. 70 to 135*, Cambridge.

mans' conflicts with the Jews, notably epitomized in the destruction of the Temple in Jerusalem (in 70 CE), might well have seemed quite meaningful as an expression of "God's will". It was obvious and easy to interpret the ruining of the Temple and the consequent weakening of the basic conditions for the Jews, as proof that the Christian organization expressed the correct interpretation of the true religion. Such a Christian perspective could, in other words, legitimize not only a distancing of oneself from the Jews, but also the launching of direct attacks against them. Judaism's lacking recognition of Jesus as the Messiah was undermining the construction of a new Christian identity. Therefore, continuing to weaken the Jewish faith and the conditions its practitioners lived under might lead to the greater promulgation and consolidation of Christianity and of a Christian identity – in various guises.

This is the wider tapestry before which we must hold up Augustine's portrayal of Seneca – that is, still assuming that Augustine is actually quoting Seneca's original wording. An interpretation of Augustine's entire passage about Seneca as expressing a particular constructed religious enemy therefore appears to hang by just a few tenuous threads of substantiated reasoning. On the other hand, Augustine's use of Seneca unmistakably replicates a recurring pattern in the greater tapestry, consisting of later and more systematic constructions of enemy images on the part of the Christians. Using Seneca as a template, Augustine constructs a religious enemy to clarify the Christian position and consolidate Christian identity: The more trouble with the Jews, the more polemic against them, and the more defeats they suffer, the greater will be the weight and truth value attributed to the Christians, or so the reasoning apparently runs. In the Rome of Augustine's day – in the late fourth century – the emperors passed laws against the Jews. Christian converts to Judaism would lose their property, for example, and members of the Jewish faith were barred from holding certain public positions. Chapter 6 discusses Augustine's construction of religious enemy images at greater length.

Nero's Christian scapegoats

The sources describe the persecution of Christians under Emperor Nero, plainly indicating that at this point the Christians are receiving attention as a group. Suetonius describes the Christians as people who were infected with a new and harmful *superstitio*, and who were subjected to rigorous punishments during Nero's reign.[142] Among other things, Christians were accused of starting the great fire of Rome in 64 CE, even though according to the historian Tacitus the conflagration begun with a fateful accident, or was started by Emperor Nero himself. In his *Annales*, Tacitus writes about the fire:[143]

> A disaster followed, whether accidental or treacherously contrived by the emperor is uncertain, as authors have given both accounts, worse, however, and more dreadful than any which have ever happened to this city by the violence of fire.

In order to put an end to the stubborn rumour that he was actually the one who had set the great city ablaze, Nero attempted to cast the Christians as scapegoats. Tacitus continues:[144]

> Consequently, to get rid of the report, Nero fastened the guilt and inflicted the most exquisite tortures on a class hated for their abominations, called Christians by the populace. Christus, from whom the name had its origin, suffered the extreme penalty during the reign of Tiberius at the hands of one of our procurators, Pontius Pilatus, and a most mischievous superstition, thus checked for the moment, again broke out not only in Judaea, the first source of the evil, but even in Rome, where all things hideous and shameful from every part of the world find their centre and become popular. Accordingly, an arrest was first made of all who pleaded guilty; then, upon their information,

---

142 Suetonius, *Nero* 16.
143 Tacitus, *Annales* 15.38.
144 Tacitus, *Annales* 15.44.

> an immense multitude was convicted, not so much of the crime of firing the city, as of hatred against mankind.

According to our historian, Nero did not find it sufficient to simply arrest the Christians. Some he had crucified; others he covered in animal skins and had torn apart by hounds; yet others were set alight, like living torches that lit up the night. On this basis, Tacitus concludes:[145]

> Hence, even for criminals who deserved extreme and exemplary punishment, there arose a feeling of compassion; for it was not, as it seemed, for the public good, but to glut one man's cruelty, that they were being destroyed.

So even though Tacitus represented the Christians as blameless in the burning of Rome, some people still regarded them as a sort of asocial criminals. And it was precisely these notions of Christians – as delinquents who kept to themselves and conspired against the state and against humanity at large – that would become one of the linchpins around which the subsequent and periodical rounds of Christian persecutions would revolve.

To sum up: Warfare and the making of an empire with a significant concentration of wealth and power in Rome brought about an influx of foreigners, creating a huge heterogeneous and cosmopolitan population of perhaps a million or so in the first century CE. The Roman terms *religio* and *superstitio* were two dynamic key words that the Roman religio-political elite could apply when debating the nature of proper and improper religious behaviour, thereby constructing a vital part of Roman and non-Roman identity. This dichotomy seems to function as an important mechanism operating in a number of religious tension-filled or conflictual interactions that we can discern in the antique evidence. The two terms express tensions between Roman and foreign religion; friction and dynamics between cultural flow and religio-political closure; resistance and chafing generated by the "flux" and "fix" of Romanization processes. And the cases examined in this chapter, focusing on the Roman control of foreign influences through

---

145 Tacitus, *Annales* 15.44.

patterns of expulsion, demonstrate how these tensions played out in ancient Rome.

Unfortunately, our knowledge and understanding of the Roman policies, attitudes, and actions towards Jews and Christians in Rome is very limited and based on fragmentary sources. However, even though Romans initially categorized both Judaism and Christianity as *superstitio* in the various streams of acculturation, certain differences can be observed in Rome's treatment of the Jews and Christians living there. The sources leave the general impression that the Romans were largely tolerant of Jews, despite their *superstitio* and peculiar customs relating to circumcision, the sabbath, culinary taboos, et cetera. It seems that to a certain extent these customs were simply ignored. But they were also made the object of wonder and of ridicule, and even of disdain when it came to their *superstitio* – and occasionally some of the Jews were also booted out. Still, there is not much to suggest that the Romans generally considered the Jews a particular threat in a way that warranted any particularly distinctive, permanent, or systematic construction of a religious enemy. Conversely, it is noteworthy that for some time the Romans tolerated the fact that Roman Jews refused to worship any other gods than Yahweh – Jehovah – the One God worshipped at the Temple in Jerusalem.

This stands in stark contrast to Rome's failure to accept the Christians' refusal to participate in official state and imperial cult practices; an issue that will be treated in the next chapter. This contrast witnesses a brand of "special treatment" that is quite interesting seen from a modern perspective – and perhaps also somewhat paradoxical.[146] The difference in attitude should most probably be regarded in light of the fact that although the cult of Judaism could seem rather peculiar to Roman eyes, at least it had a Temple, a sacred place, as well as an age-old tradition. So the cult of the Jews was associated with a historic location, and unlike the Christ cult's similar prohibition against worshipping other gods, the doctrine of the One God in Judaism was at least historically founded. To the Roman mindset, the Jewish argument of complying with the traditions and laws of their

---

146 Josephus, *Antiquitates Judaicae* (*Jewish Antiquities*) 18.257-258; Goodman (2007) pp. 392-393; M. Goodman (2011) "Josephus and Variety in First-Century Judaism" in North & Price (2011) pp. 419-434.

ancient ancestors was an understandable point of reference – despite its peculiarities – focusing as it did upon the significance of the customs of one's forefathers. To a certain extent, Judaism could therefore be legitimized by virtue of its cultic location and historic dimension – which did not even remotely apply to the circumstances surrounding the cult of Christ.

As already stressed in Chapter 1, the Christians had done quite the opposite, abandoning the ideas and rituals of their forefathers, and establishing a new and – to Roman eyes – even more peculiar cult. Bear in mind that the Christ cult had no other cultic location it could offer as an alternative to the Temple in Jerusalem, and to make matters even worse the Christians claimed that the temple of God lay not in Jerusalem, but within Jesus and his followers.[147] Furthermore, the Christians' situation could hardly have been improved by their reputation for gathering in secret, and for doing so to worship a man who had been executed at the behest of a Roman governor. Finally, through the Jewish people's belief in its own election and the adherence to the Jewish law, the Jews isolated themselves from others, whereas the Christian missionary attitude and strategy excluded everyone who refused to take up the invitation to Christianity. This difference between a Jewish self-imposed isolation and a – more aggressive – Christian mission and claim to universalism, probably also influenced Rome's initial reactions towards Jews and Christians, respectively.

The Jewish uprising

Palestine came under de facto Roman rule when it was conquered, along with Syria, in 63 BCE by the Roman general Pompey. In 40 BCE the Roman Senate declared Herod the Great, an Idumean by birth, as King of Judaea. Herod's rule in Jerusalem was dependent on Roman power from 37 BCE, when Roman legions conquered the city on his behalf. Various ill-advised decisions on his part – which included stripping the highest Jewish council (Sanhedrin) of its powers – led to unrest and opposition movements among the Jewish people. Finally, when Herod died, the Jews openly rebelled and Ju-

---

147 Cf. Paul, *1 Cor.* 3:16-17; *Gospel of John* 2:18-22; 4:19-26.

daea was reorganized as an independent province ruled directly from Rome. Although Rome wielded direct power, the Jewish Sanhedrin re-established a measure of its authority, serving as the legislative body in internal Jewish matters. Still, religious tensions between the successive Roman procurators and the Jewish people gradually built. According to the Jewish writer Josephus, the reign of Emperor Tiberius saw serious religious clashes unfold between Romans and Jews in Jerusalem.[148] The sight of Roman troops marching through the streets of the city, with their standards portraying the emperor held high, led to riots. It was also regarded as a religious violation of Jewish law that Pontius Pilate, the governor of Judaea, used money from the Jewish temple to pay for the construction of an aqueduct to improve the water supply to Jerusalem. Predictably, matters were not improved by Emperor Caligula's demand that the Jews were to worship him as a deity as well, or his desire to have a statue of himself erected in the Jewish temple in Jerusalem.

Besides all this, in the years prior to the uprising much disorder was caused in Judaea not by the Romans, but by internal Jewish power struggles. Under the Roman governor, Gessius Florus, relations between the Roman administration and the Jewish institutions broke down completely, culminating in the year 66 CE with the onset of the Judaeo–Roman war – in which Titus ultimately conquered the city in 70 CE. The temple of the city was destroyed – either on purpose, according to Titus's plan, or by an accidental fire. This detail remains unclear, but it was certainly not Roman standard practice to destroy enemy temples.[149]

At any rate, the great temple in Jerusalem was the very image and physical epitome of Judaism's continuity, and so its destruction must have been perceived as a devastating blow, not just for the Jews living in Jerusalem but for Jews throughout the Roman Empire. One consequence of the war was that the special status Jews enjoyed in Rome was sorely damaged. Another was that many Jews must have subsequently come to regard Roman rule as brutal and destructive. After Rome quashed the Jewish uprising

---

148 Josephus, *AJ* 18.55-62; *BJ* 2.196-201. Cf. Goodman (2007) pp. 397-422.
149 Josephus, *Bellum Judaicum* (*The Jewish War*) 2.266-407; 6.252-266. Cf. E.M. Smallwood (1981) *The Jews under Roman Rule from Pompey to Diocletian*, Leiden; Goodman (2007) pp. 422-444.

Fig. 6. The arch of Titus in Rome was erected c. 82 CE to commemorate the victories of Emperor Titus, including the Siege of Jerusalem in 70 CE. The south panel of the arch shows the triumphal procession in Rome, carrying spoils taken from the Temple in Jerusalem. The scene gives striking prominence to the religious objects of the Jews (the seven-branched candlestick, an offering table, two vessels, and two trumpets).

Jerusalem's status was that of a city under siege – and it seems that the emperors Vespasian and Titus ruled all of Judaea directly, meaning without any Jewish leaders acting as intermediaries. Furthermore, the Roman state did not allow the Temple in Jerusalem to be rebuilt, and this was indeed a new Roman religio-political attitude and manifestation, preventing the Jews from participating in their ancestral temple cult. Such obstructing of people's performance of traditional temple practices indicates a radical shift in official Roman religio-politics.

Another factor that came into play at that time, and which is important to the issue at hand, is that Vespasian ordered a special tax to be paid annually by all Jews in the Roman Empire, with the proceeds earmarked for the Roman deity Jupiter Capitolinus. The aim was to finance the reconstruction of the Jupiter temple in Rome, which had burned down in the great fire of 69 CE.[150] This manifestation on the part of the Roman rulers was, in

---

150 Josephus, *BJ* 7.218; Cassius Dio, *HR* 66.7.2.

essence, a collective punishment for the uprising in Jerusalem, meted out against all Jews throughout the empire. The punishment was in fact dual, and decidedly religious in nature. First, the emperor would not allow the Jews to reconstruct the temple in Jerusalem. And second, the Jews of the Roman Empire – who had previously sent regular contributions to support their own temple in Jerusalem – were now forced to financially support the state cult at Rome.[151]

This constituted a drastic change in the way Rome treated the Jews, not just in Jerusalem but across the empire. Even today the military and religious significance of this shift can be seen, chiselled upon the honorific Arch of Titus in Rome. The monument portrays Roman soldiers triumphantly carrying off Judaism's most sacred treasures as the spoils of war, highlighting Rome's assumption of supreme religio-political power and asserting, once and for all, the ultimate repression of the Jewish uprising against Rome.

---

151 Josephus, *BJ* 7.160-162. The fact that Jews in Italy and the Roman provinces sent annual contributions to Jerusalem is substantiated in several sources, including Cicero, *Pro Flacco* 67.

Chapter 4

The Dialectics of Cultural Flux and Fix – Religious Romanization and The Making of Martyrs

As far back as we can historically trace it, Roman religion was distinctly multicultural. There is archaeological evidence of Etruscan, Greek, and Carthaginian influences, testifying to the fact that right from the outset Roman religion was the product of an ongoing acculturation process. There were, of course, many differences between the hamlet of the eighth century BCE located by the marshy banks of the Tiber, and the pulsating, pluralistic, multicultural metropolis of the Late Republic and Imperial Rome.

Yet although Rome's religious life changed over the centuries, her rituals and festivals continuously served as a cornerstone in Roman society. Consequently, Rome's rise to power and eventual world supremacy was explained and legitimized by way of religious institutions. One of these institutions was cultic worship of the emperor through a variety of rituals designed to associate him with the gods, or developed over time to incorporate him into religious ceremonies that already existed. These would include the reigning emperor's birthday and the dates of his most notable military victories, which were commemorated with sacrifices and celebrations like the festivals held for specific gods. A formal procedure for the deification of deceased emperors also gradually evolved. The Senate would decide whether an emperor was to be recognized as a god or not. If deified, the emperor was then assigned the additional title of *divus* and had temples, priests, and annual public sacrifices consecrated in his honour. Inscriptions, coins, and other sources show how the emperor figure was incorporated into public cult with specially designated shrines, priests, and ceremonies spread across Roman territory.

In some instances the emperor was apparently treated explicitly as a god, while in other instances sacrifices were offered not directly to the emperor's person, but to his *numen*, his *lares*, or his *genius*. It thus seems that in certain official contexts a distinction was maintained between the cult of deceased and deified emperors, who were worshipped as gods, and the living emperor, whose position and well-being, symbolizing imperial power and unity, were venerated with sacrifices and celebrations.[152] We are unable to precisely reconstruct the subtle boundary between the revered status of some emperors as "godlike" and the status of others as "unequivocally divine". Nevertheless, as the supreme commander of the armed forces and the unrivalled holder of the premier position in Rome's social, political, and religious hierarchy, the emperor provided a strong religious focal point upon which the eyes of the whole empire could fix. That is why his figure and his person played such a key role in the process of religious Romanization.

There is no doubt that imperial power had an impact on religious and cultural life across the imperial territories. Conversely, the Roman provinces also, to a greater or lesser degree, exerted an influence on the religions of Rome. Alas, it is all but impossible to reliably generalize about the complex and varied processes and degrees of Romanization, given that it took on many different forms depending on the place, the period, and the concrete cultural and religious context in question.

As described in Chapter 1, local gods were reinterpreted, transformed, and integrated into the Roman pantheon. The regional elites out in the provinces also seemed to pay considerable attention to the Roman gods, probably because stressing one's connections with these deities was a good way of acquiring prestige and displaying one's social and political prowess, both within and outside the immediate community. Accordingly, the Roman authorities generally did not seek to undermine or eradicate local cults as part of religious Romanization, and many local gods were reinterpreted or replaced, resulting in novel or hybrid deities.

On the other hand, as described in Chapter 3, this certainly did not prevent Rome from striking back against localized unrest that was religio-political in nature and was debated and categorized by the Roman authorities as *superstitio*. We find examples of local religious traditions and priesthoods

---

152 See, for instance, Beard, North & Price (1998) pp. 245-363; I. Gradel (2002) *Emperor Worship and Roman Religion*, Oxford; Rives (2007); R. Gordon (2011) "The Roman Imperial Cult and the Question of Power" in North & Price (2011) pp. 37-70.

stimulating insurrection against Roman rule, such as the Jewish revolt against Rome (66-70 CE, described earlier), which was sparked by religious conflicts and multiple internal and external power struggles.[153]

Pursuing this theme further, the present chapter focuses on the construction of identity among Christians and among Romans, and on the making of Christian martyrs as an example of a religious opposition manifested against Roman religio-politics. In considering this aspect of religious Romanization, it is worth noting that from the early second century CE onwards, the use of the term *superstitio* seems to increase when the sources are referring to the religious practices of foreign peoples. As described in previous chapters, this term is used to define and reject various kinds of improper religious behaviour, and the intensified focus on *superstitio* in the imperial period no doubt reflects the shifting dynamics in the religious Romanization process.

From a sociological point of view, it is obvious that we should consider the conflicts between Roman authorities and Christians, which resulted in the construction of religious enemies in both camps, as a question of constructing and reconstructing identity. Increased religio-political use of the term *superstitio* could very well be symptomatic of a growing interest in consolidating Roman identity and creating coherence in a geographically widespread multicultural empire. After all, Roman religion defined Roman identity and consolidated the status of the Roman elite in relation to the provinces and the empire's many local elites. The foreign cult of Christ was not merely disturbing the peace and the established order of things when its members refused to sacrifice to the Roman gods and the emperor's health. The Christ cult was regarded as a new and disruptive sort of *superstitio* that opposed the ancient and honourable traditions of Roman *religio*. And this Roman *religio* was not only the foundation of the history and the city of Rome, but also of the entire Roman Empire. The *superstitio* of the Christians was therefore perceived as a serious obstruction to the traditional religion that was embedded in Roman society, and which safeguarded both Roman identity and the prosperity of the Roman Empire.

In this light, Rome's increased use of the term *superstitio* and the growing conflicts between Roman authorities and Christians appear to represent a

---

153 Cf. Goodman (2007) pp. 7-29.

certain aspect of two (contradictory) religio-political trends that I term the "flux" and the "fix" of Romanization. These signify, respectively: the trend towards "global" cultural flow and interchange of Romanization, and the trend towards (Roman) cultural closure and the fixing, or consolidation, of a (Roman) identity encompassing the whole empire. As I explain in Chapter 7, thinking in such terms helps to accentuate the similarities with certain trends observable in the globalization processes taking place in the world today.

Martyrdom defined

If we define martyrdom as a willingness, perhaps even a striving or longing, to sacrifice oneself and die for a religious cause in order to achieve personal salvation, then the appearance of the Christian martyr was certainly a hitherto unseen phenomenon in the ancient world. Actually the concept of martyrdom is – and has always been – a controversial topic in the research history.[154] It is nonetheless irrefutable that Christian martyrdom in its capacity as a new institution went against the very grain of the most deep-seated Graeco-Roman norms, values, and modes of action in matters concerning religion, social behaviour, and philosophy. As demonstrated below, Christian martyrdom provoked a wide range of sentiments among the empire's Roman communities, ranging from bewildered astonishment across revulsion to anger and downright frustration. And these sentiments are evidenced in Christian and non-Christian sources alike.

Ancient sources and modern research history both occasionally interpret the famed philosopher Socrates, who was condemned to death in 399 BCE, as an example of a pre-Christian, prototypical martyr. In this context, the term "martyr" means a person who is unjustly found guilty of religiously founded accusations, and who dies for their cause. Note, however, that the circumstances in the case against Socrates were substantively different than the circumstances in later cases brought against Christians. One very sig-

---

[154] See, for instance, Fox (1986) pp. 419-492; G.W. Bowersock (2002) *Martyrdom & Rome*, Cambridge (1st ed. 1995); E. Castelli (2004) *Martyrdom and Memory. Early Christian Culture Making*, Columbia; Clark (2004) pp. 38-59.

nificant difference was Socrates' uncertainty as to the outcome of death, as opposed to the Christian martyrs who, thanks to their faith, held a firm conviction that death would lead them to ultimate salvation in the afterlife.

One of the main themes in Plato's dialogue *Phaedo* is Socrates' attitude towards death. In Plato's work, the old philosopher's friend and student Phaedo describes the condemned Socrates as a happy man who faces death fearlessly and with eyes wide open. During the dialogue, related by Phaedo, Socrates says that actually a philosopher is constantly practicing dying, and that being dead is not something that frightens him.[155] A philosopher grapples with his corporeality in all respects, endeavouring to disassociate his soul as much as possible from his physical body. According to Socrates, then, it would be completely illogical if, as the time of death drew near, the philosopher became terrified and completely beside himself. On the contrary, the philosopher ought to be happy at this point because he finds himself on the verge of being released from the thing he has been grappling with, and because he can now hope to achieve what he has been longing for his entire life: insight and understanding.

In Plato's *Apology of Socrates*, the author repeatedly has Socrates point out that he does not know whether death is a good thing or a bad thing. And in concluding the speech in his own defence, Socrates underscores the uncertainty relating to the consequences of death, addressing the judges as follows:[156]

> And now it really is time to depart, I to be executed and you to continue living. But which of us goes to a better life is unclear to everyone except the god.

Pliny the Younger and Emperor Trajan

Rome's persecution of Christians, most notably its nature and scope, has been fiercely debated ever since such activities began in the ancient world. These debates have led to a number of very different (and often contradic-

---

155 Plato, *Phaedo* 12.
156 Plato, *The Apology of Socrates* 42a.

tory) interpretations and questions that we remain unable to answer, even to this day. Regrettably, the sources dealing with Christian persecution are very fragmentary, and it is important to emphasize that the Roman harassment of Christians has varied over time depending on the historical and religio-political context. As the various examples in this chapter will show, the spates of ruthless persecution that we know of have been defined by specific times and places and by the prevalence of the cult of Christ, the local resentment against and clashes with Christians, and the individual tempers and inclinations of the emperors and provincial governors in power at any given time. The examples, taken from both Christian and non-Christian sources, highlight two crucial issues relating to Christian persecution. The first concerns the precautions that Rome sought to take vis-à-vis the Christians. The second concerns the methods that the Romans could employ to test Christian identity – and as it turned out, the acid test of Christian faith was one's (lacking) readiness to sacrifice to Rome's gods and to effigies of her emperor.

One of the most important and most controversial sources on the Roman authorities' treatment of Christians is Pliny's correspondence with the Emperor Trajan while he was governor over the province of Pontus-Bithynia around 110 CE. Pliny writes to Trajan, asking how he is to deal with the Christians in his province. He describes Christianity as foolish and exaggerated *superstitio*, and he continues:[157]

> As I have never taken part in a trial of Christians, I do not know what it is customary to investigate nor how far the penalty should be applied. I hesitated not a little as to whether there should be any distinction drawn between them on grounds of age, or whether rather the young and their elders should be treated alike; whether repentance should lead to a pardon, or whether rather it should not avail those who had once been Christians to have renounced it; and whether the name itself should be punished even if there were no criminal acts, or whether rather the criminal acts associated with the name should be punished. In the mean time, I have employed the following procedure

---

157 Pliny the Younger, *Epistulae* (*Letters*) X.96-97. Translations taken from Beard, North & Price (1998) vol. II, pp. 277-278.

in relation to those who were denounced to me as Christians. I asked them in person whether they were Christians. If they confessed it, I repeated the question a second and third time, threatening them with capital punishment; those who persisted, I ordered to be executed. For I had no hesitation, whatever the nature of their confession, that that stubbornness and rigid obstinacy should certainly be punished. There were others similarly fanatical whom, because they were Roman citizens, I have put on the list of persons to be sent to the city [of Rome].

As governor, Pliny obviously lacks clear guidelines he can follow when assessing and punishing the Christians in his province, and so it would certainly seem that there was no fixed legal basis prior to this time. It is worth noting that Pliny would evidently prefer not to have to discipline these obdurate Christians, whom he gives a second and even a third chance to avoid punishment. The reader senses not only his astonishment and his patience, but also a certain mental fatigue at ultimately finding himself obliged to punish the Christians – more because of their (mulish) obstinacy than because of their (superstitious) faith. However, the absolutely crucial test in Pliny's assessment and treatment of the Christians is whether he can move them to make offerings to the Roman gods and to an effigy of the emperor. Pliny goes on: [158]

> An anonymous pamphlet was laid before me containing many people's names. Those mentioned there who denied that they were or had been Christians, I thought should be released, when they repeated after me an invocation to the gods and made a *supplicatio* of wine and incense to your image, which I had ordered for this purpose to be placed with the statues of the gods, and in addition cursed Christ, all things which those who are true Christians, it is said, cannot be brought to.

Emperor Trajan wrote Pliny the following reply:[159]

---

158 Pliny the Younger, *Epistulae* X. 96-97.
159 Pliny the Younger, *Epistulae* XCVIII.

> You have followed, my dear Secundus [that is, Pliny], the proper procedures in investigating the cases of those denounced to you as Christians. For no general rule can be laid down to a fixed formula. They are not to be sought out; if they are denounced and found guilty, they are to be punished; but those who deny that they are Christians and make that absolutely clear in practice, that is by making a *supplicatio* to our gods, even if they had incurred suspicion in the past, they should obtain an acquittal as a result of their repentance. Anonymous pamphlets laid before you should have no role in any accusation. They are an extremely bad precedent and out of keeping with our age.

Here we see, above all, that Pliny is confirmed in having employed the correct method, the test being whether those accused of being Christians are willing to bring sacrifices to the Roman deities. Secondly, the Christians are not to be actively persecuted in the sense of being hunted down. Thirdly, it is considered completely inappropriate to act upon anonymous accusations. If someone wants a Christian to be condemned for their faith, that person must drag the accused Christian to court themselves. This correspondence between Governor Pliny and Rome's Emperor Trajan makes it clear that Roman citizens who repeatedly claimed to be Christians were ordered to be sent to Rome for trial, whilst non-citizens were ordered to be executed on location. However, it is likely that practices varied in different provinces, and the emperor's response to Pliny has validity only for Pliny's province of Pontus-Bithynia in the early second century CE.

Eusebius and the martyrs of Lyons

According to the accounts in the Christian sources the nature of the persecution of Christians in the late second century was far more radical and brutal. The drama and violence portrayed in the Christian accounts is quite distinctive. Yet when throwing Christian martyrdom into relief, one must recall the intentions of these sources: to relate in detail the cruelties that Christians suffered at the hands of Romans, and to illustrate the martyrs' dogged courage and final redemption as a result of their faith in the True Teaching.

Sources Christian and non-Christian demonstrate that martyrdom was an extremely important element in the institutionalization of Christianity. It defined and delineated the Christian doctrine in a new and, literally, very spectacular way. It illustrated in no uncertain terms the raw power embodied in Christian faith, and in Christian behaviour and identity as compared with other religious and philosophical movements of that age. One source where this is remarkably clear is the narratives of the church historian Eusebius (circa 260-340 CE), who was bishop of Caesarea in Palestine during the rule of Constantine the Great. After Emperor Constantine's death in 337 CE the prolific Eusebius wrote about his life in *Vita Constantini* (*Life of Constantine*), but the author is actually best known for being "the Father of Church History" by virtue of his *Historia Ecclesiastica* (*Ecclesiastical History*), the work that marks the establishment of church history as an actual genre.[160]

The *Historia Ecclesiastica* is a many-faceted work. One facet is its positive staging of Christianity as a success story. A story of religious hardship, struggle, and victory. A struggle against enemies of various kinds: pagans, who were enemies because of their idolatrous beliefs; heretics (such as Gnostics), who were enemies because they distorted the True Doctrine; and Jews, who were enemies because of their attacks against the Saviour and the Church.[161] If we regard Eusebius' writings and his success-story staging based on a very narrow historical criticism of their credibility as sources, it will inevitably give rise to numerous points that seem at best questionable and at worst completely unreliable. On the other hand, if we regard his works in the broader perspective of acculturation, they often prove to be extremely valuable sources, revealing much about the Christians' perception of themselves, of "the others", and of their interaction with the non-Christian world around them.

The fact that Eusebius' history of the Church (and also his work about Constantine) in several places exhibits a bombastic, aggrandizing construction of ecclesiastical success and excellence, as opposed to the fiascos of

---

160 Cf. Drobner (2007) pp. 223-235. Eusebius wrote quite a large number of pieces that can fairly be termed "apologetic" in the sense that they responded to questions, objections, and accusations raised against Christianity. Eusebius himself underscores that, broadly speaking, the term *apologiai* covers writings that fall within several different literary genres; see Frede (1999) pp. 223-250.
161 Eusebius, *Historia Ecclesiastica* 1.2. Especially the initial books of this work define very precisely the opponents of Christianity.

the heathens, certainly compromises his credibility on certain issues, strictly speaking. But this does not necessarily make him a worthless source or discredit him from a sociological point of view. The author himself describes his account as a representation of historical facts, and an edifying one at that.[162] The circumstance that this very edification – from a more sober-minded perspective – consists precisely in his own extremely subjective and grandiloquent approach to the topics at hand becomes eminently apparent in much of Eusebius' work.

The *Historia Ecclesiastica* reproduces a letter describing events that befell Christian congregations in the Gallic towns of Vienne and Lyons in the year 177 during the reign of Emperor Marcus Aurelius. The original letter (now lost), written by the two Gallic congregations to fellow Christians in Asia Minor,[163] recounts the ruthless treatment Christians suffered at the hands of the local population and the Roman authorities, and of the martyrs this produced. Based on Eusebius' reproduction of the letter, the course of events can be reconstructed under these main headings:

1. A furious mob of heathens attack the Christians, showering them with insults and stones, and beating and robbing them. Subjecting them quite simply to: "all things which an infuriated mob delight in inflicting on enemies and adversaries."[164]

2. The Christians are interrogated in public, in the presence of the agitated mob. This results in numerous confessions and the imprisonment of those who affirm their faith in Jesus Christ. The governor is expected to arrive shortly.

3. The governor arrives, and a young spokesman by the name of Vettius Epagathus steps forward, wishing to intercede on behalf of the Christians. The governor asks the young man whether he is a Christian, and when he answers "Yes" for all to hear, he too is thrown into prison.

---

162 Eusebius, *HE* introduction to Book 5.
163 Eusebius, *HE* 5.1-5.2. There were age-old links between the South of France and Asia Minor, as Marseille was originally a colony of Asia Minor.
164 Eusebius, *HE* 5.1.7.

4. Non-Christian slaves from Christian households are also jailed. These servants level a number of false accusations against their Christian masters involving incest, cannibalism, and other unspeakable crimes. The reasons given for these accusations are that the slaves are "ensnared by Satan, and fearing for themselves the tortures which they beheld the saints endure."[165]

5. The letter also makes it obvious that the authorities were uncertain of how to deal with those Christians who held Roman citizenship. The authorities await a response from the emperor.[166]

6. The response from the emperor commands, firstly, that the Christians are to be tortured to death unless they deny Jesus Christ. If they deny him, they are to be set free. Secondly, it commands that the Christians holding Roman citizenship are to be beheaded, whereas the others are to be thrown to the wild beasts for public sport.

7. This response leads to the governor having the Christians taken before the court and interrogated again, and then dealt with according to the emperor's orders.

The letter as presented by Eusebius portrays a number of significant features, the sum of which amounts to what can fairly be called the *Idealtypus* of the martyr; the idea-construct for a "pure type" of Christian martyrdom.[167] By this I mean the particularly emphasized qualities and personality traits and "pure" patterns of reaction that the letter associates with the various types of torment and suffering inflicted upon the Christians. This especially applies to a pattern of uncompromising confession and commitment to one's personal faith in Jesus Christ; physical and mental stamina and courage; obstinacy in the face of Roman authority; rejection of Roman religion; and

---

165 Eusebius, *HE* 5.1.14.
166 Eusebius, *HE* 5.1.44.
167 Cf. M. Weber (1904) "Die 'Objektivität' sozialwissenschaftlicher und sozialpolitischer Erkenntnis", *Archiv für Sozialwissenschaft und Sozialpolitik*, XIX. Band, 1 Heft, pp. 22-87, Tübingen. English translation: M. Weber (2012) "The "Objectivity" of knowledge in social science and social policy" in H.H. Bruun & S. Whimster (eds) *Max Weber. Collected methodological writings*, pp.100-138. Translated by H.H. Bruun, London 2012.

a longing for Christian martyrdom as the ultimate release and fulfilment.

Examples of such features are found in the letter's description of the Christian woman Blandina, who, despite her initially weak constitution and her tortured and broken body, gains new strength "like a noble athlete" when confessing her faith, exclaiming before the court: "I am a Christian, and there is nothing vile done by us."[168]

The same is true of Sanctus, whose bravery and steadfastness are praised. When interrogated as to his identity, name, native town, and status as slave or free and answers, simply: "I am a Christian."[169] His unbending determination drives the Roman governor into a frenzy, and so he is tortured with red-hot copper plates but stands his ground. The letter describes how Sanctus is brought up and tortured a second time, on the expectation that his physical abuse and death at the hands of his captors will serve as a horrifying example to his fellow Christians. The Romans' intentions are put to shame, however, and Sanctus does not die. His body instead straightens up and remains standing during the torments that follow. Sanctus later regains his physical abilities, and according to the account the torture therefore does not serve as a punishment but rather as an act of healing by the grace of Jesus Christ.[170]

Similarly, features of the Christian martyr as *Idealtypus* are found in Biblias, a woman who stubbornly opposes the authorities and defends the Christians against the accusation of cannibalism levelled against them by the non-Christian community. "How could those eat children who do not think it lawful to taste the blood even of irrational animals?" Biblias asks.[171] She confesses her Christian faith and gains a place among the holy martyrs. Finally, consider the exemplary Christian reaction in the description of Pothinus, the Bishop of Lyons, who was over 90 years old at the time of the persecutions. Although weakened by age and infirmity, he is imbued with new energy as a result of his longing for martyrdom. The Roman soldiers bring Pothinus before the court, and with the incensed mob shouting insults

---

168 Eusebius, *HE* 5.1.19.
169 Eusebius, *HE* 5.1.20.
170 Eusebius, *HE* 5.1.20-24.
171 Eusebius, *HE* 5.1.25.

all around him, the bishop confesses his faith in Christ. When the governor asks him who the God of the Christians is, the bishop calmly replies:[172]

"If you are worthy, you shall know."

People in the enraged crowd react by battering away at the aged bishop, after which, more dead than alive, he is thrown into prison where he gives up the ghost two days later.

What is particularly noteworthy in the context of constructed enemy images is the fact that the contents of the letter, as quoted by Eusebius, link the persecution of Christians to the heathen mobs as well as the Roman governor in Lyons and the emperor in Rome. Yet the letter does not mention any sort of formal, legal procedure for the prosecution of Christians to the effect that they could only be tried on the basis of personal accusations (as in the correspondence, described earlier, between Pliny the Younger and Emperor Trajan). The reason for this omission may be that the formal requirements to that part of the legal procedure simply were not followed in the persecutions in Lyons. But it is equally possible that those writing the letter intentionally omitted this particular information to reinforce the sense of drama, brutality, and injustice in the way the authorities treated the Christians of Lyons. Whatever the case may be, my errand here is not to dwell upon whether these accounts are credible as statements of historical or religio-historical fact. My errand is to emphasize the actual intention behind the letter's accounts and testimonies, and to point out their relevant ideal-typical points of orientation and significance in relation to Christian identity. In other words, the letter could be viewed as a source from which to extract a (Weberian) theoretical construction within a particular social and religio-political situation: Christian martyrdom.

Max Weber's methodology includes the concept of the *Idealtypus* or "pure type" as a sort of one-sided exaggeration of certain significant aspects of a given "reality", which can then be compared with various empirical "realities". Thus, the *Idealtypus* is not a depiction of a "reality", but a kind of utopia that attempts to grasp the character or the "essence" of, for

---

172 Eusebius, *HE* 5.1.31.

Fig. 7. The Roman aqueduct Pont du Gard in southern France, built in the first century CE.

example, a religion. In this case, we seek to grasp the "essence" of Christianity and Christian martyrdom in the cultural clash between Christians and non-Christians.

Again, as concerns the contemporary status report from Lyons in 177 CE, I shall not attempt to assess the empirical validity of that specific "reality" and its many miraculous events. Here, I find the symbolic truth more interesting than the possible historical truth. The salient points in this connection are the depiction of the occurrence of Christian martyrdom as an outcome of a religio-political clash, and the text's intention as a targeted act of communication relating to a pattern for Christian comportment. This means the cultivation – to a state of perfection – of a certain pure (Christian) approach to life and death. Our essential concern here is how the text and its message are perceived by its recipients, and how the contents of the text represented a model for Christian behaviour and the "essence" of Christianity. It is, significantly, on this point that we can proceed to examine the letter's illustration of certain religious attitudes and reactions in an ideal-typical light.

According to the letter, the fury and outrage of the townspeople are presented as one of the most important motivations behind the persecution of Christians in Lyons. The letter also states the religious justification for the people's anger: The reason why the heathen mob attacks the bishop is their conviction that if, as pagans, they fail to react to his defiance, then they will be violating their own deities, which in turn will punish them.[173] This reasoning is fully concordant with the fact that it is perceived as a serious religious violation when the Christians refuse to comply with the imperial authority's demands that they sacrifice to the traditional deities to ensure the health and well-being of Rome and her emperor and empire. This, then, is effectively the issue that lies at the crux of the Christian persecutions; a claim that is further substantiated by the above-mentioned example of the Christian spokesman, Vettius Epagathus, whose well-reasoned (and vain) defence of the imprisoned Christians attempts to refute the accusations of ungodliness and impiety.[174] Hence, we find that the Roman perception of Christian attitudes and behaviours as a violation of traditional Roman religion is confirmed, not only by non-Christian sources such as the Pliny–Trajan correspondence, but also by Christian sources such as the letter dealing with the martyrs of Lyons.

According to Eusebius, this entire period is characterized by the brutal persecution of Christians across the Roman Empire, and when explaining the upsurge of violence he specifically emphasizes a widespread opposition, not only among the Roman authorities but also among the common people, against adherents of the Christian faith.[175] From a Christian point of view, the assaults by the aggressive mob are perceived as a result of the Devil's work and ultimately as a test of their Christian faith. To the persevering Christians, martyrdom transforms evil into good because persecution leads to martyrdom, punishment to healing, helplessness to empowerment, suffering to release, and defeat to victory. The Christians' trials and tribulations clarify the struggle between those who are good (the righteous Christians) and those who are evil (the unrighteous pagans). The problems presented by this particular clash of religions naturally include the huge differences between traditional Roman and Christian thinking, not merely regarding

---

173 Eusebius, *HE* 5.1.31.
174 Eusebius, *HE* 5.1.9.
175 Eusebius, *HE* introduction to Book 5. Here the author refers to another work that he wrote to deal specifically with the martyrs. This work has since been lost.

the concept of God/gods, but also regarding the whole attitude towards life and death, "good" and "evil", and the actual essence of the struggle between good and evil. Christian ideas are anchored in a clear-cut dualism between good and evil, whereas the traditional Roman mind held different ideas about the contents and the implications of these concepts.

The meditations of Marcus Aurelius

According to Eusebius, the persecutions in Lyons took place while Marcus Aurelius reigned as emperor (161-180 CE), and the latter's position on Christians has long been discussed among scholars and researchers.[176] Ideas of justice, equal rights, freedom of speech, and the freedom of the governed were matters of great concern to Aurelius, who also gave much thought to improving the legal status of women, slaves, and other vulnerable groups in society.[177] One reason for this special interest was the trend in philosophical Stoicism of seeing an equality in the innate dignity of all people, irrespective of their gender, social status, distinction, or nationality. However, this Stoic interest in equality does not directly correspond with the Christian concept of equality. In Christian terms, equality did not consist in a common "dignity", but in a common "indignity" resulting from humankind's common Original Sin. Furthermore, equality in Christian terms was based on the death suffered by Jesus Christ for the sake of all people, whereas in Stoic terms the fundamental equality among people sprang from the idea that the essence of being human is decisively constituted by divine reason (*logos*). Stoics saw all people as equal in the sense that all human beings are based on reason – although they did concede that there was a gap between the wise man and the fool. Not all men are wise, but all men share the seed of divine reason. Stoics were obliged to take care of their fellow man because human beings and gods populate a shared world where each

---

176 Cf. A. Birley (1987) *Marcus Aurelius. A Biography*, 2nd revised ed. (1st ed. 1966), London, pp. 202-203; 256-265; Castelli (2004).
177 Marcus Aurelius, *Meditations* I.14; II.5. Cf. A.L.S. Farquharson (1944) *The Meditations of the Emperor Marcus Antoninus* I–II, Oxford; R.B. Rutherford (1989) *The Meditations of Marcus Aurelius. A Study*, Oxford; Birley (1987).

individual has obligations towards the community and towards the weak.[178] In keeping with this approach, Marcus Aurelius the Roman, the Stoic, the Emperor, could not permit the Christians – when they staunchly refused to sacrifice to the Roman gods and the emperor's well-being – to undermine the religio-political practices, community, and collective identity of the empire.

During his imperial reign Aurelius was constantly afield on military campaigns. In his spare time he would write down comments and thoughts addressed to himself, which reflect his views on people, society, religion, and philosophy. He often reflects on life as an individual, as a world citizen, and as emperor, and his *Meditations* exhibit a decidedly Stoic view of humanity, a strong sense of his imperial duty, and not a little *Weltschmerz*. To Aurelius, philosophy was a lifeline:[179]

> Of man's life, his time is a tiny point, his existence a flux, his sensation is clouded, his whole body's composition swiftly corruptible, his vital spirit an eddy, his fortune hard to predict, his fame uncertain. To put it briefly: all the things of the body, a river; all the things of the spirit, dream and delirium; life a warfare and a sojourn in a strange land: and as for renown hereafter, it is oblivion. What then can be man's escort through life? One thing only, philosophy.

Furthermore, as emperor one must wake up each morning prepared to meet brutal, scheming, selfish people. But the evil in these people is caused by ignorance, and consequently cannot hurt you – according to Aurelius, who also stresses that he who errs is acting out of ignorance; that often you yourself also act wrongly; and that what hurts you is not what the others do, but what you think about what they do.[180] To a stoically inclined emperor such as Aurelius, the world (*cosmos*) was a coherent, interlinked whole. This whole is also called "god", which does not prevent Stoics from simultaneously speaking of "gods" in the plural, since various gods represent different

---

178 Cf. Cicero, *De Officiis* III.27; *De Finibus* III.64; *De Republica* III.33; *De legibus* I.28.
179 Marcus Aurelius, *Meditations* II.17. Translation taken from Rutherford (1989) p. 236.
180 Marcus Aurelius, *Med.* II.1; XI.18. Cf. XII.26.

aspects of the divine cosmos.¹⁸¹ In a theoretical, philosophical, and religious sense the world is perfect and complete, because nothing exists outside the world. Also, the world is good, for if it were not good, then it would not be perfect and complete.¹⁸² That which appears to be imperfect or unhappy is therefore either an illusion or, in reality, a benefit to the cosmos. Put differently, a so-called "evil" can be beneficial to the cosmos because "good" needs its opposite to complement it and make it whole.

The good human being – which to Aurelius meant "the Stoic" – is someone who is satisfied because they have recognized and acknowledged that this is the way things are. A good person acknowledges that they are a small piece in the great puzzle that makes up the cosmos: a citizen alongside gods and fellow men in the state of being that is cosmos.¹⁸³ A good person therefore also accepts the lot in life that they are accorded by Fate, without discontent, reluctance, or fear. To the Stoic, attempting to defy or deny one's fate is an expression of stupidity, or more specifically "ignorance". As Aurelius sees it, a citizen of the world in the cosmic community has an obligation to understand the conditions and events that they encounter in life – in the sense of seeing through them and comprehending the true nature of things – rather than simply being contented with illusions or being influenced by the opinions of others. One has a duty to act according to one's knowledge and convictions when dealing with issues that are within one's power to affect. And one also has a duty to accept one's fate in life with equanimity.¹⁸⁴ That is why the Stoic does not quail at the prospect of death.

In his personal writings Aurelius reflects quite a bit upon the prospect of death, and he also mentions the willingness of the Christians to maintain their faith, even until death.¹⁸⁵ He seems to find this Christian eagerness to suffer and die distasteful. The decision to be prepared to meet death should not be the result of intransigence or some rebellious religious manifestation, but should instead rest upon a process of deliberation that is dignified,

---

181 Marcus Aurelius, *Med.* I.10; I.17; XII.28.
182 Marcus Aurelius, *Med.* VIII.50; V.30; XII.5; VII.9.
183 Marcus Aurelius, *Med.* X.1-10. Cf. V.27; II.16; IV.40.
184 Marcus Aurelius, *Med.* VI.41. Cf. II.17; IV.48; VI.49; V.31.
185 Marcus Aurelius, *Med.* XI.3.

personal, and free of theatrical posing. It seems that the approach Marcus Aurelius took towards Christians was largely in line with the Greek philosopher Epictetus (circa 55-135 CE), an important representative of Late Stoicism.

Epictetus, a native of Asia Minor, was born a slave but was later freed, so it is probably no coincidence that his philosophical thinking revolves around the concept of freedom. On the topic of being free of fear, Epictetus states that madness and desperation can lead to fearlessness in the face of death, as in the case of persecuted Christians.[186] What Epictetus wishes to demonstrate in this context is how the recognition of philosophical knowledge can neutralize fear. Epictetus, who is fond of propounding his views through fictitious conversations full of questions and inquiry, therefore asks what might enable, say, a tyrant to prompt fear. One obvious answer – still according to Epictetus – is that what causes such fear is the tyrant's guards with their long, sharp swords.[187] However, the philosopher's ensuing chain of inquiries concludes that when a person has understood, once and for all, that what has come into existence must also be extinguished in order that the cosmos should not stand still, then it does not make any difference to that person whether he is killed by a fever, or by a loose roofing tile falling on his head, or by guards with long, sharp swords. Nevertheless, as Epictetus adds, if he himself were forced to compare the alternatives, he would have no doubt that the guards would make a quicker and more painless job of it.

Both for Epictetus and for Marcus Aurelius the important thing was to free oneself of fear through philosophical recognition of the cosmos. Similarly, to the Stoic thinker Seneca the freedom of humankind was underscored by the option of committing suicide. As he so succinctly put it:[188]

The way of escape lies open before you.

In a letter, Seneca also writes that the person who asks one to ponder death is also obliging one to ponder freedom.[189] He also finds it important to re-

---

186 Epictetus, *Discourses* IV.7.6.
187 Epictetus, *Discourses* IV.7.4; IV.7.25-28.
188 Seneca, *On Providence* 6.7.
189 Seneca, *Epistulae* 26.10.

member that love of life certainly should not be squandered, but that it ought to be mitigated, such that if at some point circumstances make it necessary, then nothing should prevent one from being ready to take one's own life.

So here it is not the religious motives that are at stake, fuelling one's contempt of death or legitimizing the taking of one's own life. For the Christian martyrs, on the other hand, what mainly fuelled their contempt of death was the fear of religious condemnation combined with the fight for religious truth and longing for religious salvation and life eternal. About twenty years after the persecutions in Lyons, the church father Tertullian described Christian martyrdom as follows:[190]

> While thus, then, we spread ourselves before God, let the hooks pierce us, the crosses suspend us, the fires play upon us, the swords gash our throats, the beasts leap on us. The very posture of the Christian at prayer is readiness for any torture.

Tertullian describes the Roman view of these Christian martyrs, as well as the Christians' own perception of their persecution and martyrdom as the ultimate religious victory:[191]

> "Then," you [the Romans] say, "why complain that we persecute you, if you wish to suffer? You ought to love those who secure that you suffer what you wish!" ... Our battle consists in being challenged to face the tribunals; that there, in peril of life, we may fight it out for truth. Victory is the achievement of the thing for which you have fought. Our victory means the glory of pleasing God, and the spoils are eternal life. But we are condemned. Yes, when we have achieved our purpose. So we have conquered when we are killed; we escape when we are condemned. So you may now call us "faggot-fellows" and "half-axel-men", because we are tied to a half-axle-post, the faggots are piled round us, and we are burnt. This is our garb of victory, the robe embroidered with the palm; this our triumphal chariot.

---

190 Tertullian, *Apologeticum* 30.7.
191 Tertullian, *Apol.* 50.1-3.

The triumphant tones sung in praise of the Christian martyrs amount to a real victory for the Christians, causing a considerable amount of religious, social, and political unrest that the Roman authorities had to deal with. In his apologetic piece *To Scapula*, Tertullian addresses the Roman governor of Carthage in the year 212. He depicts a slightly threatening scenario in which thousands of Carthaginians, good Christian men and women of all ages and from all walks of life, line up to die as martyrs.[192] The church father particularly draws the governor's attention to two circumstances: firstly the scenario's social chaos and its potential consequences for Carthage; and secondly the governor's personal dilemma when he discovers that senators and other prominent figures within the aristocracy step forward as Christians, fully prepared to suffer a martyr's fate. Tertullian also refers to the story of a Roman governor in the province of Asia, who in the late 180s was contacted by a number of people who voluntarily declared themselves to be Christians. When the crowd encouraged the governor to punish the Christians with death he had a couple of them executed. But finding that this merely spurred the other Christians on to enthusiastically confess their faith, he lost his temper and shouted at them, infuriated, "You miserable lot! If you want to die, there are cliffs you can jump off, and ropes you can use to hang yourselves with!"[193]

Tertullian mentions in several instances the fact that Christians refused to revere Rome's deities. He describes the situation by enumerating various local cults that exist freely and openly in different places across the empire without Roman intervention, concluding:[194]

> But we alone [the Christians] are forbidden a religion of our own.
> We injure the Romans, we are reckoned not to be Romans, because we do not worship the god of the Romans.

This conclusion very precisely pinpoints the dilemma of this acculturation process, this clash of cultures, detailing the sometimes brutal Roman reactions to what was perceived as a grave infringement in contravention of

---

192 Tertullian, *Ad Scapulam* 5.
193 Tertullian, *Ad Scap.* 5.
194 Tertullian, *Apol.* 24.9.

Roman cultic practices. What is more, Tertullian's conclusion clearly bears witness to two key issues: His statement firstly confirms that local cults in the empire were generally able to carry on with limited interference, existing side by side with Roman cult. Secondly, it is evident that participating in Roman cultic activities defined "being Roman" within the sphere of the great, multicultural Roman Empire. Besides citizenship status, Roman identity consisted first and foremost in actively participating in Roman rituals, since upholding the traditional Roman cult insured the entire empire's welfare and cultural continuity.

In the year 212, Emperor Caracalla decided to extend Roman citizenship to almost all free men in the empire. Whatever his reasons for doing this, the edict in question stressed the interrelation between the Roman gods and the Roman Empire.[195] Consequently, Caracalla's considerable extension of Roman citizenship may very well have intensified the religious conflicts and the identity gap between Christians and non-Christians in the empire. In any case, imperial regulations during the periods that followed shone a much sharper spotlight on Christian *superstitio* and on Christians as enemies of the Roman deities and rites.

Around the year 250, Emperor Decius initiated the first systematic persecution of Christians throughout the empire. He issued an imperial edict ordering the entire population in every corner of the empire to make sacrifices to the gods. Special commissions were appointed to oversee the sacrifices in every town and city. Those who were professed or suspected Christians were able to obtain an official certificate in writing once they had publicly performed their sacrifice, proving that they had complied with the edict.[196] In this way, Decius sought to employ a religio-political strategy to unify a vast and multicultural empire by the compulsory performance of Roman rituals and traditional sacrifices.

Later spates of systematic persecution were instituted by Emperor Diocletian (who reigned 284-305). He implemented radical and far-reaching reforms of the Roman Empire aimed at re-establishing its military, financial, political, and religious stability. This included financing a number of mo-

---

195 Cf. Beard, North & Price (1998) vol. 1, p. 241.
196 Cf. Beard, North & Price (1998) vol. 2, p. 165; Fox (1986) pp. 450-462; J.B. Rives (1999) "The Decree of Decius and the Religion of Empire", *JRS* 89 (1999); Castelli (2004).

mentous construction projects and reinforcing the military by introducing new types of fortifications and new strategies. Furthermore, to maintain a grip on the far-flung empire Diocletian also introduced the Tetrarchic system: Management of the empire was divided between two senior Emperors, who handled the eastern and western parts, respectively, and each of these had one junior Caesar beneath him. In religio-political matters, Diocletian consolidated his supreme status in this imperial college by styling himself "Son of Jupiter".[197]

In other words, various types of religious legitimization and consolidation went hand in hand with the empire's military and political reforms – and this was presumably the backdrop for the extensive and systematic persecution of Christians that Diocletian initiated in 303. He refused to stand idly by while the growing number of Christians obstructed the veneration of traditional Roman deities (and imperial power), undermining the stability of the newly reformed Roman Empire. Orders were issued demanding that Christian congregations were to be dissolved, churches torn down, sacred manuscripts burned. Many Christians who refused to sacrifice to the Roman gods were imprisoned, tortured, enslaved, or killed. However, apparently Diocletian's successor, Emperor Galerius (who reigned 305-311), gave up persecuting Christians, although he did maintain that Christianity was destabilizing and detrimental to society.

Precisely why the persecution of Christians lost momentum at this juncture is hard to say with any certainty. The Christians, of course, believed that the Word of the One True God would inevitably prevail. Yet it also seems that credit is owed to the remarkable effects of the martyring of Christians. As reasoned above, in the experience of the Roman authorities such persecution, while certainly resulting in the execution and torture of the faithful, thereby momentarily reducing their numbers, those Christians who steadfastly opposed the authorities greatly promoted the Christian cause. So in effect, the contempt that the martyrs showed for suffering and death was able to arouse interest and spread the Christian message, thereby causing outcomes that were converse to what the Romans had intended. Hence, the persecution reinvigorated the minority movement's religious

---

[197] Cf. Wissowa G. (1971) *Religion und Kultus der Römer*, Munich (1st ed. 1912), p. 94; S. Williams (1985) *Diocletian and the Roman Recovery*, New York NY.

identity, group spirit, and religious ideals and zeal, which in turn increased its influence and swelled the ranks of Christian believers.

***

To summarize: As the examples in this chapter show, Christian persecution and martyrdom became pivotal issues in the context of constructing enemy images as acculturation played out in the Roman Empire. Generally speaking, the Christians interpreted the entire acculturation process, complete with religious conflicts and periodic persecutions, as a test of their faith. For those Christians martyrs who unswervingly stood by their faith, evil was transmuted into good: Persecution was transformed into martyrdom, punishment into healing, weakness into strength, failure into victory, and suffering into redemption. In a manner of speaking, it was through martyrdom that the Christian battle against paganism and evil reached its zenith. The Christians' trials and tribulations were regarded as the Devil's attempt to get the faithful to deny Jesus Christ as their Saviour. Those who rejected this diabolical offer and instead died as martyrs were following the example of Jesus Christ.

However, it will also have become evident by now that from a general Roman perspective, Christian martyrdom was a foreign, unfathomable, seditious, and undermining factor lodged within the framework of the norms and practices of the non-Christian world. In the context of the ritual sacrificial practices of the imperial age, Roman cult and the imperial throne and the future of the empire were three equivalent pillars supporting and upholding one great, common cause – and they must all be safeguarded and cultivated alongside whatever various local cults might exist throughout the empire's domain. Precisely because Christians refused to recognize the value of the Roman ritual practices and were prepared to lay down their lives for their convictions, their martyrdom was an ever-more maddening thorn in the side of the Roman authorities, and an aggravation to some local populations as well. What is more, the contempt that Christians exhibited in the face of death was perceived as a sort of rash, theatrical, rebellious attention-seeking that stood in stark contrast to, for instance, the seriousness and befitting composure with which a Stoic would ideally face death.

Fig. 8. Roman temple in Nîmes, southern France. Built by Marcus Agrippa, c. 20 BCE, this temple is one of the best-preserved Roman temples to be found anywhere in the former territories of the Roman Empire. The temple owes its excellent upkeep to the fact that it was reconsecrated as a Christian church in the late fourth century, thereby avoiding the destruction of pagan temples that ensued when Christianity became the only officially permitted religion in the empire.

As a rhetorical *topos*, the letter presented by Eusebius demonstrates that the martyr was an important example of how distinctive religious enemy images arose in a meeting between two extremely different modes of thinking and acting. The differences were striking, not just in the individual's relation to their gods or God, but also in their relation to the establishment and the state, to their immediate surroundings and the world around them, and to themselves. From a Christian point of view, martyrdom demonstrated the power of the One True Way and the path to redemption. From a non-Christian point of view, martyrdom displayed an abominable and erroneous sort of *superstitio* and constituted a stubborn and scandalous obstruction of Rome's imperial powers, threatening to rock the very foundations of the empire itself.

Interestingly, however, despite their huge differences and conflicting ways of thinking and acting, the construction of religious enemies in both camps was apparently motivated by a very basic and shared anxiety: fear of losing one's religion, identity, and culture. The Christian minority struggled to attain social and religious recognition in a hostile world, fearing all the while that they would be forced to give up their Christian faith. The Roman majority, including the imperial establishment, feared a weakening of their empire and the dissolution of the traditional religious practices that helped to consolidate imperial status and prestige, gluing together the innumerable tiles that made up the expansive and extremely heterogeneous mosaic that was the Roman Empire. From this perspective, the logical intention behind the periodic persecution of Christians was to counteract the threat that their new faith posed, not only to Roman power and identity, but to the empire's religious stability and cultural continuity.

In terms of flux and fix, the persecutions were Rome's attempt to contain the small but swelling wave of Christianity by launching a process of religious Romanization. When this Roman strategy failed, it brought about the opposite result – the making of Christian martyrs – and thereby effectively reinforced the momentum of the Christian movement.

Chapter 5

Some Religio-Political Trends – Worship of The Emperor, The Sun, and The Saviour

Augustus

After Rome's system of political government transformed from republic into empire, her successive emperors became the uncontested rulers of the entire Roman-dominated world. In 42 BCE the Senate officially elevated the deceased emperor Julius Caesar to the status of a divinity, granting him the title of *divus*. Caesar's will stipulated that his sole heir was to be Octavian, the nineteen-year-old son of his sister's daughter – which made this youth the adopted son of a divine being. This would prove to be very important for the religio-political power and leadership strategy of this young man, later renowned as Augustus (ruler of Rome from 27 BCE to 14 CE).

A copy of Augustus's own account of his *Achievements* has survived, found inscribed on a wall of the temple of Rome and Augustus in Ankara. This text, which according to Augustus's own wishes was to be inscribed and displayed in front of his mausoleum, portrays him as he wished to be remembered: the great statesman who brought an end to civil wars, reintroduced the traditional establishment, and remade Rome as a world power. In his *Achievements*, Augustus meticulously lists the political and religious offices he held, the huge costs he personally paid on behalf of the Roman state, and the admirable results he achieved as conqueror and peacemaker. He enumerates the many edifices he had built or restored during his reign (including 82 temples) and the many honorary titles and commendations he received – as well as those he refused. Once he had ended the many civil wars that beset the realm, he relinquished all his exceptional powers and mandates. That was when the Senate conferred upon him the religious title *Augustus*, which was just one of many honorifics paying tribute to his personal courage, clemency, piety, fairness, and integrity.[198] Augustus had undoubtedly learned a thing or two from observing the fate of his predecessor and great-uncle Julius Caesar, and – at least formally – he deftly avoided anything that might be perceived as reminiscent of former dictators or kings.

A decisive element in the power Augustus wielded was, of course, his status as *imperator*, and the position this gave him as supreme commander of the Roman war machine was not something he was willing to give up.

Augustus wisely preserved the Republic's institutions, but the system's senior officials could now be controlled through his own financial experts. And even though he emphasized the importance of respecting the Senate, in reality its political power was diminished. Senators became dependent on the emperor's good graces. What is more, foreign policy, which during the Republic had been one of the Senate's most important responsibilities, was now subsumed under the emperor's authority. The Senate did retain control of the state treasury, but state funds were scarce. The imperial coffers and a growing bureaucracy consequently took over more and more tasks in the administration of the empire.

In another new development, Augustus himself held important positions in multiple Roman priesthoods. During the Republic it was rare for any one member of the religio-political elite to hold more than a single important religious position. In other words, we find traces during the Augustan reign of a certain duality; a balancing between a Republican institutional façade and what was, in practice, an exceptionally high concentration of positions in which the emperor wielded actual religious and political power.

A further manifestation of the distinctive links between religious and political power on the one hand and the authority seated in the imperial office on the other is the huge number of temples, forums, aqueducts, baths, bridges, and roads that Augustus restored and built while in power. He expressly stated that his goal in rebuilding the city was to revive Rome's traditions, culture, and respect for its glorious past. In the lavishly furnished square Forum Augustum, for instance, he built a temple dedicated to Mars Ultor (Mars the Avenger), which he had vowed to erect after taking revenge

---

198 On Augustus's *Achievements* and the religions of imperial Rome, see, for instance, Beard, North & Price (1998) vol. I, pp. 167-312; Gradel (2002); Rives (2007).

on Julius Caesar's assassins.[199] At the same time, the great Mars Ultor temple was also a religious and political monument commemorating the emperor's victory over Parthia, a kingdom that was Rome's arch-enemy and represented one of the most pressing foreign-policy problems of his time. The Parthians had repeatedly humiliated the Roman army by capturing their battle standards, and after Augustus finally succeeded in getting the standards back he put them on show in front of the Mars Ultor temple. The fact that recapturing these standards was considered a great triumph is something that Augustus himself stresses in his *Achievements*, according to which he forced the Parthians to return booty and battle standards taken from no fewer than three Roman armies.

Following the Battle of Actium (31 BCE) and Rome's victory over the armies of Cleopatra and Mark Antony, the Senate was able to vote on 11 January 29 BCE that the doors of the Temple of Janus were to be closed. This was an event that tradition dictated could only take place when peace reigned at all of Rome's borders, and as such it was a decisive religio-political milestone for Augustus. Besides closing the temple doors the Senate decided to erect the *Ara Pacis* (Altar of Peace), in the Field of Mars in honour of Augustus and the Augustan Peace.

The friezes that embellish the enclosure surrounding the altar are related in various ways to Augustus and his activities, and to important myths and rites in Roman religion. The altar illustrates offerings and sacrificial processions featuring the Emperor, his family, and Roman officials. Other figures include attendants and sacrificial animals, and also a bearded man in a toga (often presumed to be Aeneas, the mythical progenitor of the Romans) who is preparing a sacrifice. The *Ara Pacis* clearly shows its viewers the rituals of a mythical past, the meanings of which are revived and renewed through the sacrifices Augustus himself makes at the peace altar. This establishes a mythico-historical line that runs directly from the earliest foundations of the city of Rome and all the way up to the Augustan Peace and the foundation of the Roman Empire. The altar's mythical references and depictions link Rome's glorious past with a great present and the hope of an even grander future. In short, the *Ara Pacis* demonstrates that religion is the fundamental

---

199 For details on the temple of Mars Ultor, see Beard, North & Price (1998) vol. II, pp. 80-83.

Fig. 9. A goddess of fertility and prosperity. Relief from the *Ara Pacis Augustae* in Rome, 13-9 BCE.

element in Roman history, in the world-spanning Roman Empire, and in Roman identity.

Much literary and archaeological evidence bears testimony to the close connections between religion and questions of war and peace in Roman culture. What is particularly interesting and decisive in the context we are presently discussing is that although there is a rich gallery of enemy images throughout the entire history of Rome, these enemy images are primarily linked to political and military affairs, meaning the internal and external conflicts of Rome and her empire, and to the emperor's institutional status. So historically speaking, enemies constructed by the Romans were not primarily related to religious affairs – at least not until Rome came face to face with Christianity.

Fig. 10. Processional frieze from the *Ara Pacis*.

Emperor worship

From the Roman Empire's inception, its history was characterized by a range of practices that scholars of Antiquity have referred to under the umbrella term "imperial cult" or "emperor worship". From a religio-historical point of view, however, this term does not cover just one type of devotion towards imperial power. It embraces a wide array of dissimilar phenomena, the shapes and meanings of which are dependent upon time, place, and varying religio-political situations. It is therefore no surprise that modern scholars disagree on how to most appropriately perceive and employ the concept of "Roman emperor worship". The abundance of definitions and interpretations that exist are based on very different sources, which are often viewed separately, outside of their original historical and cultural contexts. Also, the acts of veneration dedicated to living emperors are sometimes intermixed with the cultic worship of deceased emperors, contributing further to the confusion on this issue.[200] Just as today we have a wide variety of modern perceptions of emperor worship, various groups of Roman (and non-Roman) citizens in ancient societies presumably held very different views concerning the divine status of the emperor's person. What is more doubtful is that the common man in Antiquity contemplated any of the finer points being argued in today's subtle theoretical debates on this topic.

The literary sources and also the monuments, statues, reliefs, inscriptions, and coins that have survived indicate that Emperor Augustus was a great and gifted ruler, peacemaker, and reconstructor. He is portrayed as nothing less than a new and divinely legitimized reinventer of Rome and the founder of Roman world dominion in terms of religion and politics – even though contemporary interpretations of Augustus and the monuments lauding him obviously depend upon the beholder and his or her social position in the Roman Empire.

In connection with the transition from Republic to Empire the worship of the emperor in Rome itself can, in a certain sense, be perceived as both a religio-political problem and an religio-political solution. The "problem" is that Roman state cult is the preserve of deities and the divine sphere. This means that having a living person serve as the object of cultic worship appears to be contrary to traditional religious practices in Rome. Nevertheless, a more pragmatic solution comes into view when one takes the perspective that given that the Roman Republic was, for all intents and purposes, ruined beyond repair, it was necessary to provide divine cultic guarantees for a new form of government, and to undergird the power of a new ruler. Imperial rule backed by divine justification was therefore preferable by far to a monarchy based on the traditional model; a model which had actually been banned throughout Roman history. In his capacity as emperor, Augustus played a role in numerous religious institutions, ceremonies, and rites. Striking an appropriate balance between mortality and divinity was undoubtedly a difficult task. This is also clearly evident in the ongoing discussions among scholars and researchers, who still cannot agree on Augustus's status and the nature and extent of his self-styling.

Some of the sources suggest that Augustus tried to avoid becoming the

---

200 The death of an emperor would greatly simplify the issue of his divinity, and formally it was the Senate that was authorized to posthumously deify him.

object of the sort of divine cultic veneration that would traditionally befit a deity, at least within the confines of Rome itself. The fate of Julius Caesar may well have weighed on his mind. In the city of Rome various aspects of the emperor were the object of devotion: his *lares* (house or patron deities), his *genius* (life-force), and his *numen* (divine power).[201] In the Roman religious tradition this did not make the living emperor an official god. What it did do, however, was to clearly underline that there was a divine legitimization behind the Roman Emperor's status as the ruler of Rome and the Empire. It marked off the emperor's uniquely superior position in the secular and the religious sphere. Not so in the provinces.

Sources from the Roman dominions (including decrees of gratitude, honorary inscriptions, and temples expressly consecrated to Augustus) clearly indicate that the living emperor himself was worshipped in the same fashion as the traditional deities. These indications should probably be seen in light of the fact that the provinces often benefited very tangibly from the emperor's reforms, and so a reinforced and more direct brand of emperor worship would almost certainly have strengthened the ties between the provinces and the Roman Emperor. Temples in his honour were built far and wide, greatly helping to consolidate his position as ruler over the various dominions, and also helping to establish religio-political cohesion and thereby to "Romanize" a huge and extremely diverse empire, as described in Chapter 4.

Generally, emperor worship in its various forms provided a strong focus that converged on the Roman Emperor as the figure with the greatest authority over the armed forces and the highest position in the social, political, and religious hierarchy.

In cultic practices centred around the living emperor, it predominantly seems to be the office of emperor that is venerated rather than the person himself. It is the potency and prestige of the *imperator* to which divine character and strength are attributed. This is linked to the traditional belief that the benevolence of the Roman gods was a precondition for governing the Roman Empire. Political and military successes therefore demonstrated that the gods were favourably inclined. By inference, as part of the divine

---

201 Cf. Gradel (2002); Beard, North & Price (1998) vol. 1, pp. 206-210.

governance of the world the office of the Roman Emperor was raised up to become a vital ritual hub between gods and mortals.

Elagabalus, god and emperor: the acculturation of the Syrian sun-god

The sun-god Sol Invictus ("The Invincible Sun") was one of several rivals to the cult of Christ, and this deity came to play an important role during the Roman Empire, not least during the reign of Emperor Aurelian. It must be emphasized, however, that generally the various ancient sun cults are intermixed almost to the point of indistinguishability in a body of sources that is complicated and fragmentary, and which primarily consists of inscriptions and images that are widely dispersed in time and place. We do know, though, that about 50 years before the rise of Emperor Aurelian's cult of Sol Invictus, a relatively brief but nonetheless quite remarkable example of acculturation took place on Roman soil. It is a convoluted and rather odd course of events that precedes and in a sense presages the Sol Invictus cult, and which relates to Emperor Marcus Aurelius Antoninus and the Syrian sun-god Elagabalus.

The story runs as follows: Julia Domna, the wife of Emperor Severus and mother of their two sons Geta and Caracalla, was born the daughter of the priest-king who served the sun-god Elagabalus in the Syrian city of Emesa (modern-day Homs). Julia Domna came to hold a key position in the power structure after Caracalla ascended the imperial throne, and after he was assassinated in 217 CE she committed suicide. But Julia Domna had a sister, Julia Maesa, who was able to manoeuvre her daughter's son into a position that would make him the successor of Caracalla. Julia Maesa's plan succeeded, and her very young grandson became Emperor under the official name of Marcus Aurelius Antoninus (reign 218-222 CE).

This emperor is better known as Elagabalus, a name he was given after his death. It is actually the name of the Syrian sun-god that was the principal deity of the city of Emesa, and to whose priests the emperor's bloodline was related. The surviving sources – which remain the object of intense debate – are full of outrageous stories about Elagabalus the emperor, who also served as the sun-god's high priest.[202] Whether the accounts of his lavishness and excesses (priestly and carnal) are true or not, they contain interesting thoughts on the issues of extreme behaviour, acculturation, religious pluralism, and cultural continuity. These colourful stories (which may or may not be spiced with fictitious elements) indicate potential reactions to, and ways of handling, situations where cultures meet and religions conflict. They also illustrate which types of foreign and extreme social and religious ideas and behaviours were able to create cultural and religious discord, thereby rousing the levels of indignation and debate among Rome's populace and politicians to great heights – even while exerting a certain fascination on the city's people, and on chroniclers.

Elagabalus was declared emperor while he was still residing in Emesa, and the Greek historian Herodian, who wrote of the events just after the reign of Elagabalus ended, provides an intriguing account of the meeting between religions and cultures.[203] Herodian writes of how, right from the very start, Elagabalus introduced Rome to a religiously and culturally innovative and utterly immoderate style. Prior to his arrival at Rome the new emperor wished to test the reactions of the senators and the people. He therefore had a portrait made of himself in Emesa, clad in the full glory of his colourful Oriental priestly garb and standing next to the deity Elagabalus, making a sacrificial offering. He then sent this portrait to Rome, ordering that it be hung in the Senate above the head of the statue of Victory – precisely the place where the senators would offer wine and incense when entering the building. He also ordered that all Roman magistrates and others performing public sacrifices were to invoke the new deity, Elagabalus, before invoking the other gods. And so, if we are to believe Herodian, when the new emperor finally arrived in Rome wearing the strange vestments of his foreign priestly

---

202 Cf. G. W. Bowersock (1975) "Herodian and Elagabalus", *Yale Class. Stud.* 24 (1975) p. 229-236; R. Turcan (1985) *Héliogabale et le sacré du soleil*, Paris; M. Frey (1989) *Untersuchungen zur Religion und zur Religionspolitik des Kaisers Elagabal* (*Historia* Supp. 62) Stuttgart; Beard, North & Price (1998) vol.1, pp. 255-256; Wissowa (1971) pp. 365-368.
203 Herodian, *Hist*ory V.5.5-7. Cf. Beard, North & Price (1998) vol. II, pp. 206-207. On Emperor Elagabalus, see also Historia Augusta (Augustan History), *Life of Elagabalus*, though note that researchers strongly debate the reliability of this portrayal.

office, the Romans had already become so thoroughly used to this sight that not a single eyebrow was raised.

Apparently the young Elagabalus considered himself to be not only a representative of the sun-god but also an actual incarnation of the sun-god. In addition, he also struck upon a fresh new religio-political idea: to make Elagabalus the principal deity for all of Rome's many and varied cults, and for Jews and Christians as well. To do this he had the deity Elagabalus – which was worshiped in Emesa in the form of a conical black stone – physically transported to Rome in 219 CE. The emperor had the god/stone placed in a newly built temple on the Palatine, close to his own imperial palace, and also built a summer residence to accommodate it east of the city.[204] Twice a year the cone-shaped deity was moved from one location to the other in a special procession, riding upon the Chariot of the Sun, which was drawn by a team of snow-white horses. The emperor additionally had sacred images and other cultic objects removed from Rome's numerous other temples and transferred to the new Elagabalus temple. As it turned out, putting the unfamiliar Syrian god above all other deities, including Jupiter himself, was a religious innovation that gave rise to considerable resentment amongst the Roman community.

Many of the new emperor's personal habits were perceived as extremely exotic: It was said that he never took a bath without pouring the most exquisite perfumes into his bathwater, and he filled his belly with sophisticated dishes like flamingo brains and nightingale and peacock tongues.[205] Clearly the emperor's behaviour was a source of resentment and fascination. By Roman standards he was rather effeminate: He was fond of dancing and spinning wool; wore a hair net and dressed in colourful silken garments; accessorized his outfits with long necklaces, jangling bracelets, and soft slippers; and made up his face with white-lead ointment. Some of these features undoubtedly came with his status as high priest, for the cultic costume was very colourful and made of gold-embroidered silk. According to Syrian custom he was also circumcised and refrained from eating pork. These things

---

204 Cf. Beard, North & Price (1998) vol. 1, p. 256; F. Chausson (1995) "Vel Iovi vel Soli: Quatre études autour de la Vigna Barberini (191-354)" MEFRA (1995) 107, pp. 661-765.
205 Herodian, *Hist.* V.5.5-7. Hist. Aug., *Life of Elagabalus* 20.

caused a good deal of revulsion and surprise, respectively, but being based on cultic requirements they could be tolerated, at least to a certain degree. Nevertheless, something that apparently could and did cause strong resentment among born-and-bred Romans was that the Emperor would wear his outlandish outfits for official occasions – situations in which Roman custom required the emperor to wear the Roman toga.

Another serious religious infringement arose when Elagabalus sought to link his new sun cult to the traditional cult of Vesta by marrying Aquilia, a most highly revered Vestal virgin of Rome. The nuptials were officially celebrated with great pomp and circumstance. According to Roman practices such an action was a severe religious breach, violating the vow of chastity taken by the Vestal virgins. In fact, under normal circumstances the punishment would involve burying the priestess alive and publicly flogging the guilty man in the Forum Romanum. Yet it seems that Aquilia avoided the traditional punishment. No one knows why. Perhaps because she was forced into the marriage. Perhaps because her vow of chastity had not been broken in the technical sense. The first wife of Elagabalus was said to be a virgin even after their divorce, and the sources strongly indicate that the emperor preferred rest and recreation in the company of men rather than women.

Another of his bright new cultic ideas was to bring Tanit, the patron goddess of Carthage, to Rome (as Regina Caelestis, the heavenly queen). Here, in an extravagant wedding ceremony, Tanit was married to the god Elagabalus and neatly installed in his temple.[206]

Emperor Elagabalus allegedly held boat races at the Circus in channels filled with wine, and at festivals he would sometimes toss violets and other blossoms on his guests – in such heaps that some of them were asphyxiated as a result. Other accounts say that he delighted the people of the city with invitations to enormous drinking binges, and by setting up lotteries where participants could win all sorts of prizes, ranging from 10 camels or 10 pounds of gold to 10 mice, 10 flies, 10 heads of lettuce, or a dead dog. He kept tame lions, leopards, and bears as pets, and he found it incredibly amusing to let them loose among his friends as they lay in a stupor after a night of heavy drinking.[207]

---

206 Cassius Dio, *HR* LXXIX.12; Herodian, *Hist.* V.6.4-6.5.
207 Hist. Aug., *Life of Elagabalus* 21-23; 25.

All in all, the sources on the reign of Elagabalus draw a picture – probably somewhat exaggerated – of a young man who lived out debauchery and vice to the fullest extent, freely indulging his own religious eccentricities, obscene habits, lustful promiscuity, and extravagance, and exhibiting a remarkable irresponsibility in matters of government. Rather than making appointments based on political experience and qualifications, Elagabalus seems to have assembled his staff on the merit of their excesses. He surrounded himself with a veritable army of whores, pimps, and fancy-boys, and his highest-ranking imperial officials included a dancer, a barber, a donkey-driver, a cook, and a blacksmith.[208]

Needless to say, this intriguing religio-political leadership strategy was not tenable in the long run, and finally it became too much to bear even for the emperor's own maternal grandmother, Julia Maesa. It was she who had originally brought him to the imperial throne, and she who orchestrated his murder. The deity Elagabalus was banned from Rome along with its entire cult, and the conical black stone was sent packing, back to Emesa.

Compared with the way Augustus governed as emperor, as initially described in this chapter, the colourful stories of Emperor Elagabalus and his religious and personal excesses underscore how different the manifestations and the outcomes of religious encounters and conflicts in Rome could be. Foreign rites playing out at the highest levels of the religious and political hierarchy could produce very different reactions in the various layers of Roman society, ranging from fascination to outrage, from acceptance to expulsion. Regardless of its potentially fictitious elements, the many tales of the enigmatic rule of Emperor Elagabalus, and of the Syrian sun-god's banishment to Emesa, remind us that it was certainly possible to transport or transplant foreign cultures to Rome, but also that it was equally possible to kick them out of the city again if they threatened or undermined the emperor's power and status or Rome's state religion.

Whilst the colourful cult of Elagabalus was evicted, what became of the much less colourful cult of Christ is quite a different story. This cult was neither ready nor willing to leave town, and at one point it was even identified with the cult of Sol Invictus, as described below.

---

208 Hist. Aug., *Life of Elagabalus* 12.

Emperor Aurelian and Sol Invictus

Following a period that left the empire weakened by plagues, civil wars, invasions, political chaos, internal strife, and power struggles, Emperor Aurelian (a native of Illyria who reigned 270-275) succeeded in once again consolidating the Roman Empire. After many hard-won battles against the Germanic tribes Aurelian went on a campaign eastwards, to the region where Queen Zenobia had had her son proclaimed emperor and herself proclaimed empress in 271 CE. Aurelian crushed Zenobia's army in a bloody battle fought in Syria, and after a brief siege her city of Palmyra surrendered. Despite her attempts to escape, Queen Zenobia was captured and taken to Rome, where she was paraded in front of the people as part of Aurelian's triumphal procession.

To symbolize his victory and imperial consolidation, Emperor Aurelian summoned up the cult of the invincible sun, Sol Invictus. Using this sun cult he could seek to forge links between the many different cultures in the Roman Empire and dissolve the tensions and hostility that existed between its Eastern and Western parts. In 274 CE, Aurelian inaugurated a great temple to Sol Invictus and instituted a new Roman priesthood (*pontifices Solis*) along the lines of the traditional Roman priesthoods. The date December 25 marked the Festival of Sol Invictus and also celebrated the consecration of the temple, which was famed for its elaborate decorations – enabled in no small part by the treasures that the victorious Aurelian had brought home from Palmyra as the spoils of war. That is why this temple, in particular, was associated with the cult of the Syrian sun-god Ba'al of Palmyra.[209]

From an acculturation perspective, however, it is obvious to regard the cult of Sol Invictus in a wider religio-political, multicultural, and syncretistic context. In the same way as the Roman Empire encompassed numerous and very diverse peoples, this sun cult was an obvious choice as a deity that could bring together and encompass a number of different sun-god images and ultimately roll them into one: It was relatively easy to identify Latin, Greek, Syrian, Egyptian, Gallic, Germanic, Anatolian, and Illyrian sun-gods with Emperor Aurelian's version of Sol Invictus. At the same

---

209 Wissowa (1971) p. 367, note 3; Beard, North & Price (1998) vol. 1, p. 259.

time, the rootedness and the anchoring of the cult in Roman tradition was highlighted when Aurelian instituted a new Roman priesthood to serve this sun-god, thereby refraining from bringing the deity's Palmyran priests to Rome – perhaps with the still-vivid stories of Elagabalus and his vanquished sun-god in mind.

The designation *invictus* has been applied to several different mythical sun-gods of varying origins, and it reflects a well-known religio-historical tendency to confuse, blend, and mutually identify deities that resemble one another. In this syncretistic process many conceptions merged into one another and, in this case, became associated with a larger and much loftier god than the original sacred figures. What happened was that over time the divine title of Deus Sol Invictus took on an identity of its own, achieving the status of the Roman Empire's supreme deity. Aurelian's successors perpetuated the cult of Sol Invictus, and we have testimony that priests of Sol Invictus existed as late as the 390s.

Nevertheless, as posterity has shown us even the great Sol Invictus did not remain undefeated. Perhaps as the decades rolled by Sol Invictus was gradually subdued by the power of the Christian establishment's emphasis on internal organization, centralization, and control? Whatever the reasons, we know that by the advent of the third century CE the Bishop of Rome had become an exceedingly powerful figure. We might get some idea of just how powerful he was from Bishop Cyprian's remark that Emperor Decius was more afraid to hear about the election of a new bishop of Rome than about a pretender to the throne.[210]

As described in Chapter 4, around the year 250 CE, Decius introduced the first systematic persecution of Christians that covered the whole Roman Empire. This measure probably sprang not merely from his reforming of the empire, but also from his misgivings about the institutionalization of Christianity itself. In this light, his more systematic persecution would also be a response to the Christian consolidation, centralization, and control that was taking shape, partly by means of the Christians' construction of internal and external religious enemies. After Decius, there were further

---

210 Cyprian, *Epistulae* (*Letters*) 55.9.

outbreaks of persecution and imperial regulations against the Christians. In 257 the Emperor Valerian ordered all to perform Roman rites, and Christian bishops, presbyters and deacons who failed to do this were exiled. The following year, those who refused to sacrifice became liable to execution. Among those executed under Valerian were Cyprian, bishop of Carthage, who was declared an enemy of the Roman gods and rites.[211] However, the persecution of the Christians was not a continuous process. Valerian was killed in 260 and – according to the Christian bishop Eusebius – the son and co-emperor, Gallienus, reversed his fathers persecution of Christians and directed the bishops to perform their customary duties in freedom.[212] But in 303, as described in Chapter 4, Emperor Diocletian initiated an extensive and systematic persecution of Christians. The political ideology of the Diocletianic Tetrarchy was rooted in traditional Roman religious practice and values. Christianity was undermining the stability of the newly reformed Roman Empire and orders were issued demanding that Christian congregations were to be dissolved. Christians who refused to sacrifice to the Roman gods were imprisoned, tortured, enslaved, or killed.

The controversial conversion of Constantine

Towards the end of the third century and into the early fourth century, Rome gradually ceased to be the emperor's primary residence and the centre of imperial government. The Eternal City's importance as the fulcrum of the empire waned as Rome's dominions and authority were divided between East and West. This radically altered the course of imperial history, setting the scene for a series of far-reaching changes on Rome's religio-political stage. These changes took place during the fourth century, and the most well-known and remarkable shift – the recognition of Christianity as a state religion – was initiated by Emperor Constantine the Great.

But in looking at Constantine we face certain questions relating to an extremely controversial figure's even more controversial conversion to Christianity. The discussions about Constantine and the sources describing his

---

211 Cf. W.H.C. Frend (1965) *Martyrdom and Persecution in the Early Church*, Oxford, p. 327.
212 Eusebius, *HE* 7.13.

life and deeds, not to mention the impact they had, seem to be endless.[213] The following treatment therefore considers only a few aspects that hold particular relevance for the issues of acculturation, religious pluralism, and freedom of religion.

Constantine interpreted his military victory in 312 at Pons Milvius in Rome as a Christian victory. According to the Christian bishop Eusebius, who knew and admired Constantine, the emperor himself related several years later what had happened. The reason for his sudden change of heart was a portent: Before the battle of the Milvian Bridge, Constantine had a vision, seeing in the heavens a sign of the cross inscribed with the words "By this, conquer", and the following night Christ appeared to Constantine in a dream.[214] The emperor's about-face and subsequent position in favour of Christianity is therefore inscribed in the history of religion as a decisive turning-point.[215] According to the Christian writer Lactantius, however, Constantine was already a protector of Christianity from the moment he became an Augustus in 306.[216]

The principal source on Constantine's controversial conversion is the account that Eusebius wrote about him. This account of Constantine's life is, at the same time, an account that reflects the bishop's own extremely subjective perception of Constantine, which is intimately intertwined with the bishop's subjective glorification of Christianity as a conquering force.[217] If, despite these acknowledged weaknesses, one still chooses to accept Eu-

---

213 See, for instance, N.H. Baynes (1972) *Constantine and the Christian Church*, 2nd ed., London; T.D. Barnes (1981) *Constantine and Eusebius*, Cambridge MA; T.D. Barnes (2011) *Constantine: Dynasty, Religion and Power in the Later Roman Empire*, Malden MA; S.N.C. Lieu & D. Montserrat (1998) *Constantine. History, Historiography and Legend*, London; H.A. Drake (2000) *Constantine and the Bishops. The Politics of Intolerance*, Baltimore MD; Clark (2004) pp. 93-117; R. Van Dam (2007), *The Roman Revolution of Constantine*, Cambridge.
214 Eusebius, *Vita Constantini* 1.28-1.29; Lactantius, *De Mortibus Persecutorum* 44.5; Cf. Barnes (2011) pp. 61-89.
215 Cf. G.B. Millar (1992) "The Jews of the Graeco-Roman Diaspora between Paganism and Christianity, AD 312-438" in Lieu, North & Rajak (1992) pp. 97-123; T. Barnes (1998) "Constantine, Athanasius and the Christian Church" in Lieu & Montserrat (1998) pp. 7-20; Barnes (2011).
216 Lactantius, *De Mort. Pers.* 24.9, cf. Barnes (2011) p.65.
217 Cf. Eusebius, *HE* 10.8.

Fig. 11. Head of the Colossus of Constantine the Great (emperor, 306-337 CE). This and other fragments of the Colossus are in the Palazzo dei Conservatori, Musei Capitolini, in Rome.

sebius's writings as a reliable account, the questions follow thick and fast: What role did the emperor's vision play? How was it interpreted by contemporary Christians, and by non-Christian Romans? What did people whisper behind closed doors about this matter? And what did the senators think of it, given that on Constantine's triumphal arch in Rome they authorized the (discreet) attributing of his victory to "the inspiration of the divine", without specifying which divinity was responsible?[218] What significance lay in the fact that after his victory Constantine did not sacrifice at the temple of Jupiter on the Capitoline, as victors customarily did? Did Constantine really abandon the traditional Roman gods from one day to the next? Could his motives have been more tactical and political than religious? The list of question goes on.

---

218 *Inscriptiones Latinae Selectae* (1892-1916) edited by H. Dessau, Berlin, 694.

Unfortunately, we can only speculate on the answers to these and other questions about the workings of Constantine's mind. But we do know that a meeting took place in Milan in February of 313, and that during this meeting Constantine and Licinius, his co-emperor, laid down a general policy on religion. Scholars disagree about the details, but based on the meeting in Milan a letter was later sent from Licinius to the Roman governors in the eastern provinces setting out guidelines for dealing with Christians. This letter (quoted in Lactantius) classifies both the cult of Christ and the cults of non-Christians as *religio*, underscoring that everyone has the right to openly and freely practice devotion to any cult:[219]

> When I, Constantine Augustus, and I, Licinius Augustus happily met at Milan and had under consideration everything which related to public convenience and security, we thought that, among other matters which would benefit most people, arrangements particularly needed to be made to ensure respect for the divinity, so that we should grant both to Christians and to all people freedom to follow whatever *religio* each one wished, whereby whatever divinity exists in the celestial abode can be placated and propitious to us and all who are placed under our power. ...

This shows that the agenda for the meeting in Milan not only dealt with Christianity in particular, but also with freedom (or toleration) of religion in general.

The essential point here is that Christianity was officially redefined from *superstitio* to *religio*, and that Christians were not to be regarded and treated as enemies of Roman religion and the Roman state. It is also worth noting that the letter reflects consideration for the individual's rights to choose to practice this or that type of *religio*. The framework of traditional Roman religion already allowed a range of choices as to cultic worship, but the

---

219 Eusebius, *HE* 10.5.4; Lactantius, *De Mort. Pers.* 48.2-12. Translation taken from Beard, North & Price (1998) vol. II, p. 283. Concerning the misleading application of the term "Edict of Milan" to the letter, see Barnes (2011) pp. 93-97. Cf. Drake (2000); U. Berner (2008) "Early Christianity as a Global Religion" in A.W. Geertz & M. Warburg (2008) *New Religions and Globalization*, Aarhus.

collective dimension of official religion was still a key feature. *Religio* was, above all, concerned with ensuring the continuity, fecundity, and welfare of the entire society (*salus publica*). And although the letter concerns a kind of "general freedom of religion" without therefore taking steps to eradicate pagan cultic practices, Constantine initiated a religious and sociological shift that led to a new and less prominent status for the ancient Roman religious practices as a matter of collective importance.

This shift in the foundations of religion – from its being a primarily collective matter towards becoming a matter of personal choice – would prove to be decisive to the perception of the links between religion, society, and identity. With the passing of time the collective worship of the Roman deities lost its function as a specific precondition for the welfare of the Roman Empire. Hence, in the long run it ceased to be the trait that primarily characterized Roman identity at a micro level and a macro level. That is why the letter mentioned above seemingly heralds a landmark shift in the basic paradigm. Still, the question of how the guidelines set out in the letter to the eastern provinces were actually administered *in practice* is an altogether different matter, and there may well have been considerable variations between one area or one governor and another. At any rate, the shift came about through a very slow process, as exemplified in the matter of Bishop Gelasius and the pagan Lupercalia festival. This celebration was still going on in Rome as late as 495, as described further on in this chapter.

What is indisputable is that during his rule Constantine began to actively support Christianity in a manner that was hitherto unseen. From 313 onwards he supported the building of Christian churches and Christian authorities throughout the Roman Empire by means of huge donations and tax exemptions. In addition Constantine himself had various churches built, and in Rome alone he financed the construction of five or six new churches.[220] Though previous emperors had ended persecution of Christians, no previous emperor had officially redefined Christianity from *superstitio* to *religio* and made huge donations from the imperial treasury to the Christian authorities. No previous emperor had founded or endowed churches. This is indeed a religio-political turning-point, initiated at the meeting in Milan and

---

220 Eusebius, *HE* 10.6; cf. Beard, North & Price (1998) vol. I, pp. 364-388; Barnes (2011) pp. 85-89.

reflected in the letter to the eastern provinces. In this fashion Constantine very visibly initiated a religio-political process in which Christianity was increasingly favoured by the imperial office. At the same time, however, this process shows signs of merging and shifting between pagan and Christian ideas. One instance of this is Constantine's appearance alongside Sol Invictus (though he did not appear alongside any other Roman deities) on coins dating well into the 320s. And along this same line, there is the necropolis beneath the Basilica of Saint Peter, where Christ is depicted as the sun-god Sol Invictus, who with the sun's rays shining about his head drives his team of horses across the arc of the heavens.

Whatever his motivations, Constantine apparently found the cult of Christ to be more powerful than the cult of Sol Invictus. After this point it would primarily be the cult of Christ that guaranteed the existence and the welfare of the Roman Empire, and Constantine's about-face gave the emperor control of the Christian Church as an organization and as a force to be reckoned with. This made the emperor an important player in the process that redefined the Christian Church: What was formerly a suspicious and socially detrimental organization was on its way to becoming a well-reputed, top-down-managed organization that consolidated power and was seen as a pillar of society. From a religio-historical point of view, however, this process was rather protracted, and was influenced by shifting religio-political and identity-related interests, conflicts, and battles for social and religious recognition. During the process, the Christian emperors in certain respects also acted as leaders of the Christian Church, in that they would summon the parties to meetings and also approve or reject various types of decisions concerning, say, the validity of battling Christian factions. The early history of Christianity shows that constructions of religious enemies were also based on numerous internal discussions and battles with (and on the persecution of) so-called heretical sects. From the time of Emperor Constantine onwards we see Rome's emperors prohibiting such sects by law. In this way the successive emperors came to play an active role in establishing Christian orthodoxy in its various and changing forms.[221] Furthermore, from Constantine

---

221 Cf. Beard, North & Price (1998) vol. 1, pp. 369-375; S.G. Hall (1991) *Doctrine and Practice in the Early Church*, London.

Fig. 12. Mosaic of Christ as *Sol Invictus*, from the necropolis beneath Saint Peter's Basilica in Rome. Early Christian and pagan beliefs come together in this third-century mosaic of Christ represented as a sun-god.

onwards there are several examples of imperial laws limiting Judaism. Such laws caused Christians who converted to Judaism to forfeit their personal property and prohibited Jews from holding certain civic offices.

Finally, Constantine prohibited *superstitio*, which especially targeted non-official rituals concerning divination. As discussed in the preceding chapters, however, this sort of activity was strongly frowned upon even in pre-Christian times. In connection with the traditional Roman institution of public portents Emperor Constantine would still permit, for instance, that prodigious events such as lightning striking public buildings were to be interpreted by the priesthood of the *haruspices*, as tradition prescribed.[222] This is clear evidence of Constantine's acceptance of an undeniably pagan practice and of a likewise undeniably pagan priesthood. It is also worth noting here that Constantine himself, like the emperors before him, held the office of *pontifex maximus* – the high priest of Rome's public religion.

***

From a consistently Christian point of view, in the long term naturally Christianity could not simply be incorporated side by side with other religions in the multicultural Roman Empire – which was, in fact, the gist of the above-mentioned letter that was issued to the governors in the East. From a Christian – and ultimately also a Constantinian – perspective, the faithful could not merely regard Christianity as one brand of *religio* among many. The opposite of Christianity was not other religions but heresy and paganism, in short: *superstitio*. As stressed repeatedly in the preceding chapters, the Christian religion had a new and uncompromising requirement that was absolute, implying that Christianity fundamentally rejected all other religions.[223] And as mentioned, such a requirement of religious "absoluteness" must still have seemed unprecedented and subversive based on traditional Roman ways of thinking and acting.

On this basis it is evident that the religious pluralism of the Roman Empire was, and continued to be, an unresolved problem of (religious) acculturation for the Christian emperors: They issued numerous and repetitive regulations against the traditional cults. And in 391 and 392 the Emperor Theodosius prohibited all sacrifices, closed all temples, and threatened Roman magistrates with penalties if they broke the ban. Ultimately, the Christian perspective was that only a single state cult could be tolerated,

---

222 Cf. Beard, North & Price (1998) vol. I, pp. 372-373; Rasmussen (2003) pp. 35-182.
223 Cf. H.C. Brennecke (1995) "Der Absolutheitsanspruch des Christentums und die religiösen Angebote der Alten Welt" in J. Mehlhausen (ed.) (1995) *Pluralismus und Identität*, pp. 380-397.

namely the Christian Church. This religious conflict is reflected in sources dating well into the fifth century, and it is clearly illustrated by accounts like that of the internal quarrel between Gelasius, the Bishop of Rome, and certain Christians in the city: The Bishop issued a harsh letter attacking and condemning Christians for celebrating the ancient Roman fertility festival of Lupercalia.[224] From the letter it is evident that around the year 495 this festival was still celebrated not only by pagan Romans but also by certain Christians, whom Bishop Gelasius felt obliged to prohibit from participating in the festival. Incidentally, it is noteworthy that the bishop's prohibition evidently caused great opposition among the Christians of the Roman elite, who felt that the city's traditional cultic rites ought to be carried out as was customary, out of regard for the welfare of Roman society.

The bishop's letter tells us several things. Firstly, it testifies to the tenacity of non-Christian rituals and beliefs, pitting a Christian bishop against a pagan festival that simply refused to die, and this at a time when the church fathers had been thundering against paganism for 300 years or so. Secondly, it reflects the perception among Romans, Christian and pagan alike, that the Lupercalia was not merely a cornerstone of Roman culture, but also an irreplaceable precondition for the continued existence of that culture. To the traditional Roman mind the city's future quite simply hinged on the performance of these rites, even though Christianity at that time was the official religion of the city. In other words, as late as 495 CE paganism was still a living (and highly controversial) focal point for Rome's past, present, and future. The legendary, time-honoured festival of Lupercalia could not simply be written off, even by those who might well confess their faith in the Christian God and religion with its dogmas and its particular tenet of monotheism.

This example eloquently demonstrates how tough and tenacious traditional religious thoughts and actions were, and also how religion was the glue that held Roman society together and was, decisively, able to dictate on questions of identity in the ancient world. In short, the entire affair of Bishop Gelasius and the Lupercalia was about asserting the identity and

---

224 Cf. Beard, North & Price (1998) vol. II, pp. 123-124.

Fig. 13. The remains of the temple of Saturn (god of agriculture and wealth) in the Forum Romanum. The temple is said to have been founded in the last years of the monarchy or the early years of the Republic. The temple of Saturn housed the state treasury of Rome. It was completely rebuilt in 42 BCE, then rebuilt again under Emperor Diocletian after a fire in 283 CE.

the future of the Romans and the city of Rome, the question being: If the ancient deities, cults, and festivals were abolished, could Roman society even continue to exist?

Chapter 6

God's Great Olive-Press – from Augustine to Huntington?

Augustine and Manichaeism

According to the renowned theologian and thinker Saint Augustine of Hippo (354-430), who was the most influential of the Latin church fathers, we are all little olives that must go through God's great olive-press. The aim of this processing, as Augustine saw it, is to separate the droplets of pure oil in the true believers from the dregs of blasphemy and non-belief.[225] In keeping with this view Augustine expended a large part of his formidable strength in fighting the dregs of blasphemy, heresy, and sacrilege. This is suggested by the many titles in his huge body of work that begin with or contain the word *contra*, one notable example being his magnum opus *De Civitate Dei contra Paganos* (*The City of God against the Pagans*). There is no doubt that in his own day and in later times Augustine exerted a strong influence when it came to determining what was "proper Christian doctrine" and what was false doctrine. It was precisely by delimiting and fighting against heresies that the True Faith could be thrown into relief and true believers recognized and separated from the heretics. This was, quite simply, Augustine's basic view:[226]

---

225 Augustine, *Epistulae* 111.2 "… so that under this great pressure, as it were, in the olive-press of the Lord our God, although there be the dregs of unbelieving murmurs and blasphemies there is also a steady outflowing of pure oil in the confessions and prayers of believers."
226 Augustine, *Confessions* 7.19.

> For the disapproval of heretics makes the tenets of Your Church and sound doctrine to stand out boldly. For there must be also heresies, that the approved may be made manifest among the weak.

It is also clear from Augustine's work *Confessiones* that fighting false doctrines was a preoccupation that shaped his personal development. Parts of this work describe how, as a young man, his philosophical mind had been awakened by reading the work of Cicero, and how in disappointment over the Bible he had turned to philosophical scepticism.[227] In religious matters he was seriously attracted to Manichaeism, and by his own accounts he adhered to this school of thought for nine years:[228]

> During this space of nine years, then, from my nineteenth to my eight and twentieth year, we went on seduced and seducing, deceived and deceiving, in various lusts; publicly, by sciences which they style liberal – secretly, with a falsity called religion. Here proud, there superstitious, everywhere vain! Here, striving after the emptiness of popular fame, even to theatrical applauses, and poetic contests, and strifes for grassy garlands, and the follies of shows and the intemperance of desire.

Manichaeism, which was a Gnostic and syncretistic school that arose in the third century CE, was named after its founder – Mani (216-276 CE) – who regarded himself as the heir of Zoroaster, Buddha, and Jesus Christ. The Manichaeist ideas originated in the Persian Empire, growing from the dualism that stressed how there is an absolute contradiction between the Kingdom of Light (good) and the Kingdom of Darkness (evil), which are both eternal.

The dualistic system in Manichaeism divides the world into good and evil, spirit and matter. The spiritual part includes light, life, truth, and goodness, whereas the material part includes darkness, death, lies, and evil, and Mani's religion proclaims a cosmic conflict between light and darkness. All things living contain something material and something spiritual, with spiritual particles called "light-particles" that are bound to material bodies. According

---

227 Augustine, *Conf.* 5.19.
228 Augustine, *Conf.* 4.1., cf. 5.3-5.14.

to Manichaean thinking what needs to be done is to free the light-particles from this binding. The worlds of good and evil are, in their origins and their nature, completely independent and diametrically opposed worlds. But the Manichaean myths explain how light and darkness, good and evil, the divine and the demonic, became intermixed.[229] Indeed, the very aim of Manichaean cult and mythology was to identify and separate the constituents in this enigmatic cocktail. The mythical liberation of light-particles is facilitated by divine beings, who fight to free the light-particles that are trapped and at the mercy of the dark powers of matter. The ritual liberation of light-particles includes taking a sacramental meal in which "the Elect" (*electi* – the chosen inner circle of the Manichaeans) eat what the "the hearers" (*auditores*) bring to them, absorbing the light to bring it back to God's world. Other central cultic elements are the singing of psalms, fasting, prayer, and confession and penance.[230]

In Manichaean mythology the various deities are, in a certain sense, identical, as they are all expressions of the same Divine Father. Humankind was created out of a mixture of Satanic matter and Divine goodness, and the human soul is therefore a part of divine life and salvation. For the individual, salvation consists in acquiring the Manichaean knowledge (*gnosis*) and living in accordance with this knowledge, thereby eventually returning to the realm of light. It is through *gnosis* that the slumbering humans shall awaken and recognize their own true being, and know that they are of the house of God.

Augustine writes that in Rome there lived, in secret, a considerable number of Manichaeans, whose religious ideas he shared. He was particularly taken with their concepts of sin, which rested on the belief that the dualism between good and evil is a cosmic dualism that removes personal responsibility and guilt. As he retrospectively writes in his *Confessiones*:[231]

---

229 Cf. G.G. Stroumsa (2011) "Purification and its Discontents. Mani's Rejection of Baptism" in North & Price (2011) pp. 460-478.
230 The Manichaean eschatology says that the final liberation from matter will take place in "the great war", "the return of Jesus Christ", and "the great fire" that will last for 1468 years, cf. N.A. Pedersen (1996) *Studies in the Sermon on the Great War. Investigations on a Manichaean-Coptic Text from the 4th Century*, Aarhus.
231 Augustine, *Conf.* 5.10; 5.9.

> And even then at Rome I joined those deluding and deluded "saints"; not their "hearers" only – of the number of whom was he in whose house I had fallen ill, and had recovered – but those also whom they designate "the Elect". For it still seemed to me that it was not we that sin, but that I know not what other nature sinned in us. And it gratified my pride to be free from blame and, after I had committed any fault, not to acknowledge that I had done any – that You might heal my soul because it had sinned against You; but I loved to excuse it, and to accuse something else (I know not what) which was with me, but was not I. But assuredly it was wholly I, and my impiety had divided me against myself; and that sin was all the more incurable in that I did not deem myself a sinner.

It was understandable that Augustine was attracted to this dualistic Manichaean thinking, for the ideas described the split between good and evil that he experienced in his own life, as he mentions several times in *Confessiones*. This thinking enabled him to deal with, and live with, past experiences of negative forces such as evil, death, and pain by attributing their origins to another source, separate from the source from which all good is said to originate. And yet Augustine ended up refuting Manichaeism and travelling to Milan to teach rhetoric. Here he met Bishop Ambrosius, and this encounter led to what is probably the most significant event in Augustine's religious and philosophical development: his conversion from Manichaeism to neo-Platonic Christianity, which he became familiar with through the sermons of Ambrosius.[232] This meeting with Bishop Ambrosius's Christian thinking and congregation led Augustine to undergo a process of doubt, crisis, and personal revelation.[233]

---

[232] Augustine, *Conf.* 5.13-5.14. In his religio-philosophical and apologetic work *De Vera Religione*, Augustine turns against Manichaeism in particular. He also refutes his former faith in a work against Faustus the Manichaean, responding to his polemical writing against the Christian interpretation of the Old Testament, the birth of Christ, and the epistles of Paul.

[233] Augustin, *Conf.* 5.14; 6.

The Fall of Rome – and two opposing standpoints

In 410 CE the Goths captured the city of Rome. Even though at this point Rome was no longer a seat of great political power, the city was still a central seat of religion, culture, and identity, and it was a horrible shock when it fell into the hands of Christian barbarians under the leadership of King Alaric. Even though by this time Rome's Christian community had grown considerably in size, many important public offices were still held by non-Christians – and in their traditional view the sack of Rome represented the annihilation of the entire world's cultural heritage. Many Christians probably also saw the fall of Rome as a catastrophe, both in general terms and in a specifically religious sense, but mainly because the city was home to the graves of numerous Christian apostles and martyrs. At any rate, Christians and non-Christians alike were badly traumatized, and this seems to have caused the religious conflicts between the two groups to flare up, creating two opposing views that were based, respectively, on Christian and non-Christian standpoints.

In a non-Christian religio-political perspective it was obvious that the terrible fate that befell Rome could be explained by two root causes, which were also related. First, the Romans themselves had allowed traditional Roman cult to fall into neglect. Second, the Christians had to bear most of the responsibility for the atrocious situation, since the neglect of Roman cult was, of course, due to the infiltration of Christianity into Rome, and to its gradual ascent to a dominant position. Such views intensified the religious strife between pagans and Christians, which is what provided Augustine with the external justification for writing his great work *De Civitate Dei*. As the author himself wrote by way of explanation shortly before his death:[234]

> Meanwhile, Rome was devastated in a crushing attack when the Goths invaded the city under the command of King Alaric. Those who worship many false gods, and whom we name "pagans" in common parlance, attempted to lay the blame for this catastrophe upon the Christian religion and began to blaspheme more bitterly and more scornfully against the True God than usual. Therefore, inflamed by

---

[234] Augustine, *Retractationes* (*The Retractions*) 2.43 (my own translation from the Latin found at www.augustinus.it/latino/ritrattazioni/index2.htm).

zeal for [defending] the House of God, I undertook to write the books "On the City of God" against their blasphemies or errors.

In other words, Augustine formulates his reasons for writing this determining work as an intention to defend the Christians and the City of God (using "*civitas Dei*" in the sense "God's community") in the fight against the ungodly pagans. With *De Civitate Dei*, Augustine develops the extreme Christian standpoint in the religious struggle between Christianity and paganism. He also comprehensively develops his entire perception of religion and civic responsibility, taking an ideal view in outlining the model relationship between the earthly city (*civitas terrena*) and the divine city (*civitas Dei*). Thus, Augustine's thinking on Christianity and his defence of it rests upon a fundamental (counter)attack against traditional Roman religion and culture, which he rejects completely. His aim is to undermine, once and for all, the religious and cultural foundations of non-Christian society.

He begins this project by seeking to refute the idea that Roman religion would have been able to ensure Rome's future. To Augustine, Rome as *civitas terrena* was merely one of many secular states, as opposed to the city of heaven, which was not a power of this world but a community whose existence cut across secular boundaries.[235] In one sermon Augustine posed the rhetorical question "What is Rome, but the Romans?"[236] In *De Civitate Dei* he applies two views on history: His primary view relates to sacral history, which begins with Creation and the Fall and the development of the two *civitates*, and which ends with the division of the two *civitates*, the Day of Judgement, and life everlasting. Parallel to this, however, Augustine takes a secular view of history, which completely denies that Rome has any special status in the eyes of the gods, or holds any particular importance in the ebb and flow of history. "The eternal city" is not Rome, but rather the City of God. Such a categorically Christian view would naturally have been offensive to non-Christian Romans, for whom Rome had for centuries been the very height of a religiously founded culture that shaped world history on the grandest scale.

This is also why, according to the Christian viewpoint in this cultural col-

---

235 Cf. Augustine, *De Civ. Dei* 18.2; 18.21; 19.24.
236 Augustine, *Sermones* (*Sermons*). 31.9.

lision and also to the literary strategy that Augustine follows in *De Civitate Dei*, the sack and downfall of Rome appear to be especially well-suited for legitimizing and consolidating the status of the Christian doctrine as the world's true *religio*. Moreover, Augustine sees the fall of Rome as a further impetus behind the growth of Christianity. In this context the religious enemy images vilifying Roman religion are (re)born and reinforced.

From a strictly historical point of view one could naturally discuss the significance of the Fall of Rome at this particular point in time – as has indeed been done on many occasions. Could Rome's defeat have been overdramatized? Was it truly such a horrendous and catastrophic event? Was it actually the final straw that broke the back of Roman tradition and led to Christianity's ultimate victory? Though all of these points could be debated, in the context of constructing enemy images it is not critically important to establish whether the defeat and the shock and the contemporary rows over Roman deities versus the Christian God were exaggerated in the sources, or in various scholarly interpretations of the sources. Nor is it decisive to determine whether there might be a direct causal relationship between the Fall of Rome and the growth of Christianity. What is important from a sociological perspective is that Augustine's work demonstrates that at this juncture Christianity still lacked religious and historical legitimacy both internally to keep Christians from lapsing, and externally in relation to certain non-Christian Roman circles. In short, Christianity still needed to construct enemies. This is one reason why the Fall of Rome would become an absolutely pivotal and strongly motivational element in Augustine's literary strategy. From a Christian point of view, the destruction of Rome could serve to legitimize and consolidate Christianity's truth, victory, and further expansion.

Augustine describes the most important difference between the City of God and the earthly city as the difference between humility (*humilitas*) and haughtiness (*superbia*). This difference is emphasized very early on, in the preface to his *De Civitate Dei*, where he begins by looking at the history of Rome as recounted in Virgil's great national epic, the *Aeneid*. In Augustine's view, this work blatantly reveals the pride and arrogance of the Romans in claiming that their role is to conquer those who are proud and to protect those whom they have subjugated. In his epos Virgil lets the character of the father, Anchises, remind his son Aeneas of the Romans' historic role as world leaders and peacemakers:

> You, Roman, be sure to rule the world (be these your arts), to crown peace with justice, to spare the vanquished and to crush the proud.[237]

But only God can conquer pride, Augustine declares, and the Romans have haughtily put themselves in God's place, erroneously attributing divine status to the city of Rome. One could certainly argue both ways about whose tone is the haughtiest. But quite apart from that, the account of Roman history given in *Aeneid* serves in this way as a backdrop for Augustine's initial enemy construction in his attack on Roman culture. By going straight for the jugular vein that carried the life-blood of Rome's mythical past – Virgil's heroic and patriotic *Aeneid* – Augustine is assailing one of the most important and most identity-creating works in the Roman tradition. Pursuing this line of thought, he asserts that one main point in the constructed enemy is that it was foolish of the Romans to deal themselves a losing hand back in mythical times by originally putting the household gods (*penates*) in charge of protecting the Roman people. As he points out: The *penates* themselves had been vanquished at Troy.[238] With this argument Augustine once again turns tooth and claw against a fundamental element in Roman culture, given that the *penates* played a very prominent role in Roman religion, history, and identity. Roman legend tells how the Romans themselves were descended from the Trojan hero Aeneas, who fled the burning city of Troy carrying his father Anchises on his back. Aeneas also succeeded in saving the household gods from the flames, just in the nick of time. And as Aeneas continued his journey it was the *penates* he had saved who pointed him in the right direction, towards Italy, where he would eventually settle and become a mythical ancestor of the Roman people.

Augustine also points to the defeats that the Romans suffered during the Punic Wars, which were neither avoided nor alleviated by their invocations of the Roman deities, enabling the author to conclude that the Roman rituals were ineffectual and ridiculous.[239] He goes on to list the many misfortunes that beset Rome and its dominions throughout the course of history without her deities having intervened to prevent them: Social War, slave uprisings,

---

237 Virgil, *Aeneid* 6.851-853.
238 Augustine, *De Civ. Dei* 1.3; 3.2.
239 Augustine, *De Civ. Dei* 3.28.

Fig. 14. Roman Republican coin (47-46 BCE). *Obverse*: Diademed head of the goddess Venus, who was regarded as the mother of Aeneas and hence an ancestress of the Romans. *Reverse*: The hero Aeneas escaping from the burning city of Troy, carrying his father and the household gods.

and civil wars.[240] Augustine's conclusion is quite simple: Having revealed that the pagan gods are worthless, he argues, it must be clear to all that unlike the God of the Christians these pagan deities are unable to grant anyone eternal life, being incapable of any beneficial intervention in the course of earthly events.[241]

Benighted philosophers

The next important point in Augustine's construction of a pagan enemy is that he associates his rebuttal of heathen religions with a rebuttal of non-Christian philosophy.[242] As explained in Chapter 1 and elsewhere, his *De Civitate Dei* is characterized by an underlying polemical debate with the pagan philosophers. In certain respects Augustine agrees with the Platonic school of thought, but he also criticizes it for not appropriately distancing

---

240 Augustine, *De Civ. Dei* 3.23.
241 Augustine, *De Civ. Dei* 6.12.
242 Augustine, *De Civ. Dei* 6-10.

itself from polytheism, and for other flaws.[243] He describes the adherents of Platonism as people who know the destination of their journey, but who are ignorant of the way[244] (as explained in the section on Augustine and Porphyry in Chapter 1). One thing that Augustine finds most sorely lacking in the conceited philosophers is the fear of God.[245] Recurring elements in Augustine's descriptions of the philosophers are their impiety, conceit, duplicity, and darkness of the mind and soul:[246]

> Nor do You [Lord] draw near but to the contrite heart, nor are You found by the proud … [And] by an impious pride, departing from You, and forsaking Your light, they foretell a failure of the sun's light, which is likely to occur so long before, but see not their own, which is now present. … This [Your] way they knew not, and they think themselves exalted with the stars … changing Your truth into a lie, and worshipping and serving the creature more than the Creator.

Augustine rebukes the philosophers for not recognizing the Incarnation, and he zealously debates their teachings on the soul.[247] He sweeps aside these teachings with the great trump card of Christianity: the alluring promise of eternal life:[248]

> Christ, however, promises life eternal; and therefore to Him the world flocks, greatly to your indignation, greatly also to your astonishment and confusion.

In Augustine's treatment of the two types of societies or communities – the earthly and the heavenly – there is a stark contrast between the philosophers' illusions, emptiness, false happiness, and lies on the one hand, and the Christian doctrine's truth, hope, and God-given joy on the other.[249]

---

243 Cf. Augustine, *De Civ. Dei* 8.1; 8.5; 10.1; 10.26; 10.29.
244 Augustine, *Conf.* 7.20; Cf. Augustine, *De Civ. Dei* 8.9-10.
245 Augustine, *De Civ. Dei* 10.27; cf. *Conf.* 7.21.
246 Augustine, *Conf.* 5.3.
247 Augustine, *De Civ. Dei* 10.29.
248 Augustine, *De Civ. Dei* 10.27.
249 See, for instance, Augustine, *De Civ. Dei* 19.1; 19.4.

Another important difference here is that the members of the two *civitates* have different goals in their lives, depending on whether they seek happiness in this physical life or in the afterlife. The motivation for worshipping the God of the Christians is not to attain earthly pleasures or contentment, but to ascend to perpetual heavenly bliss. In Augustine's view, the idea of earthly happiness is an illusion. The question of the individual human being's happiness, or unhappiness, revolves around whether a person directs their love and devotion towards God. Augustine distinguishes between two types of love relating to the earthly and to the heavenly city: love of self, and love of God. In the city built on self-love and selfishness the qualities that will thrive are hunger for power, pride, and injustice. Conversely, in the city built on the love of God people will serve one another in charity, humility, and peace.[250]

Augustine sees humankind as created to live in obedience to God and receive eternal life. Meanwhile, Man has turned against God in sin, chiefly expressed in vanity and desire. Satan succeeds in deceiving Adam, and because of his downfall Adam's love of God is transformed into selfishness. This Fall tainted the entire race of Adam, dooming his kind forever. According to Augustine, all of humanity is nothing but dust, bound to emptiness and sin, and the only path away from perdition and towards salvation is the grace of God.[251] So Man is nothing in and of himself, and this world is merely a pitiful likeness of a higher world. God's work can only be recognized by humans through the interpretation of His signs, and by means of will and faith. God communicates with and shows Himself to human beings through Christ, who became a man of flesh and blood. And Christ in turn conquered Satan and overcame the pride of Man, giving Himself as a sacrifice in mankind's stead to atone for human sins. This concept of the divine remakes humankind anew, but not everyone is redeemed. God chooses a certain number among the masses of the damned. All people are called to God, but not all are chosen. By means of divine grace the chosen are led to the deliverance that awaits beyond. The Church acts as an institution of salvation, and for Augustine the Church is also the community of the holy, of those who are predestined

---

250 Augustine, *De Civ. Dei* 14.28.
251 Augustine, *Conf.* 1.6; 1.7.

to be saved. For those who stand outside the Church, there is no salvation. Only damnation and eternal darkness.

Let us briefly recapitulate: When considering the construction of enemies it is worth noting that Augustine's religious views and moral judgments concerning himself and others clearly spring from his own personal development and the conceptual horizons that this defined. Furthermore, in a certain sense Augustine's development and works reflect key historical and religio-historical processes that lay at the root of the Christian construction of enemies and of the blossoming of Christianity itself. This is true of the conflicts with pagan religion and philosophy; of his meeting with and rejection of Manichaeism; and of the Christian mingling of religion and morals, one result of which was a use of the concepts *religio* and *superstitio* that turned the traditional religious and moral universes of Antiquity upside down.

These circumstances are evident in Augustine's literary manoeuvres and strategies, for instance when he describes the virtues and vices he sees in himself and others, Christians or not. A good example of this is found in his *Confessiones*, where Augustine moves on two interwoven planes: one that is autobiographical and directed towards the reader, and another that is conversational and directed towards (glorifying) God. In baring to God and his readership his own pagan past with all its weaknesses, ignorance, falsehood, vanity, impiety, superstitiousness, pride, and desires – his life prior to his conversion to the True Faith – Augustine the Christian simultaneously assembles the scaffolding of a religious enemy. In one fell swoop he attacks all the characteristics of the pagan lifestyle and the pagan world and all the flawed interpretations of Christianity, of which Manichaeism is but one. On the other hand, when describing his conversion to Christianity, salvation, truth, patience, piety, humility, love, forgiveness, and obedience to God, Augustine simultaneously portrays and praises the world's one true religion as the absolute opposite of the religious enemy he has sketched out. In this way, Augustine himself is employing the very dualism (essentially Manichaean, and definitely absolute) that typifies the construction of enemies.

When faced with Augustine's high praises of the Christian virtues, a typical non-Christian Roman would obviously be quick to regard Christian humility and patience as nothing but fear and cowardice. A pagan Roman would also be quick to perceive Christian obedience to God as a sort of abject submission that was not only inappropriate but downright contemptible. And to the pagan mind, such submission was the result of a distorted, misconceived kind of worship – which was, simply, *superstitio*.

***

Universal values – the regimen of the West in a multicultural world?

It is striking that some of the most pivotal issues and trends of demonization in the acculturation processes of Antiquity seem so easily recognizable in the current public debate, not least in connection with the catchphrase "clash of civilizations". Both the phrase and this angle of the debate were thrown into focus with the publication of the influential American political thinker Samuel Huntington's hypothesis and presumption that the conflicts unfolding in today's world are increasingly caused by differences in culture and religion rather than differences in ideology or economics.[252] According to Huntington, in the future the boundaries that define civilizations will be the most important lines of engagement, and cultural identifications and discrepancies will play a substantial role in when, where, and how civilizations will clash.

Mainly seeing cultural disputes as the driving force behind contemporary conflicts, Huntington expects that the greatest challenge of the twenty-first century will be the clash between the West and Islam. Nation-states will continue to be the most powerful players in world politics, he argues, but even on that stage the most serious conflicts will arise between nations and groups that belong to different spheres of civilization. Regardless of the arguments – some justifiable – that one could present against the various elements in Huntington's hypothesis (his civilization paradigm, concept of culture, portrayal of religion, and various interpretations of international politics), it is certainly true that Huntington focused the spotlight on the

---

252 S.P. Huntington (2002) *The Clash of Civilizations and the Remaking of the World Order* (1st ed. 1996), London.

necessity of including, in our discussion of conflicts, the importance of acculturation and issues of religion and identity. But although Huntington asserts that religion plays an absolutely crucial role in various conflicts and clashes, his analyses unfortunately lack systematic considerations of the dynamic interactions going on between religion and society in the cultures he discusses. Consequently, parts of Huntington's hypothesis are anchored in a construction of religious enemies, which in certain respects calls to mind the arguments of Augustine and other church fathers.

On the topic of constructed enemy images, Huntington's influential work actually contributed to the consolidation of religious enemies in the Western World, and several of Huntington's views are still very much alive in certain American and European circles. These views basically revolve around two seminal passages in Huntington's book:[253]

> Western Culture is challenged by groups within Western societies. One such challenge comes from immigrants from other civilizations who reject assimilation and continue to adhere to and to propagate the values, customs, and cultures of their home societies. This phenomenon is most notable among Muslims in Europe, who are, however, a small minority.
>
> So long as Islam remains Islam (which it will) and the West remains the West (which is more dubious), this fundamental conflict between two great civilizations and ways of life will continue to define their relations in the future even as it has defined them for the past fourteen centuries.

With this dictum as his starting point, Huntington played a role in propagating some rather biased, static, generalizing, stereotypical views on cultural encounters and religious disputes in Western societies: Viewing assimilation as the only path for the future, he presents Muslims and Islam as static and monolithic factors, unable to interact with Western societies without creating unresolvable conflicts. It is beyond question that Huntington put import-

---

253 Huntington (2002) pp. 304-305 and 212.

ant topics on the global agenda. Nevertheless, in light of his considerable impact as a political thinker and theorist it is somewhat problematic that several of his views are not only simplified but also misleading, both from a religio-historical and a sociological perspective.

However, there can hardly be any doubt that Huntington's book from 1996 represents a model of interpretation that seemed acceptable and rational in the immediate aftermath of the appalling terrorist attack on 11 September 2001: The book could be read as presaging and explaining the almost incomprehensible circumstances of this act of violence. In that sense the world felt a need for Huntington's analyses. But as the passages above and the rest of the book shows, in hindsight and in a broader perspective parts of Huntington's world-view could, at the same time and in themselves, be seen to stimulate the religious conflicts of our own age and reinforce the underlying enemy images. Today, more than a decade later, it is not unreasonable to interpret Huntington's hypothesis and his thinking as a barometer that gauged the prevalent thinking behind the world's reactions to, and its handling of, the conflicts taking place in the Western World. Aspects of this topic will be treated in Chapter 7.

Huntington emphasises that enemies are an essential tool when people and nations are seeking to establish an identity.[254] Clearly this mechanism is also a defining trait in Huntington's own brusquely formulated opinions. Or as Augustine the church father put it (as expressed in the first quote in this chapter): There must also be heresies, so that the approved may be made manifest among the weak.

Surely Huntington does have a point, although establishing an identity is about much more than merely identifying one's opposite in a negative, belligerent light. Another salient point in his theoretical thinking, and one that goes more to the heart of the matter at hand, is his cautionary presentation of the West's perception of Western culture as a universal culture that ought to be propagated throughout the world.[255] Referring to peers and predecessors who have pointed out the West's illusions as to its own superiority, Huntington notes that these old delusions of Western grandeur began to thrive again in the late twentieth century, and that they naively,

---

254 Huntington (2002) pp. 125-126.
255 Huntington (2002) pp. 53-55.

arrogantly, and myopically agree that the European model of Western civilization represents universal ideals and values. But as Huntington writes, the West hardly won the world over because of its superior ideas and values. Rather, it won because of its superior ability to apply organized violence.[256] He concludes:[257]

> In the emerging world of ethnic conflict and civilizational clash, Western belief in the universality of Western culture suffers three problems: it is false; it is immoral; and it is dangerous.

I find it odd that in this context Huntington does not mention the fact that this very Western culture stands firmly planted in a Christian missionary religion, with its corresponding ideas of universal applicability and the obligation to disseminate specific cultural ideas across the length and breadth of the globe. Even so, I daresay it would be worth our while to ponder the potential internal links between the various Western cultures' (neo)evolutionist and/or (neo)liberalist views and inherited Christian ideas about the universal applicability of (Christian) values. In other words: Might not the West's naive, arrogant, myopic unanimity regarding its own superiority and the universal applicability of Western values be rooted, to a very great extent, in the culture of Christianity? And might not Augustine's principal thoughts and enemy images still be making themselves felt in Europe in relation to issues of religious pluralism and cultural continuity? Perhaps the venerable church father's ideas of the Lord's great olive-press – which we must all pass through to make the noble oil rise and the waste products fall away – has simply been refinished with a nice, thick layer of (neo)evolutionist lacquer? This question is a basic theme in the following chapter.

---

256 Huntington (2002) p. 51.
257 Huntington (2002) p. 310.

Chapter 7

Cultural Flux and Fix – Perspectives on Religious Enemies in Contemporary Europe

Globalization and religious pluralism

As described and explored in the previous chapters, in the world of Antiquity the meeting between Roman religion and Christianity revealed significant points of conflict and brought about the construction of very clear religious enemy images. And as discussed, these conflicts were particularly related to questions of identity, religious pluralism, and cultural continuity. In many ways the same can be said of the culture contacts and the religious conflicts and the enemy images of today. Religious pluralism was a cornerstone in traditional Roman culture, and it clashed with Christianity's insistence that one path – and only one – leads to God and to salvation. With the Christian doctrine assuming the position of a universal truth, the ancient sources demonstrate a new way of thinking: that religious diversity in a multicultural world cannot, will not, be tolerated. This led to the construction of a new and conspicuous religious enemy, operating on the basis of rigid perceptions about cultural and religious opposites, and on a simplified division of the world into true believers (who must be protected) and pagans (who must be converted, and whose depraved culture must be brought to an end).

The Christ cult's religious and cultural approach to the world was in discord with the general, fundamental assumption that typified the Roman empire (and indeed typifies our own modern globalized world): that there are many different cultures, which classify themselves differently and have diverging traditions and norms systems, but which find themselves progressively obliged to coexist.

In contemporary Europe the questions of identity and religious pluralism are inextricably linked to questions relating to globalization processes. Obviously, globalization is a hotly debated and very broad concept that can cover many different aspects, but which always revolves around growth and interaction that oversteps politically defined national and regional boundaries. This applies to a wide variety of political, financial, social, and cultural activities, relations, and interdependencies that can be linked to factors like increased migration, information technology, global production systems, and so on. Nevertheless, despite the broad scope of the definitions and analyses of globalization and its consequences, it is still fairly rare to see religion subjected to systematic analysis in a globalization perspective – even in studies that focus very precisely on the cultural rather than the financial dimensions of these processes.[258]

As for the ancient world, the rise of the Roman Empire could be regarded as "globalization" from several different angles. One angle has to do with the empire's extensive intracultural contacts and communication; its common language and economic system; its cultural diversity and religious pluralism; the intensification of trade, commerce, production, and distribution networks; and the Romans' (further) refining of particular religio-political institutions and (power) structures, which were systematically copied throughout the imperial provinces, and which were a strong cohesive force throughout the Romanized world.

If one views this ancient meeting between Roman religion and Christianity in light of these parallels between Antiquity and modern-day globalization processes, there are two trends that become especially prominent and relevant in the context of this book. On the one hand there is a Roman desire to consistently manifest and consolidate traditional Roman norms, values, and practices, while on the other hand there is a general desire to create a "global" Roman culture with new and expanded versions of local/global identities, which are founded in fragments of traditional Roman practices. As previously discussed, religion comes to play such an absolutely crucial role precisely when the issue is (re)constructing, consolidating, negotiating, and (re)defining local *and* global aspects. Consider, by way of example, the official Roman rituals and sacrifices carried out not only by the Ro-

---

258 Beckford (2003) p. 104. Cf. Geertz & Warburg (2008). For the concept of religious pluralism, see the analysis in Beckford (2003) pp. 73-102.

man Emperor himself, but across the cities of the empire. This was a key component meant to underscore the emperor's personal power as well as the identity, unity, and strength of the Roman Empire. In other words, the unity of the empire was defined religio-politically by means of rituals, and religion became a powerful identity marker in the new "globalized" Roman world – and obviously to the Graeco-Roman mind the Roman Empire *was* the (entire) world. So interestingly, at the same time as the Roman world was increasingly being perceived as "one single place", which is a distinctive feature of globalization,[259] we also see a growing tendency to strive towards a clearer, more solid line of demarcation between Roman *religio* and foreign *superstitio*.

To a certain degree these very striking and contradictory tendencies in Antiquity can be compared with observations of contemporary globalization with its (slightly paradoxical) tendencies to encompass both "global flow" and "cultural closure".[260] Such globalization trends, which I refer to as "flux" and "fix", seem to be extremely characteristic of contemporary Europe and are manifested as insecurity and fear in the face of foreign religions and cultures, and in the face of Europeans' own unstable identity constructions. Not only in Antiquity but also in contemporary Europe we find, on the one hand, a desire to participate in the global flow and, on the other hand, a desire to fix this flow by consolidating traditional identity, norms, values, and practices.

We have already established that issues relating to *religio* and *superstitio* were absolutely pivotal in the encounters and clashes that took place during Antiquity between Roman religion and Christianity. It is true that in varying measure the powerful members of the Roman establishment felt annoyed,

---

259 R. Robertson (1992) *Globalization. Social Theory and Global Culture*, London, p. 6; P. Beyer (1994) *Religion and Globalization*, London.

260 See B. Meyer & P. Geschiere (1999) *Globalization and Identity: Dialectics of Flow and Closure*, Oxford, p. 2: "There is much empirical evidence that people's awareness of being involved in open-ended global flows seems to trigger a search for fixed orientation points and action frames, as well as determined efforts to affirm old and construct new boundaries." Cf. I.S. Gilhus (2008) "*Orbis terrarum Romanorum est*: Globalization Processes in the Roman Empire" in Geertz & Warburg (2008) pp. 131-144; U. Berner (2008) "Early Christianity as a Global Religion" in Geertz & Warburg (2008) pp. 145-161; T. Banchoff (ed.) (2008) *Religious Pluralism, Globalization and World Politics*, Oxford.

provoked, and sometimes threatened by Christianity, resulting in the periodic persecution of followers of the Christian faith. However, by professing the basic doctrine that Christianity was the one and only true and legitimate *religio* in the whole world, Christianity in fact constructed its own religious enemies. And these were far more systematically, enduringly, and consistently applied to "the others"; the heathens and the heretics with their widespread delusions and misconceptions (*superstitio*) that the Christian mind found absolutely ungodly.

As the Roman Empire grew and clashes between Roman religion and Christianity grew more frequent, one question became exceedingly urgent: What did it mean to be Roman in such a vast multicultural territory? Applying a modern angle to this question, given that cultural contacts and globalization processes are proliferating and bringing with them a demand for reinforcing the collective identities of groups and societies, we can similarly ask ourselves the pressing question: What does it mean to be, say, a Dane, or a European, today? For one thing it has become increasingly difficult to draw distinct lines to demarcate local, national, and global communities. Local phenomena can quickly become global. An excellent example of this is the budding and sudden burgeoning of the "cartoon controversy", the seeds of which were sown in Denmark (as discussed later in this chapter). Recent identity research certainly suggests that to some extent globalization destabilizes traditional collective identities. This causes certain groups in society to attempt to repair, protect, and maintain *their* collective identity by seeking to underscore the delimitations applied so far, and to focus on certain common group traits. One way of doing this is to latch onto or seek to "fix" ideas of shared roots, religion, ethnicity, or cultural heritage, which that particular group then raises up to the status of an original or genuine "core" consisting of inalterable norms and values. At the end of the day, such fixations and static ideas of originality and immutability are nonetheless illusory, from a historical and a sociological perspective.

Put differently, both in Antiquity and in today's world, a major component in the glue that binds people together is a common cultural self-perception brought about by identifying categories of strangers, "others" – including groups that are perceived as dangerous enemies against whom one must join forces. As has been made clear, religion and the rise of constructed enemies played a central role in this delimitation and self-perception for the steadily growing Roman Empire and its meeting with Christianity. But religion also plays a role as an important identity-generating factor, even in the culture contacts and globalization processes of this day and age. In this context, as Peter Berger and others have pointed out, a large number of historians, sociologists, and sociologists of religion (including Berger himself) have been wrong in their developments of various secularization theories by predicting or presuming that religion weakens in step with modernization.[261]

The modest number of investigations seeking to move on after the failure of these secularization theories by examining the relationship between religion and globalization have, thus far, primarily tended to focus on different religious behaviours subsumed under the problematic umbrella term "fundamentalism", identifying this as an expression of a religious reaction against globalization. This has caused us to overlook the existence of many other – and far less extreme – religious factors and the significance of how these factors dynamically link in with globalization processes.[262] For instance, if globalization is experienced negatively, as a threat against a religious organization, this threat may very well reinforce the organization's collective sense of "we". But if globalization is experienced as a positive force, that can also bolster the collective sense of "we" – that is, if the group focuses on the globalized world's many new opportunities to disseminate religious ideas and recruit new adherents in a worldwide religious network. So in both cases, the processes of globalization are conducive to identity construction within the religious sphere.[263]

There is no doubt that globalization has generally made people feel that

---

261 P. Berger (ed) (1999) *The Desecularizarion of the World*, Washington DC; cf. Berger, Davie & Fokas (2008). On modernization and secularization theories, see also J. Casanova (1994) *Public Religions in the Modern World*, Chicago IL, pp. 3-39; Beckford (2003) pp. 30-72; C. Taylor (2007) *A Secular Age*, London; H. Joas (2012) *Glaube als Option. Zukunftsmöglichkeiten des Christentums*, Freiburg.

262 Beckford (2003) pp. 127-149; J.A. Beckford (2008) "Religious Interaction in a Global Context" in Geertz & Warburg (2008) pp. 23-42.; M. Warburg (2008) "Religion and Globalisation, or Globalisation and Religion?" in Geertz & Warburg (2008) pp. 43-59; O. Hammer, "Purity and Mixture – Religious Plurality and the Domestication of Alterity" in Geertz & Warburg (2008) pp. 61-93.

263 In *practice*, the individual religious group or religious community will probably experience – and employ – certain aspects of globalization positively and others negatively, while other aspects appear inconsequential.

the world has become smaller and can be perceived as "one single place". Yet at the same time, today's global flux means that various smouldering conflicts that feed on religious, ethnic, political, local, and international discontent risk bursting into flames when fanned by the negotiations and/or struggles to gain identity, recognition, power, resources, and other desirables in our global village. Because religion is such a very basic element in the construction and consolidation of identity both at a micro level and at a macro level, the influences of religion continue to grow in our ever-shrinking world. And it is certainly true that an increasing number of the world's conflicts have religious overtones.

Religions are frequently used to legitimize a "cultural freeze"; a sort of cultural closure and a fixing of identities. Even so, evidently the fact that the adherents of a given religion regard their religion as being a fixed and unalterable thing certainly does not mean that religion actually *is* a fixed and unalterable thing. Quite the opposite. In a sociological perspective, religions and globalization processes are involved in dialectic and dynamic give-and-take relationship. As a result, both the intensified global communication and interaction (friendly and hostile) and our notions of globality and debates about (other people's or groups') undermining norms, values, and behaviours cause all of us, including religious organizations and communities of faith, to reconsider our place in the world. Religious organizations and communities are actively and increasingly employing global issues, such as the fight against global warming, pollution, poverty, disease, crime, terrorism, and other ills, to legitimize their religious views and objectives, and also their recruitment of new acolytes. In short, religions are not deteriorating in today's world, as secularization theories have claimed. Globalization processes act as a floodlight, illuminating the surfaces and shadows in the rich array of cultural contexts that are in fact delineated and coloured by religious norms and values.

It is occasionally emphasized that one of the many aspects of globalization is a pervasive feeling that "we are all in the same boat", seeing that all of humankind are – more or less – facing the same global problems (like those mentioned above), and that we are therefore obliged to act jointly to solve them. This does not mean, however, that globalization processes automatically steer us all towards moderation. Inversely, the constant flux of globalization in political, religious, and socio-psychological respects can

Fig. 15. *Priests*, Martin Bigum, 2003. The priests crowded into Bigum's painting at once summarize the fundamental common features of religions and show the many and varied cultural expressions of religion. The Christian minister in the foreground, surmounted by the blue cape of the figure beyond, seems to be wearing the headdress of a Hindu. Just one example in the throng of holy men that illustrates the religious contacts and potential conflicts in the globalized (and perhaps somewhat claustrophobic) world we inhabit.

increase our need to fix, or fixate on, our identity. To mark, define, and differentiate ourselves in a world where national and regional borders are becoming ever more permeable and porous. This is accompanied by an increasing need to differentiate others and to demarcate the boundaries of "the others" – and one way to do this is by constructing images of religious enemies.

***

Briefly, on a historical note

On European soil, the religious and cultural encounters between Islam and Christianity began in the seventh century. Cultural contacts were characterized by confrontations between Islamic Arabs and the Christian Byzantine Empire. The two continued to clash during the Muslim conquest of the Iberian Peninsula, which resulted in 800 years of Muslim rule in that region. The Christian Crusades were another religio-political chapter in this cultural encounter, followed by the Ottoman incursions into Europe, the expansion of the Ottoman Empire, and its ultimate demise after standing as a German ally in World War I.

It is impossible to list the countless examples of religious enemies constructed by Christians and Muslims during these historical eras, which stretch from Late Antiquity into modernity. Let me simply point out that in a historical perspective, one must not imagine that the relationship between Muslims and Christian Europeans was consistently full of conflict and governed by religious enemy images. From the earliest meetings between the two cultures there were also peaceful cultural exchanges and lively trade between the Islamic world and Christian Europe – in spite of many a papal decree prohibiting devout Christians from trading with Muslim infidels. Also, remember that many of the historical conflicts and conquests were not fostered by religion alone, but were also strongly motivated by political and economic interests. Clearly, the meeting between Christian Europe and the Islamic world was not merely a series of hostile clashes. It was also a relationship formed by peaceful interaction for the mutual benefit of both cultures, including European emperors and kings, and Islamic caliphs, sultans, and emirs.

During the latter twentieth and early twenty-first century, the cultural contact between Muslims and Christians in Europe has taken on the form of migration, notably from the Middle East, Turkey, Iraq, Iran, Pakistan, and North Africa. This massive migration has created a number of large Muslim minorities, with some 53 million Muslims living in Europe today. It is clear, then, that over the past 50 to 60 years Europe has increasingly become a central area for global immigration. Still, many European countries are finding it difficult to regard themselves as such, as opposed to countries like the United States, which sees itself as the great melting pot, and the epitome of an immigration-based society.

The distinction between citizens born in a country and immigrants (be they of the first, second, or third generation) is far more significant in various social contexts in Europe that it is in the United States. This is, of course, mainly a result of very prominent cultural and historical differences between the two continents, and their consequently diverging attitudes to waves of immigration and integration processes. There is no long-standing historical tradition of immigration in Europe. On the contrary, Europeans themselves have emigrated to other countries in droves. A rough estimate says that from 1800 to 1920, approximately 85 million Europeans left the land of their birth, with about 60 percent settling in the United States.[264]

Diverging perceptions of immigration are also a result of fundamental religious differences, however. In the United States immigrants have generally contributed to an already existing religious diversity, whereas historically in many European countries religious pluralism has been relatively limited. Religious pluralism in Europe is therefore much more quickly perceived as a threat to the existing society. This perception of religion as a threat must further be seen in light of the European traditions for having various types of secularization processes, the object of which has been – and still is – to make religion a private matter, best kept out of the public sphere.[265] Naturally one must keep in mind that there are considerable differences in secularization among the individual countries in Europe, depending on their history and political and legal systems, making any generalized statements on this issue rather problematic. Even so, it is noteworthy that a study from 2011 concludes that European populations generally exhibit a relatively uniform and quite hostile pattern in their views on Islam and the presence of Muslims in Europe.[266]

---

[264] Cf. J. Casanova (2009) "Immigration and the new religious pluralism: a European Union–United States comparison" in G.B. Levey & T. Modood (eds) (2009) *Secularism, Religion and Multicultural Citizenship*, Cambridge, pp. 139-163.

[265] Cf. T. Jelen & C. Wilcox (eds) (2002) *Religion and Politics in Comparative Perspective: the One, the Few and the Many*, Cambridge; J. Madelay & Z. Enyedi (eds) (2003) *Church and State in Contemporary Europe*, London; M.C. Nussbaum (2012) *The New Religious Intolerance. Overcoming the Politics of Fear in an Anxious Age*, London.

[266] Cf. the European enquiry from the German think-tank Friedrich-Ebert-Stiftung, also mentioned in my Introduction (http://library.fes.de/pdf-files/do/08338.pdf), and the

Fixing identity in flux

When investigating the role that religion plays in Europe, it is quite common to focus on the generally waning numbers of church-goers in Europe; a circumstance that the British sociologist of religion Grace Davie has elegantly summed up as "believing without belonging".[267] Inversely, however, if one focuses on the many Europeans who – albeit somewhat vaguely – identify themselves as belonging to a Christian culture, it seems more appropriate to apply the French sociologist Danièle Hervieu-Léger's precise characterization: "belonging without believing".[268] Both views can justifiably be argued, which only goes to show just how difficult, or how impossible, it is to assess or quantify the notion of "religiosity". What does such a concept actually mean? And can religiosity even be measured at all in any sociological sense? If so, what does one measure: a specific religious behaviour? Or religious ideas? Or both? And how does one handle incongruity between behaviour and ideas?

At any rate, the falling propensity among Europeans to attend church services does not necessarily express a general downturn in the European interest in religion, or in religious issues. More plausibly, Europe is undergoing a shift in practices and in attitudes: Once a duty, attending church has now become a personal choice. But that does not mean that Europeans want to do away with the Church as an institution. They in fact wish it to endure, as an option for fulfilling one's personal religious choices. Davie describes the general European attitude as follows:[269]

---

report "Living together: Combining diversity and freedom in 21st-century Europe", report of the Group of Eminent Persons of the Council of Europe (2011).
267 Cf. G. Davie (1994) *Religion in Britain since 1945: Believing without Belonging*, Oxford; G. Davie (1999) "Europe: The Exception That Proves the Rule?" in Berger (1999) pp. 65-83; G. Davie (2000) *Religion in Modern Europe: A Memory Mutates*, Oxford; G. Davie (2002) *Europe: The Exceptional Case. Parameters of Faith in the Modern World*, London.
268 Cf. D. Hervieu-Léger (2004) "Religion und Sozialer Zusammenhalt", *Transit: Europäische Review* (2004) 26, pp. 101-119.
269 G. Davie (2010) "An English Example: Exploring the Via Media in the Twenty-First Century" in P. Berger (ed.) (2010) *Between Relativism and Fundamentalism. Religious Resources for a Middle Position*, Cambridge, pp. 35-55. Quoted passage found on p. 42.

I go to church (or another religious organization) because I want to, maybe for a short period or maybe for longer, to fulfill a particular rather than a general need in my life and where I will continue my attachment so long as it provides what I want, but I have no *obligation* either to attend in the first place or to continue if I don't want to.

This attitude is very much in line with other trends in the globalized world that widely allow the individual to choose, compile, and replace elements in his or her own identity and life project while safely navigating the seas of globalization. To put it bluntly, one could say that while a motto for Antiquity was "know thyself", the buzzword of this day and age could be "design yourself". And in the context of self-expression and self-realization, religion is only one of many components when modern individuals design one or multiple identities to steer by in the swirling waters of the globalized world.

But this fluctuating field of identity and culture also exhibits tendencies of cultural closure and a fixing of identity – "fixing an identity in flux" so to speak. And these signs of European fluctuating identities and cultural closures become much clearer and stronger when contact with Islam as a religion, and with people of the Muslim faith, takes place within Europe's borders. One result of this is that parts of the specific European societies (and the EU) have difficulty deciding whether European interaction with foreign cultures should primarily define itself in terms of its common Christian heritage, or whether it should define itself by basing its self-perception on such qualities as secular, liberalist values, ideas of modern democracy, universal human rights, or a society modelled on multicultural principles, complete with religious tolerance.[270]

The identity construction in European societies certainly seems to be in flux, oscillating as it is drawn by the opposing forces of freedom of religion (on the personal and the societal level) and the hesitations and difficulties associated with consistently recognizing the role of religions in public life and their significance for establishing collective identities. That is why Muslim

---

270 Cf. Casanova (2009) pp.139-163; Hansen (2010) *Demokrati som styreform og som ideologi*, Copenhagen, pp. 7-57, 321-372; T. Banchoff (ed.) (2007) *Democracy and the New Religious Pluralism*, Oxford; Z. Bauman (2004) *Europe. An Unfinished Adv enture*, Cambridge; J.-W. Müller (2010) *Verfassungspatriotismus*, Berlin.

Fig. 16.

immigration into Europe has reignited the old debates about religion's role in society – similarly (re)introducing questions that many thought had been answered and resolved long ago in a European context. Most particularly these questions concern the proper place of religion in the private versus the public sphere; social recognition and religious tolerance; secularism as a viable path in and through a multicultural European landscape; and the search to determine general European norms and values and related (attempts at) identity construction. For historical reasons the borders of Europe as a continent are blurred or imaginary, and they are constantly being reinterpreted as historical, political, and economic circumstances change. This is clearly discernible in the intense efforts to discover an effective adhesive force that can glue together the many countries that are currently involved in "the EU Project". There are several factors hampering these endeavours. Certain difficulties relate specifically to questions of definition, given that Europeans themselves cannot answer clearly when asked where Europe begins and ends. Other difficulties stem from the fact that the EU Project lacks a clear direction and clear goals. What the EU presumably needs is some sort of "core identity", which at the same time is capable of accommodating the differences between the individual countries' cultural identities within the European framework.

In European debates about the role of religion in society, the argument is often aired that secularism as an ideological dividing line between religion and politics (as discussed later in this chapter) is one feature that defines Europe and binds its countries together – unlike the United States, for instance, or the Islamic world. In the present context it is nevertheless difficult – and would be a grave error – to ignore the importance of factors like the numerous discussions currently going on about the role of Turkey and Islam in Europe.[271] The debate about whether Turkey ought to become a member of the EU or not vividly demonstrates the mixing of religion and politics on European territory. These particular discussions show that the various brands of Christianity, implicit and explicit, have a power that can be used to define and legitimize. Christian norms and values influence the political agenda as today's EU seeks to define (and redefine) its position in relation to various globalization processes. Its discussions are a cocktail of identity-related, cultural, and religio-political fillers, mixers, and special twists: Does the EU want to grant Turkey membership into the Euro-Christian club? Is the EU prepared to accept Turkey based on arguments of timely, pragmatic global political thinking, or will it reject Turkey by invoking arguments hauled from the abysmal chasms of history, cultural heritage, traditions, and – not least – religion? In an EU context it is not unusual to regard Turkey as "the Non-European Other".[272]

Whether one wishes to promote secularism as a particular characteristic and foundation of a sort of European identity or not, the immigration of Muslims into Europe has sharpened the focus on religion and identity on both sides of the debate. Both among the new Muslim minority groups

---

271 On this aspect of secularism, an important discussion is the one initiated with an article on Europe by Jacques Derrida and Jürgen Habermas, which appeared in the Frankfurter Allgemeine Zeitung on 31 May 2003. Cf. J. Habermas & J. Derrida (2003) *Philosophy in a time of terror. Dialogues with Jürgen Habermas and Jacques Derrida*, Chicago IL; T.G. Ash (2004) *Free World: America, Europe and the surprising future of the West*, New York NY, pp. 46-83; J.-W. Müller (2010) pp. 114-123; E. Mendieta & J. Van Antwerpen (eds) (2011) *The Power of Religion in the Public Sphere*, New York NY.

272 Moïsi (2009) pp. 105; cf. U. Østergård (1998) *Europa. Identitet og identitetspolitik*, Copenhagen, pp. 133-184, 381-389.

and in the European societies where they settle, religion has come to play a prominent role in the assertion of identity. The fact that religion can also become more important than ethnicity is supported by a study done among young people of Pakistani extraction living in the United Kingdom.

The study shows that these young people clearly distinguish between religion and ethnicity as identity-generating factors, and as an identity marker they indicate religion as being the more important of the two.[273] One reason for the stronger focus on religion among Muslims in Europe is their struggle for recognition and identity in the face of challenging integration processes. Muslim residents in European countries have a significant risk of ending up in a situation where they do not (yet) feel acknowledged in Europe while at the same time feeling alienated vis-à-vis their (parental) country of origin. In such a situation one is often troubled by cultural insecurity, and a feeling that "if nothing else", one can identify oneself as a Muslim.[274] Greater focus on religion in the European countries where Muslims settle is also caused by fear and insecurity; feelings that partly arise because native Europeans lack knowledge of Islam, and/or despise or fear Muslims. Feelings such as contempt, disgust, and anxiety are closely linked when people wish to protect their own identity against foreign influences. As the French politologist Dominique Moïsi describes this exaggerated European fear factor:[275]

---

[273] J. Jacobson (1997) "Religion and ethnicity: dual alternative sources of identity among young British Pakistanis" in *Ethnic and Racial Studies* 20; 2, pp. 238-256; cf. J. Jacobson (1998) *Islam in Transition: Religion and Identity among British Pakistani Youth*, London. For similar results from studies of young Muslims in France, see F. Khosrokhavar (1997) *L'Islam des Jeunes*, Paris.

[274] Moïsi (2009) pp. 78-89; cf. O. Roy (2007) *Secularism Confronts Islam*, New York NY; O. Roy (2004) *Globalized Islam. The Search for a New Ummah*, New York NY. Not surprisingly, the body of material on Islam in Europe is rapidly growing. Newer contributions include, for instance, J. Nielsen (2004) *Muslims in Western Europe*, Edinburgh; J. Cesari & S. McLoughlin (eds) (2005) *European Muslims and the Secular State*, Aldershot; J. Klausen (2005) *The Islamic Challenge: Politics and Religion in Western Europe*, Oxford; A. Al-Azmeh & E. Fokas (eds) (2007) *Islam in Europe: Diversity, Identity and Influence*, Cambridge.

[275] Moïsi (2009) pp. 101-102. As concerns unwarranted European fear of a "Eurabia" in the making, cf. J. Laurence & J. Vaisse (2006) *Integrating Islam: Political and Religious Challenges in Contemporary France*, Washington DC.

> In the minds of many Europeans, the barbarians are not only at the gates but have already swarmed over the walls and are permanently transforming our society. ... In the minds of the most fearful Europeans, fear of the Other expands to include actual conquest by the Islamic world – the possibility that Europe will be demographically and religiously conquered by "them" and transformed into "Eurabia".

However, it is also important to consider the predicaments of European identity in a broader historical perspective, as a reaction not only to immigration, but also to other remarkable and profound historical and political changes on the international scene, including the end of the Cold War, the fall of the Berlin Wall, the dissolution of the Soviet Union, and the conflicts in former Yugoslavia. As an expression of an emerging European identity crisis, the 1990s witnessed the infancy and increasingly rapid growth of a European insecurity and fear of "the other", accompanied by a distinct rise in neonationalist trends in a number of European countries. The terrorist attacks in the United States (in 2001) and Europe (Madrid in 2005 and London in 2006) generously fed these fears, and the threat of terrorism grew to dominate the agenda in the Western World.

However, in our fearful minds terrorism has a host of other siblings: global warming, pandemics, natural and environmental disasters, unemployment, financial crises, and economic collapse, just to mention the most prominent members of the family. If fear acts as a catalyst, mobilizing energy and leading to constructive thoughts and actions, then naturally it is a positive thing, but if fear leads to paralysis, it can be destructive and even fatal. As Moïsi points out, it is precisely this atmosphere of paralysing fear that has been so typical of Europe in recent years, although he does underscore that each country has its own particular culture and climate of fear.[276] As a politologist Moïsi does not examine the role of religion as his primary field of interest when exploring a Europe in the grip of paralysis,

---

276 Moïsi (2009) p. 97: "Of course Europe remains a collection of countries with distinct political and social cultures, and each European country represents a unique case. Thus French fear is not to be confused with British fear, or Polish fear with German fear. Yet, it remains true that fear today is Europe's 'dominant colour'."

and so there is an urgent need for new, systematic studies that thoroughly investigate the religious aspect of this situation. Nevertheless, there can be no doubt that the fear and insecurity existing in Europe today are a source of nourishment for, and are nourished by, the construction of religious enemies. Nor can there be any doubt that religious conflicts play an increasingly large role in modern democracies.[277]

The most fundamental underlying idea for any liberal democracy is respect for the individual's autonomy. However, fear as a governing force can be used to achieve social control, thereby exerting a destructive influence on the autonomy of the individual. Societies that are constantly (re)constructing an exaggerated impression of fear, for example in connection with the idea of an Islamic "takeover" of Europe or threats of terrorist attacks, will have populations that live in fear. This limits the freedom of a country's citizens. A society that achieves the obedience of its citizens through fear will undermine the freedom that lies at the very core of democracy, so if one wishes to prevent fear from undermining freedom, then the climate of fear that currently dominates the Western world must be not promoted, but defused and dissolved.

Rival definitions of reality

The fear of an Islamic "takeover" in Europe was a major element in the justification given by the Norwegian right-wing extremist Anders Behring Breivik in defence of his horrific deeds on 22 July 2011, which left 77 people dead in central Oslo and the outlying island of Utøya. After the combined bombing and massacre, heated discussions have continued as to whether Breivik's fanatical acts of violence and his 1,518-page manifesto should be seen in a wider European political context or should be seen as a singular – and singularly tragic – course of events resulting from the deranged workings of a clinically insane mind.[278] The Norwegian authorities' first forensic

---

[277] Hansen (2010) p. 8. Cf. M.C. Nussbaum (2012) *The New Religious Intolerance. Overcoming the Politics of Fear in an Anxious Age*, London.

[278] Cf. R. Just & G.R. Schor (eds) (2011) *Vorboten der Barbarei. Zum Massaker von Utøya*, Hamburg; Nussbaum (2012) pp. 48-58.

psychiatric evaluation of the perpetrator concluded that he was suffering from paranoid schizophrenia and was not of sound mind, and hence unfit to serve a prison sentence. This evaluation triggered vehement reactions resulting, for one thing, in widespread public debate about how this blatantly went against the people's sense of decency and justice, and about whether it can be demoralizing that manifestos or actions of a violent, terrorist nature are officially found to be the result of an illness, which would put a lid on any detailed investigations into the political motives and consequences of the violence committed. This was followed by a new evaluation and report, which went against the conclusions of the first one: Breivik was found to be of sound mind and therefore fit for punishment.

Whether or not this particular offender was clinically insane and in possession of his faculties at the time he committed his atrocities, his lengthy manifesto does not exist in a social vacuum. There seems to be a real need for more closely examining the connections between the extreme violence that was committed and the extremist political statements and motives invoked by this homicidal native Norwegian. One aspect reflected in his motives and his manifesto revolves around existing extreme right-wing nationalist views and ideas that are in circulation among various populist politicians and various nationalist circles across Europe. Furthermore, Breivik was clearly proud of his Christian affiliation and considered his attack as part of a "holy war" against Muslims residing in Europe. In other words, Breivik's ideas and imaginings are a blend of already existing hatred, hysteria, paranoia, and religious enemy images, which casts the tragic events in a pan-European light. With its intensely emotional and irrational brew of aggression, hate, and fear, the manifesto to some degree consists of familiar constructions of enemies; constructed images that have been growing more socially acceptable in relation to Muslims on European soil.[279]

It is essential to note, however, that Breivik's enemy images not only include Muslims, but also Europeans who are claimed to represent a brand of "cultural Marxism and multiculturalism", which according to Breivik's

---

[279] See, for instance, the European enquiry mentioned earlier, conducted by the German think-tank Friedrich-Ebert-Stiftung (http://library.fes.de/pdf-files/do/08338.pdf).

perception of reality will lead to Europe's demise. And that is precisely why, on 22 July 2011, he did not attack Muslims but his own native Norwegian compatriots, whom he accused of being far too tolerant towards the presence of Muslims in Norway, and in Europe as a whole. Breivik was certainly not the only person to think such thoughts, although those who shared his opinions in theory would never, in practice, move to the tangible conclusions that Breivik reached with his attacks. Even so, this theoretical meeting of the minds emphasizes how the background for the irrational fear and aggression currently dominating Europe should not be swept into the corner, but laid bare and meticulously scrutinized.

So it is that the conflicts and enemy images we are discussing not only have to do with the arrival of foreigners. They are equally concerned with Europeans' self-perceptions and definitions of reality. The conflicts and enemy images are not merely a question of contact and clashes between different cultures. They are equally concerned with the different perceptions of how cultures can and should coexist within the confines of Europe. The inconceivable tragedy of Norway's 22 July brutally shoved to the top of the agenda such fundamental questions as rival definitions of reality; cultural diversity and cultural continuity in modern democracies; and religious pluralism and religion as identity markers. In short, intercultural conflict and coexistence, and the construction of religious enemies in Europe.

European secularism

It has often been asserted that the objective of secularism is to have a neutral and total division of religious and political affairs, the aim being to protect both. It is, however, illusory to believe that secularism is a politically neutral phenomenon, and it likewise seems naive to imagine that the concept of secularism can, in itself, constitute a modern brand of tolerance.[280] On

---

280 The illusory nature of such notions is demonstrated, for instance, in Talal Asad's analysis of French secularism, T. Asad (2006) "Trying to Understand French Secularism" in H. de Vries & L.E. Sullivan (eds) (2006) *Political Theologies. Public Religions in a Post-Secular World*, New York NY, pp. 494-526. For a discussion and definition of the many meanings and hypotheses in secularization theory and secularism concepts, cf.

the contrary, European experiences and debates over recent years (for instance about Muslim women wearing the hijab, niqab, and burka) clearly demonstrate that secularism is associated with various types of political control, negotiations, and delimitations relating to identity construction in socio-political and religious matters.

As things stand, the state cannot take a neutral position on religious matters, given that it is ultimately the state that must determine the limits within which neutrality is to exist. Therefore, in practice, the government must draw the borders between religion and politics, as is clearly illustrated by the debates about female Muslim headwear in France and other European countries. Thus, the European controversies over Islamic dress are based on religio-political constructions, including a sometimes rather dogmatic understanding, an almost inflexible fixing, of a certain European way of being a modern woman. In such rigid thinking, any aberration from this European path is condemned as being old-fashioned, subversive, and dangerous. In cases like this, the modern debates seem to resemble the ancient verbal battles between *religio* and *superstitio* as seen, for instance, in the church father Tertullian's thunderous preachings against a dangerous non-Christian world. Unfortunately, in both the ancient and modern religio-political strategies, complex cultural matters are being simplified and reduced to straightforward oppositional categories of good and bad.

Liberal nations are obliged to rely upon the loyalty and solidarity of their citizens, and there seem to be two main objectives of ideological secularism: continuously testing the loyalty of the nation's citizens (most notably new citizens of non-European origin) towards national bodies and institutions; and the ongoing consolidation and (re)construction of national identity. In other words, such processes are not in themselves neutral or protective. Rather, they are dependent upon varying social, religious, and historical contexts, and upon the political cultures of the individual state. Because of this, discussions in Europe of whether countries are "for or against secularism" seem to be somewhat misconceived, since the arguments used in these discussions spring from a simplified and misleading assumption that religion and politics are static, monolithic things that can and should operate

---

Beckford (2003) pp. 30-72; Berger, Davie & Fokas (2008); C. Taylor (2009) "What is Secularism?" in the foreword to Levey & Modood (2009) pp. xi–xxii.

independently of one another – religion in the private sphere, and politics in the public sphere. Religions will, however, unavoidably exert an influence on the public sphere, including the political stage, and vice versa.[281]

In multicultural Europe, this is the case with issues such as liberal forms of government, social organization and collective identity, ongoing negotiations and delimitations of the given society's norms and values, and issues of legal and moral prescription. What is at stake here is the very drawing of boundaries in the individual societies: religion exerts an influence on society's battles or negotiations to fix the (shifting) borders between the private and the public sphere – just as society's (shifting) borders exert an influence on and define core aspects of religions. The interrelationships between religious, social, and political institutions are therefore borne onwards by dynamic processes that can hardly be separated in the real practical world.

The immigration that has taken place over the past 50 years, and which has created large minorities that adhere to the Muslim faith in Europe, combined with the growing recognition that the intermixing of religion and politics in certain areas is unavoidable (whether one finds this desirable or not), raises new questions when considering whether secularism is a viable way forwards for what is now effectively a multicultural Europe. Given that European secularism is not a neutral state of affairs that automatically protects both religion and politics from one another, but can be regarded as an expression of political control and regulation with a view to testing the loyalty that the nation's citizens feel towards the government and the state, the new questions this raises go directly to the heart of the thinking behind the liberal state. European secularism thus raises the question of whether the traditional ideas about the nature of the liberal state remain feasible.

In his book *Liberty before Liberalism*, the British politologist and historian of ideas Quentin Skinner explores and explains the conflict between two main views in the inherited ideas of how the liberal state perceives the concept of "freedom".[282] These two views share a basic premise: that one of the state's cardinal tasks is to respect and preserve the freedom of the individual citizen. But after that, the views part ways. One view holds that the state can deliver

---

281 Cf. Casanova (1994) pp. 3-39, 40-66, 211-234; Beckford (2003); Banchoff (2008); Mendieta & Van Antwerpen (2011).
282 Q. Skinner (1998) *Liberty before Liberalism*, Cambridge.

on this promise simply by ensuring that the country's citizens are not subject to any unjust or unnecessary interference in their lives. The other view, on the other hand, believes that this can never be adequate, as it will always also, and at the same time, be necessary for the state to ensure that its citizens do not end up in situations that force them to be dependent on either the good will or charity of other people. According to this second view, the state not only has a duty to liberate its citizens from various types of dependencies. The state also has a duty to prevent the establishment's own representatives from acting as all-powerful entities when subjecting the country's citizens to regulations that are put in place to control the aspects of life lived jointly.[283]

Skinner emphasizes that in the modern Western world, people and societies have chosen to base their models on the first of these views, largely ignoring the second. His analysis underscores that this was and is a matter of choice, ending with the open question of whether the Western world really has made the right choice? Skinner's analysis, and the whole intention behind his book, is not specifically related to freedom of religion. Even so, his analysis and also his concluding question seem to be extremely relevant with respect both to the construction of religious enemies in Europe and to the debates concerning (neo)liberalism and religious freedom, and the question of whether European secularism is a viable way forward for Europe's multicultural societies.[284]

Treating the same topic, the professor of politics Jan-Werner Müller has discussed the concept of European constitutional patriotism. Müller draws attention to the fact that some of the liberal integration principles currently dominant in Europe, such as requirements concerning cultural assimilation, can be regarded as a special brand of "repressive liberalism", and he holds up Denmark as an example of liberal nationalism with tendencies to exclusion.[285]

The conditions that Skinner and Müller focus on relate to the current European dilemma regarding the sometimes exclusive and repressive nature of

---

283 Skinner (1998) pp. 119-120. Cf. Hansen (2010) pp. 205-210, 281-302.
284 Cf. J. Habermas (2001) *Glauben und Wissen*, Frankfurt am Main; J. Habermas (2009) *Europe. The Faltering Project*, Cambridge; T. Byrnes & P. Katzenstein (2006) *Religion in an Expanding Europe*, Cambridge; Bauman (2004).
285 Müller (2010) p. 104, note 9, and pp. 110-114.

liberalism and liberal nationalism. In step with this "repressive liberalism", increasing globalization, and the expansion of the EU's borders, religion as an identity factor will presumably continue to increase in importance. In the worst case, this will lead to further conflicts and more enemy images, hampering successful integration. There is consequently an urgent need for modern Europe, now nearly paralysed with fear, to ask whether it ought not consider systematically and stringently seeking to (further) develop a common sort of European constitutional patriotism, as discussed by Müller. And note that here "patriotism" is to be understood as an opposite of (neo) nationalism. The main weight is placed on the antique roots of patriotism, which are sunk deep into the shared political earthworks and the sense of duty that citizens feel towards laws and conventions.[286]

Admittedly the phrase "constitutional patriotism" sounds like anything but a buzzword for the twenty-first century. It nonetheless expresses a concept that goes directly to the heart of a very pertinent question today: What overall socio-political strategies will Europe/the EU choose in a world where the global geopolitical situation is changing more rapidly and more profoundly than it has over the last several centuries?

Developing a new European constitutional patriotism would ostensibly help to establish a superordinate, coherent European "core identity" – that is, a European identity that takes into consideration multicultural issues and religious pluralism, while at the same time being capable of embodying the particular historical and political traditions and identities of the individual European countries. The thing is, the problem of modern European democracies is not religious pluralism per se, but the art of uniting this religious pluralism with a common European identity. This calls for common, shared reflections, frames of reference, and guidelines for being a citizen of Europe – the general idea being to define Europe's relations with itself and with the world around it.

Such guidelines would not be meant to focus on differences in religious and cultural norms and values. They would instead focus on concrete types

---

286 Cf. Hansen (2010) pp. 255-257. On neoliberalism, cf. P. Mirowski (2009) "Postface: Defining Neoliberalism" in P. Mirowski & D. Plehwe (eds) (2009) *The Road from Mont Pelerin. The Making of the Neoliberal Thought Collective*, Cambridge, pp. 417-456; O.K. Pedersen (2011) *Konkurrencestaten*, Copenhagen, pp. 21-33, 41-76.

of behaviour and functionalities, like whether a given behaviour goes against fundamental European rights of democracy or freedom and can therefore be rejected as incompatible with the basic functions of European societies. And behaviours that do not go against these fundamental rights and functions of society would, and will, have to be recognized in a globalized, multicultural Europe. In this context, religion and religious issues would not be silenced, ignored, or relegated to the private sphere, but would be an element that could constructively be included in a joint paradigm for European cultural diversity and coexistence.

Here, it is worth remembering that ever since the rise of the modern nation state, European countries have especially focused on blood, religion, language, and ideas of cultural homogeneity as the core elements of a national identity. Consequently, a new paradigm such as that sketched out above would function as a common European framework of understanding within which countries could meet and challenge one another, finding a viable way to unite religious pluralism with modern European identities and democracies.

At any rate, it is necessary to thoroughly reconsider the position one wishes to take in future political decision-making processes on European soil with regard to religion and religious identities in a globalized world, where the importance of religion seems to be growing. A national power that aspires to operate "neutrally" while at the same time guaranteeing the same ethical freedom for all citizens cannot, as a basic premise, deprive any religious viewpoints or persons of the right to act and to discuss in the public domain on the basis of such viewpoints. Because of this, the state power's guarantee of freedom and neutrality in the national arena turn out to be incompatible with consistently upholding a world-view that is anchored in secularism. Therefore it is not merely the situation of Islam facing Christianity that is affecting European acculturation processes. It is also – and probably even more so – the juxtapositioning of Islam facing a variety of secularist traditions (which could be gathered under the umbrella term "European secularism") that is affecting acculturation.[287] In this situation lies an important reason for the European fear of Islamically oriented collective identities, and also the relat-

---

287 Cf. Levey & Modood (2009); Berger, Davie & Fokas (2008).

ed European tendency to immediately identify Islam with fundamentalism. This is how the sociologist José Casanova describes the situation:[288]

> Anti-immigrant xenophobic nativism, secularist anti-religious prejudices, liberal-feminist critiques of Muslim patriarchal fundamentalism and the fear of Islamist terrorist networks are being fused indiscriminately throughout Europe into a uniform anti-Muslim discourse, which practically precludes the kind of mutual accommodation between immigrant groups and host societies that is necessary for successful immigrant incorporation.

In sum, today's spectral religious images wafting through the European landscape must therefore, and not least importantly, be considered in the context of a swamp of European secularism, which rests on the idea that religion is a purely private affair – and this despite the fact that from a historical, political, and sociological perspective the very nature of that idea is illusory.

Religion and identity in the United States

The American self-perception rests on the opposite of the European way of thinking, namely on the conviction that religious organizations and religious norms and values are an important and indeed essential part not only of individual identity, but also of collective identity – which is also why such norms and values necessarily saturate the fabric of public and political life. This difference between the United States and Europe is confirmed by trends observable in a variety of interview surveys relating to religion.

Investigations show, for instance, that not only do Americans go to church more often than Europeans do. The former group also exaggerates both the frequency of their church attendance and the intensity of their religious devotion. The latter group, on the other hand, underplays both their church attendance and their level of religious devotion.[289] Although one should

---

288 Casanova (2009) p. 147.
289 Cf. Casanova (2009) p. 139-163; K. Hadaway, P.L. Marler & M. Chaves (1993) "What the polls don't show: a closer look at US church attendance", *American Sociological Review*

always be wary when working with interview-based surveys of this type, there can hardly be any doubt that the general trends in these findings are reliable: In order to live up to their collective secularized self-understanding, Europeans assume that they must distance themselves from religion, at least to a degree. Americans, however, are generally predisposed to believe that they must demonstrate a certain level of religiosity in order to live up to their country's collective self-understanding, which has remarkably deep roots in religion. This is further confirmed by the way that religious organizations in the United States frequently appear to be a powerful force in people's social lives; a force that is seriously committed to affecting political processes as much as possible. In the United States, mixing religion and politics does not arouse suspicion, which it definitely does in secularized Europe. This mix is, in fact, desirable from the angle of a collective American self-perception.

Against this backdrop it is fair to conclude that this particular religious difference in collective identity formation means that the basis for creating constructed religious enemies is present in Europe on a very different scale than in the United States, where the collective self-perception in itself condones and supports the significance of religion in both the private and the public sphere. Naturally this does not mean that religious enemies are not also constructed on American soil. In the country's very recent history the construction of just such enemies can be related, among other things, to the former American president George W. Bush. It is very easy, for instance, to construe his statements on what is (somewhat confusingly) called "the war on terror" as related to an underlying perception of the battle of the good Christians against evil, in this case represented by Islam.[290] In light of

---

1993:58, pp. 741-752; K. Hadaway, P.L. Marler & M. Chaves (1998) "A Symposium on Church Attendance", *American Sociological Review* 1998:63, pp. 111-145; A.M. Greeley (1995) "The persistence of religion", *Cross Currents* 1995:45, pp. 24-41; A.M. Greeley (2003) *Religion in Europe at the End of the Second Millennium: A Sociological Profile*, New Brunswick NJ; Berger, Davie & Fokas (2008).

290 See Ash (2004); cf. B. Lincoln (2003) *Holy Terrors*, London, which contains a comparative analysis of demonizing rhetoric in statements from Osama bin Laden and George W. Bush, respectively, following the attack on 11 September 2001. Lincoln concludes in his book: "Both men constructed a Manichaean struggle, where Sons of Light confront Sons of Darkness, and all must enlist on one side or another, without possibility of neutrality, hesitation, or middle ground." (p. 20); cf. Habermas & Derrida (2003). Cf. G.W. Bush, "State of the Union Address," U.S. Department of State, 29 January

this it was worthy of note that Bush's successor, President Barack Obama, clearly wished to call off the religious collision between Christianity and Islam; the "clash of civilizations". He already underscored this during his first presidential visit to the European continent, affirming in a speech he gave in Turkey, that "the United State is not at war with Islam".[291]

Nevertheless, little doubt can remain that some of the consequences of globalization – the global flux and fix of identity – can, under certain circumstances, influence and reinforce constructed religious enemies in the same way as globalization processes can influence the dynamics of wars and conflicts. This is clear from the expression "the war on terror", which was originally carried by the idea of George W. Bush and Osama bin Laden as (the leaders of) two adversaries engaged in battle. However, one thing characteristic of the sort of terrorist activities we currently associate with the name "al-Qaeda" is the difficulty we have in identifying the enemy. Terrorism is, first and foremost, a tactic, and the diffuse nature of the enemy is accurately described in Jacques Derrida's philosophical analysis of terror today.[292]

Today's type of "borderless", unpredictable, and impalpable terror makes it even more difficult to realistically attempt to assess precisely where the terrorist threat comes from, and how dangerous such threats and enemies really are. The period that followed the terrorist attack on the Twin Towers on 11 September 2001 and later attacks on European targets was consequently suffused with anxiety, and with fears that the worst was yet to come. Incidentally, in social psychology such a vague but pervasive sense of danger is deemed to be worse than specific threats. Further to this, the

---

2002; W. Brown (2006) "Subjects of Tolerance: Why We Are Civilized and They Are the Barbarians" in de Vries & Sullivan (2006) pp. 298-317.

291 Barack Obama's speech in Ankara on 6 April 2009: "Let me say this as clearly as I can: the United States is not at war with Islam. ... I also want to be clear that America's relationship with the Muslim world cannot and will not be based on opposition to al Quaeda. Far from it. We seek broad engagement based upon mutual interests and mutual respect. We will listen carefully, bridge misunderstanding, and seek common ground. We will be respectfull, even when we do not agree. And we will convey our deep appreciation for the Islamic faith, which has done so much over so many centuries to shape the world for the better – including my own country."

292 Habermas & Derrida (2003).

anonymous and unbounded threat of terror is perceived as nothing less than a threat against that which was meant to sustain the world order as we know it; against the conditions of globalization and the existence of the world itself. These qualities in the enemy's identity – globality, elusiveness, unpredictability, and indefinability – combined with the broad scope of the danger, as well as with the fear of future attacks, are what characterize al-Qaeda and its affiliated branches of terrorist activity. At the same time these factors help to create and reinforce the fear-inducing yet fuzzy images that typify the contemporary construction of religious enemies, both in Europe and elsewhere around the world.

In a rapidly changing world such fears can feed our general insecurity about our identity, which causes us to concentrate on the questions of who we are, and who our enemies are. In the view of Dominique Moïsi, the 1900s was the century of ideologies, while the 2000s are the century of identity:[293]

> In the ideological atmosphere of the twentieth century, the world was defined by conflicting political models: socialism, fascism, and capitalism. In today's world, ideology has been replaced by the struggle for identity. In the age of globalization, when everything and everybody are connected, it is important to assert one's individuality: "I am unique, I am different, and, if necessary, I am willing to fight until you recognize my existence."

Liberal democracies and the yawning abyss

As previously discussed, the construction of religious enemy images in Europe is closely related to the activities of religions in the field that lies between the private and the public sphere. This is the field where each individual society continuously sets its limits – which are, of course, bound to vary depending upon historical traditions, legal conditions, specific socio-political circumstances, pragmatic compromises and solutions, and so forth. As

---

[293] Moïsi (2009) p. 14. Cf. p. 12: "In the Cold War period there was never any reason to ask, 'Who are we?' The answer was plainly visible on every map that depicted the two adversarial systems dividing the globe between them."

described in Chapter 6, Huntington find it logical to assume that Muslims living in Europe set their limits in one place and Christians in another, and that between these limits there lies a yawning cultural abyss. To assume this would be a gross generalization, however, and it would also be misleading. The argument is nevertheless frequently presented in European circles and in debates about religion; even in debates that are not directed by an explicit, Christian-formulated antipathy against Islam. The argument also surfaces in debates directed by ideological secularism. What I have described earlier as the swamp of ideological secularism generally seems to impede social recognition and the integration of religions into the public sphere. This situation is ultimately in conflict with one of the primary prerequisites for resolving religious problems and enemy images related to Islam in Europe: recognizing Islam as an organized religion and constructing Muslim identities as an accepted social phenomenon. From a sociological point of view it is apparent that these two preconditions are central to ensuring the integration of Muslims in European societies, and the basis for uniting religious pluralism, liberal democracy, and freedom of religion.

In spite of this there is a pronounced tendency among Western and Muslim subgroups in the populations, and also among politicians, journalists, and commentators, to dwell upon this allegedly unbreachable cultural abyss between "Muslim values" and "Western values". This gap is diligently kept open by both camps by means of stereotypical representations of "the other", and among the Western representatives the result is often a distorted image of Islam as a violent and extremist religion whose adherents are carefully working to destroy Western civilization and achieve global supremacy.[294] All in all, the notion of the yawning abyss seems to serve both as a foundation for constructing a religious enemy image and as a political launching pad for various anti-Muslim and anti-immigration elements on the European political scene.

The construct that has gained a foothold in Europe, and which depicts Islam as a violent and extremist religion, disregards a number of relevant points. First and foremost it ignores the fact that the violence, terror, and threats coming from groups and persons that harbour an assortment of

---

294 Cf. A. Saeed (2009) "Muslims in the West and their attitudes to full participation in western societies: some reflections" in Levey & Modood (2009) pp. 200-215.

distorted, militant Jihadist ideologies does not represent any widespread religio-political movement, but a handful of extremist organizations and fanatics spread across the globe. No matter how seriously we must take today's threats of terror (which are a very serious matter), terrorism can only be effectively fought if one distinguishes sharply between these small groups of dangerous extremists (who are the real enemies) and the world's more than 1.5 billion Muslims. The constructed image further ignores the fact that Islam as a religion is not a static and immutable phenomenon. It also ignores the fact that among Europe's approximately 53 million Muslims there are many different attitudes towards Western societies and values – ranging from staunch disapproval over scepticism or disregard, to hesitant recognition and even full approval.[295] Moreover, the enemy image ignores the fact that like all other people, adherents of the Muslim faith react differently depending on the various attitudes and demands to them in the individual European countries. Finally, and not least importantly, the religious enemy image ignores the existence of a new and burgeoning Western tradition of Islam, which is highly flexible and which takes a constructive approach towards a wide range of topics such as democracy, human rights, gender equality, secular laws, and freedom of expression and religion.[296]

***

As discussed in earlier chapters, one of the great themes during Antiquity in the debates about cultural contact was the question of who, or which side, was religiously and morally superior. Time and again the ancient Christian writers pointed out that a Christian life represented the highest moral standard, and that Christians not only saw clearly the Truth and Salvation, but also became better people and better citizens because of it. Here it is apposite to draw in perspectives that, to greater or lesser extent, influence the debates going on in our own time and dealing with "the clash of civilizations", the propagation of democracy and Western

---

295 See Saeed (2009) pp. 207-215, which illustrates the differences using a classification system of the varying types of Muslim identity construction.
296 Saeed (2009) pp. 207-215; cf. T. Ramadan (1999) *To be a European Muslim*, Leicester.

values, the general consequences of globalization for society, struggles for identity and recognition, and discussions about the role of religions in the postmodern world. In contemporary multicultural, religious, and political contexts Christianity and other religions are also used – implicitly or explicitly – for purposes of delimitation and exclusion to define cultural and national identity.

One of numerous examples was the so-called cartoon controversy in Denmark, which was sparked in 2005 by the newspaper Jyllands-Posten's printing of cartoons of the Prophet Muhammad. The events and repercussions of the cartoon controversy have been, and continue to be, the object of numerous analyses and debates that I shall refrain from recounting here. There are, however, two aspects that deserve special mention, and which hold a special relevance for the issue of constructing religious enemies specifically for confrontational purposes. Firstly, the cartoons themselves involved violating a well-known Islamic prohibition against portraying the Prophet Muhammad. Secondly, regardless of the original intent behind publishing the cartoons, it was clearly very easy to (mis)interpret the drawings as representations of Islam as a violent religion and Muslims as dangerous people and potential terrorists.

The cartoons represented a distorted, hostile, and stereotypical downgrading of a group of people solely on the basis of their religion. As has often been voiced in the ensuing debate, it is naturally important to maintain the principle of freedom of expression in modern democracies. But certain voices in the debate chose – and still choose – to employ their defence of freedom of expression as a weapon to attack Muslim minority cultures in Denmark and elsewhere in Europe. Ironically, by maintaining a harsh and inconsiderate rhetoric, rigidly insisting on the right to ridicule and mock those who hold different views, these new and impassioned crusaders for the freedom of speech destroy the potential for entering into a dialogue. Among many other things the cartoon controversy indicated that for portions of the Danish population, contact with foreign cultures and religions is problematic. It also showed how groups that are insecure about their own identity have a tendency to attack and/or marginalize others, motivated by an exaggerated desire to protect themselves against foreign influence. Above and beyond this it was clear that the cartoon controversy and its repercussions were a reflection of *global* problems with cultural encounters, judging from the extremely strong reactions that it provoked across large parts of the world. This also provided extra momentum for the international debates about clashes of religions and civilizations.

In Danish and European debates about the cartoons and about issues of integration and the role of religions in society, the entire cartoon controversy was – and still is – frequently represented as a clash between secularism and liberal-democratic ideas on the one hand, and (Islamic) religious norms and values on the other. Those who wish to maintain that an abyss between the two sides constitutes the actual dilemma will probably be called upon in the future debate to explicitly clarify a few things: Which of the liberal-democratic ideas said to define today's postmodern multicultural Europe rule out the possibility of demonstrating compassionate, intercultural respect and showing consideration in religious matters? And which liberal-democratic ideas prescribe the use of hostile stereotyping with a view to achieving integration? Denmark and several other European countries will have to seriously consider the proposition that the credibility of "enlightened democracies" may be completely dependent upon their will to coexist in an open and sober dialogue with people whose native cultures have a mindset that differs from the traditional European mindset.

Religion, recognition, and competition

Clearly, when debating and bickering about religious pluralism and cultural continuity we find that culture contacts and constructed religious enemies in Europe are very much associated with power struggles, fights for recognition, and mechanisms of exclusion. A very useful approach to include in historical and religio-sociological investigations of this perspective in Europe is Charles Taylor's framework of analysis, and his reference points relating to the links between negotiations of identity, social hierarchies, and politics of recognition.[297] These reference points underscore two important facts: That how others (might) see us is a step in forming an understanding of who we are, and that the groups who possess the power of definition also

---

297 Taylor (1994).

delimit and construct the hierarchies of recognition by means of dialectical processes in society.

Seen in this light, and despite marked differences in historical context, we can identify certain common traits and mechanisms shared by the constructed religious enemies of Antiquity and those of today. Such enemy images permeate the various kinds of struggles for recognition and the mechanisms of exclusion that are observed in ancient and modern cultures alike, and intend(ed) to achieve and consolidate identity, status, and religio-political power and authority. This is clearly evident, for instance, from the Romans' use of, and the Christians' adoption and adaptation of, the concepts *religio* and *superstitio*. It is also evident in the reproachful doomsday tone the church fathers used when speaking out against the depraved lifestyle of the pagans, and in the internal disagreements and commotion about Christ in Rome. And it is most certainly evident when we hear of the Roman governors throwing the "asocial" Christians to the lions.

The topics of reproach in the contemporary debates are European Muslims' religious practices, minarets, lifestyle, burkas, headscarves, views on women, and more. Mechanisms of exclusion and battles of identity and recognition also play a substantial role in contemporary debates about Turkey's potential membership of the EU, for instance, and in the squabbling about the wording of the preambles in the EU's constitution. The same battles also make their mark on a wide range of other items on the European agendas, including migration, integration, freedom of expression, and laws against blasphemy. If these debates, which are lodged within a globalized European context, are to be productive, we must do away with the frequently cited but erroneous assumption that liberalism can rightfully be thought to automatically create a neutral meeting place for different cultures – as long as religion and politics are kept separate. At this point in the process it should have become quite clear that Western liberalism – which is a product of Christianity, among other things – is the political expression of a certain type of culture and therefore *cannot* readily constitute a neutral framework within which people from all cultures can effortlessly coexist. The above-mentioned debates and legal proposals seen across Europe reflect this.

At this juncture we have reached the essence of one of the central dilemmas of liberal democracy. The consequences of this dilemma have been emphasized by the Danish historian of Antiquity, Mogens Herman Hansen, in his book about democracy as a form of government and as an ideology:[298]

> The liberal democracy's great predicament is that is must strike a balance between a state authority that is strong enough to protect the rights and interests of its citizens, but not so strong as to be able to tyrannize them. This democratic dilemma became urgent apparent after the terrorist attack on 11 September 2001. Seeking to avoid similar catastrophes in the future, most democratic nations have introduced anti-terrorist legislation that curtails the civil liberties and legal rights of their citizens.

In brief: To safeguard democracy, they have restricted precisely those freedoms that constitute democracy's core values. In connection with this, the globalization processes currently taking place are changing the world's democratic countries and the distribution of power: Nations are losing key elements in their significance and power, which in turn are being taken over by international players, corporations, and organizations, unavoidably altering the liberal democracy as a model of government. Consequently, the political necessity of extending democratic procedures beyond national borders is striking. In a European context this is pointed out by the prominent philosopher Jürgen Habermas in his notable essay on *The Crisis of the European Union*:[299]

> The increase in power of international organizations actually undermines the democratic procedures in nation states to the extent that national functions shift to the level of transnational governance.

Habermas concludes that Europe must realize its democratic potential by evolving from an international community into a cosmopolitan community. Therefore, now more than ever, Europe is a constitutional project, says

---

[298] Hansen (2010) pp. 50-51 (my translation from the Danish), cf. pp. 39-57; 201-210; 250-319. Cf. D. Held (2006) *Models of Democracy* (3rd edition), Cambridge.
[299] J. Habermas (2012) *The Crisis of the European Union. A Response*, Cambridge, p. 15. (German version 2011.)

Habermas, who furthermore hopes that in the future "the neoliberal agenda will no longer be accepted at face value but will be opened to challenge. The whole programme of an unscrupulous subordination of the lifeworld to the imperatives of the market must be subjected to scrutiny."[300] An important element in understanding and shaping the (neo)liberal democracies in modern European nations thus has to do with certain politico-economic viewpoints and consequences of globalization, or "global competition".

In his Danish book *Konkurrencestaten* ("the competitive state"), the professor of comparative political economy Ove K. Pedersen analyses central aspects of the politico-economic history of globalization and the notion of "the competition between nations".[301] The struggle to get by and do well in the current climate of international competition appears to be a battle with strategies and agendas that permeate into various political circles and clearly make their mark across all walks of life and all layers of society, and which are detectable in policies governing everything from security and commerce to labour markets and education. Pedersen points out that the international competition we see today is different than the kind of competition that came into play after World War II. Where Denmark is concerned, he operates with three different historical periods: the nation-state (1850-1950), the welfare state (1950-1990), and the competitive state (1990-present). In Pedersen's analysis the welfare state was and is a societal organization whose objective is to protect the country's population against the negative consequences of international competition. The competitive state, on the other hand, is a battle organization whose objective is to mobilize society's resources to compete with other states:[302]

---

300 Habermas (2012) p. 104, cf. pp.1-70.
301 Pedersen (2011).
302 Pedersen (2011) pp. 31-32 (my translation from the Danish). On the tripartite division, see pp.169-203. On the organization of the welfare state and the competitive state, respectively, see pp. 205-274. In the author's opinion, the development from welfare to competition state partly entails a shift in the state's objectives, organization, and legitimization: The welfare state is legitimized by democratic participation and by compensating the population for the consequences of international competition. The competition state is legitimized in its focus on private companies by ensuring that the country has a competitive edge, as a precondition enabling the country to grow and prosper (p. 206; 237).

Whereas the construction of welfare states was built upon moral-philosophical ideas about the human condition, the current construction rests upon theories about the institutional preconditions for human action. And whereas the international economy after the war was built upon objectives regarding the nation-states' protection of their "domestic markets" and the compensation by the national welfare states of their labour forces, today's international competition builds upon assumptions that nations compete by opening their economies and by mobilizing their tangible and intangible assets in competition with others. The difference thus lies in a human-based understanding versus a market-based understanding. In the time of the welfare state, a person was defined by being a unique and individual human being; in the competitive state, a person is defined by being rational and motivated by realizing their own benefits or interests.

Unlike the welfare state, the competitive state does not have creating equality as its objective, but underscores the inequalities existing in society by distributing rights, duties, and benefits aimed at achieving the most effective utilization of the labour resources of the individual. In other words, the competitive state operates not only in the sphere of politics and economy in the narrowest sense, but permeates Danish culture in its entirety and the values on which that society is based. Moreover, although the Danish welfare state has not been eliminated as such, the shift from welfare state to competitive state entails not only a change in political economy, but also changes in the way we view human beings. What is decisive here is the development of new views on concepts such as community, equality, and democracy with the goal of integrating Denmark into the new global order and drawing "Danish" values into discussions about the country's capability to compete. Pedersen demonstrates how developments in Denmark have led to values and culture being regarded today as tools that can promote competitiveness, and which the competitive state can employ in one or several ways to leverage the country's competitive advantages.[303]

---

303 Pedersen (2011) pp. 33-34, 169-203, 277-278.

Cosmos, conflict, and coexistence?

The numerous and complex questions concerning globalization and competition, religion and (neo)liberalism, secularization and European secularism, bring a number of questions to the fore that deal with the historical legacy of the Enlightenment. Research, particularly in more recent studies, has shown that Europe cannot be bundled or dealt with as a single entity. The age of Enlightenment was sparked and fuelled by a number of different ideas and traditions, and it must therefore be interpreted on the basis of a variety of historical, religio-historical, and philosophical movements and conditions across Europe.[304]

In the field of social science, the fathers of sociology – Max Weber, Emile Durkheim, and Georg Simmel – were concerned in different ways with studying the societal significance of religions and theorizing about their further destiny in "the modern world"; a world that was, at the time, undergoing profound changes due to industrialization and urbanization. The ideas of the Enlightenment were widely welcomed by the founders of sociology, but at the same time their various analyses of "modernization" drew attention to its potential dark sides and to worrying perspectives for the societies of the future. Max Weber (1864-1920) and his contemporaries certainly witnessed widespread and pervasive social, technological, and economic revolutions, along with national, religious, and ethnic conflicts springing from the trends of industrialization, urbanization, and migration. These upheavals were compounded by the political movements and ongoing power struggles between the new capitalists and the old feudalists. Furthermore, research in Weber's day into the social sciences was dominated by assumptions that information, technology, industrialization, and urbanization would drastically influence the future (whether one believed that this was beneficial or not), and that sooner or later the new trends would undermine the influence and impact of religions in "modern" society.

---

304 See, in particular, R. Porter (2000) *Enlightenment: Britain and the Creation of the Modern World*, London; G. Himmelfarb (2004) *The Roads to Modernity: The British, French and American Enlightenments*, New York NY; cf. Berger, Davie & Fokas (2008). For a "myth" of the Enlightenment, see, for instance, C. Taylor (2011) *Dilemmas and Connections*, London, pp. 326-346.

This was the context into which Weber introduced the concept of "disenchantment of the world" (*Entzauberung der Welt*), in which humankind was gradually robbed or deprived of its notions of the existence of cosmic harmony.[305] While the stoics of Antiquity recognized that they were a part of the cosmos, Weber believed that this particular knowledge and anchoring was lacking in modern human beings. They instead perceive the world as a place or a thing that is controlled by humans, and as an object that can be applied for utilitarian purposes. In principle, the disenchanted world is a place without magic; a world where no unpredictable powers exist. On the contrary, a person in such a world believes that everything can be dominated by the forces of prediction and calculation. As Weber writes of this rationalization process:[306]

In other words, increased intellectualization and rationalization do *not* bring with them a general increase in our knowledge of the conditions under which we live our lives. What they bring with them is something else: the knowledge, or the belief, that *if we wished to,* we *could* at any time learn about [the conditions of our life]; in other words: that, in principle, no mysterious and unpredictable forces play a role in that respect, but that, on the contrary, we can – in principle – *dominate*

---

305 The English word "disenchantment" is the common translation of Weber's term *Entzauberung*, which could also be rendered as "the stripping away or loss of magic".

306 M. Weber (1992) *Max Weber Gesamtausgabe: Wissenschaft als Beruf. Politik als Beruf*, W.J. Mommsen & W. Schluchter (eds), Tübingen, vol. 17, pp. 86-87 (with the author's emphasis): "Die zunehmende Intellektualisierung und Rationalisierung bedeutet also *nicht* eine zunehmende allgemeine Kenntnis der Lebensbedingungen, unter denen man steht. Sondern sie bedeutet etwas anderes: das Wissen davon oder den Glauben daran: dass man, wenn man *nur wollte*, es jederzeit erfahren *könnte*, dass es also prinzipiell keine geheimnisvollen unberechenbaren Mächte gebe, die da hineinspielen, dass man vielmehr alle Dinge – im Prinzip – durch *Berechnen beherrschen* könne. Das aber bedeutet: die Entzauberung der Welt." English translation taken from: M. Weber (2012) "Science as a profession and vocation", in H.H. Bruun & S. Whimster (eds), *Max Weber. Collected methodological writings*, p. 342. Cf. M. Weber (2011) *Max Weber Gesamtausgabe: Abriss der universalen Sozial- und Wirtschaftsgeschichte*, W. Schluchter & J. Schröder (eds), Tübingen, vol. 6, pp. 380-396; J.-W. Müller (2011) *Constesting Democracy. Political Ideas in Twentieth-Century Europe*, London, pp. 26-48.

everything by means of *calculation*. And that, in its turn, means that the world has lost its magic.

According to Weber, "the disenchantment of the world", meaning the process of rationalization that caused magic to disappear from Western culture, was already inherently present in the religion of ancient Israel, but only leapt to prominence with the Protestant Reformation. Weber saw a link between "disenchantment" and an instrumental, goal-oriented rationality (*Zweckrationalität*), which he described as a particular type of calculating rationality that characterized the organization of Western societies. Weber found this targeted rationality expressed both in enterprises of capitalism and in Christianity – the latter especially though not exclusively in Protestantism. He dealt with this topic in his widely known and now classic work *Die protestantische Ethik und der Geist des Kapitalismus* (*The Protestant Ethic and the Spirit of Capitalism*) and in other important writings as well, analysing how peoples' religiously anchored motives and views of the world interact with the general manner in which they lead their lives, even in matters of economics and finance.[307] According to Weber's groundbreaking – and highly controversial – religio-sociological hypothesis, Judaism and Christianity definitely played a huge role in establishing the rational lifestyle of the modern Western world, including the normative values of modern capitalism. He believed that one reason for this situation was the enmity that Christianity demonstrated towards non-Christian cults (which it classified as "magic").[308] Weber's conclusion was clear: The Judaeo-Christian prophesies and legitimizing miracles caused magic to be lost from the world, thereby also creating the basis for modern science, technology, and capitalism:[309]

---

307 M. Weber (1905/1992) *Die protestantische Ethik und der Geist des Kapitalismus*, Archiv für Sozialwissenschaft und Sozialpolitik, Vol. 21, Tübingen. Cf. M. Weber (1904/2012) "Die "Objektivität" sozialwissenschaftlicher und sozialpolitischer Erkenntnis", *Archiv für Sozialwissenschaft und Sozialpolitik*, Vol. 19, pp. 22-87, Tübingen, English translation: "The "Objectivity" of knowledge in social science and social policy", in H.H. Bruun & S. Whimster (2012) pp. 100-138. For Weber's ideal type, see pp. 124-131.
308 M. Weber (2011) *Max Weber Gesamtausgabe: Abriss der universalen Sozial- und Wirtschaftsgeschichte*, W. Schluchter & J. Schröder (eds), Tübingen, vol. 6, p. 388.
309 M. Weber (2011) *Max Weber Gesamtausgabe: Abriss der universalen Sozial- und Wirtschaftsgeschichte*, W. Schluchter & J. Schröder (eds), Tübingen, vol. 6, p. 389.

> Die Magie zu brechen und Rationalisierung der Lebensführung durchzusetzen, hat es zu allen Zeiten nur ein Mittel gegeben: grosse *rationale Prophetien*. Nicht jede Prophetie allerdings zerstört ihre Macht; aber es ist möglich, dass ein Prophet, der sich durch Wunder und andere Mittel legitimiert, die überkommenen heiligen Ordnungen durchbricht. Prophetien haben die Entzauberung der Welt herbeigeführt und damit auch die Grundlage für unsere moderne Wissenschaft, die Technik und den Kapitalismus geschaffen.

Inspired by Weber's ideas about "the disenchantment of the world", Charles Taylor subsequently developed the theory he calls "the Great Disembedding".[310] According to Taylor, this "disembedding" of individuals was predominantly caused by Christianity with its requirements to individual followers that they leave their traditional community of kinship to become a part of the Christian community. In doing this, Christianity rejected the traditional socio-religious affiliations and collective rituals of the Roman world. One vital element in Christianity's detachment of the individual from the larger society and from the cosmos was the Christian doctrine's absolute requirement of personal faith and devotion as the acid test of one's religious conviction. In other words, both Weber's and Taylor's theorizing is based on an absolutely fundamental significance in Christianity's particularly strong weighting of the dimension of faith, and in its categorical dismissal of all other socio-religious communities. As demonstrated in the previous chapters, these two factors – Christianity's fixation on faith, and its dismissal of other non-Christian socio-religious communities – have been expressed and acted out not least through the application of the *religio* versus *superstitio* dichotomy and through an ongoing construction of religious enemies.

According to Weber, however, the last stop for the Western world's "disenchantment", and for its targeted rationality and victorious capitalism, all founded in a Christian ethic, would be a "steel-hard casing", "ein stahlhartes Gehäuse", commonly translated as an "iron cage".[311] A cold and mindless construction typified by the loss of freedom and the loss of meaning –

---

310 C. Taylor (2004) *Modern Social Imaginaries*, London, pp. 49-67; Taylor (2007) pp. 146-158; Taylor (2011) pp. 214-302.
311 Weber (1905/1992) p. 108.

"stripped of all magic". One of the ideas behind the Enlightenment was that knowledge and science rather than religion would protect humanity against the dangers of the world. According to Weber, however, science could undermine religious beliefs, but it could not create new values: "The fate of a cultural epoch that has eaten from the tree of knowledge is that it must realize that we cannot read off the *meaning* of events in this world from the results – however complete they may be – of our scrutiny of those events, but that we ourselves must be able to create that meaning. We have to realize that the advance of empirical knowledge can never produce "world views.""[312] Science does not give an answer to the questions "What should we do? How should we live?" Science can only deliver the prediction of consequences, the means required for mastery of the external world.[313] However, let us not dwell on the specifics of the Weberian hypothesis since what is interesting in a contemporary context is really not whether Weber was right or not. The most important point is that Weber homed in on key relations between meanings, motives, and actions. He pointed to the decisive dialectic relationship between religions and societies; between the processes going on between the sacred and the secular sphere. This is a dialectic relationship that also includes religio-political power-brokering and domination processes; a dialectic relationship that surprisingly often seems to have been forgotten in present-day Europe's insistence on maintaining a rigid distinction between religion and politics.

Present-day conflicts in Europe between sacralization/religion and "disenchantment"/secularism reflect this dialectic relationship, not only in connection with European identity problems but also in the prevalent state of apprehensive paralysis in questions about globalization, religious pluralism, and cultural continuity. In this light it is worth (re)considering the Weberian approach and the various perspectives that Weber's analyses offer, for example regarding whether "disenchantment" and suppression of people in religious and religio-political matters might actually end up reestablishing

---

312 English translation taken from: M. Weber (2012) "The "objectivity" of knowledge in social science and social policy", in H.H. Bruun & S. Whimster (eds), *Max Weber. Collected methodological writings*, p. 104.

313 Cf. M. Weber (2012) "Science as a profession and vocation" in H.H. Bruun & S. Whimster (2012) p. 344-345.

and perhaps even reinforcing the very same phenomena that they originally attempted to desacralize or suppress?

From an ancient point of view, Roman suppression of the nascent Christ cult reinforced the very cult it was seeking to subdue, for instance as expressed in martyrdom. As the church father Tertullian wrote to the Roman authorities, "We multiply whenever we are mown down by you."[314] The Romans' verbal and physical attacks on Christians actually brought about a strengthening of the Christian organization. Alternatively speaking, the efforts of the Roman authorities to consolidate the collective Roman identity and state by repressing and fighting the Christian threat brought about the opposite of the desired result: the Christian minority grew stronger as traditional Roman norms, values, and identity were weakened and undermined.

Similarly in a contemporary perspective, asserting demands for rapid assimilation, ideological secularism, and disapproval and prohibitions against religious symbols in various public contexts acts as a stimulus on the construction and the importance of religious identity. Certain trends of secularism stimulate the need for religious manifestations that aim to reconstruct and reinforce religious identity. If a person is not permitted to express his or her religious convictions through interaction in the public sphere, it will ultimately result in the intensification of attitudes and actions aimed to further assert precisely that religious conviction. The political and religious desire observable in certain European countries to suppress and fight what is perceived as "the Muslim threat" ends up having the opposite effect, which is: the consolidation of religion as a marker of identity, and if worse comes to worst, it increases hardline Muslim radicalization in Europe. In this perspective, political and national bodies in Antiquity and today appear to have clear intentions to protect themselves – a stance which could ultimately prove self-destructive.

The question now is whether Europe's susceptibility to xenophobia, anxiety, and paralysis is in the process of creating a new "iron cage" within the continent's own boundaries. A seemingly paradoxical fixed construction in the flux of the globalized world. Do we really wish to cast this rigid and unseemly concrete structure made up of bureaucratization, ideological sec-

---

314 Tertullian, *Apol.* 50.13.

Fig. 17. Detail from the Forum Romanum

ularism, excluding and repressive (neo)liberalism, cynical competitiveness, and calculating, object-oriented rationality? With or without the iron cage, which may or may not be fixed in a bed of solidified concrete, Europe's intentions of self-preservation are helplessly bogged down in the quagmire of an obsolete secularization paradigm. And Europe's consternation at realizing the actual importance of religions in public life is abundantly clear. However, issues relating to religious conflicts and religious identities cannot be clarified or resolved if religion is categorically banished from the public sphere and confined to the private sphere. Only by conducting cross-disciplinary, systematic and thorough analyses of the social and identity-generating significance of religions at a micro level and a macro level can we hope to establish a broader understanding, and to find ways to handle the cultural and religious conflicts and clashes currently unfolding in the European landscape.

Conclusion

*"People are not disturbed by things,
but by the view they take of them."*

Epictetus

Generally speaking, the advent and rise of Christianity in the Roman world was clearly accompanied by a religious rivalry that sparked an extensive construction of religious enemy images in Europe. As Christianity expanded, so did its message of opposition to the long-standing acceptance of religious pluralism in the Roman Empire. As I have shown in the preceding chapters, it is essentially the same fear of losing identity and culture that lies at the core of the religious enemies built in Antiquity and those being built in contemporary Europe. What is more it was, and is, the same fear that controls the attitudes and interactions of the majority and minority camps involved in both scenarios, ancient and modern. As for the majorities (the non-Christian Roman majority in Antiquity *and* Europe's Christian majority today), their conflicts, enemy images, and antipathies towards minorities have to do with religio-political power and the fear that traditional norms, values, and modes of action will be weakened, undermined, and eventually dissolved. As for the minorities (the Christian minority in Antiquity *and* the Muslim minority in today's Europe), their conflicts, enemy images, and antipathies towards the majorities have to do, among other things, with the minority's identity formation and their quest for social and religious recognition. Another shared element in the ancient and contemporary conflicts is the majority's (more or less rigid) requirement that the minority should adapt and subordinate itself, which means the minority must partially relinquish their own religious ideas and practices. Which in turn means partially relinquishing their identity.

Let us consider for a moment the most fundamental aspirations of the camps mentioned above. What is it they seek? What do they wish for? Basically, the same thing: the defence and preservation of their particular religious and cultural identity. All four camps seek cultural continuity. And as part of this continuity, their religions are carried forwards by social, political, and religious factors that are interdependent and constantly interacting. This makes them incredibly difficult to separate, whether we are trying to analyse ancient or modern practices.

When cultural encounters and religious clashes occur, they throw the norms, values, and behaviours of the involved parties into relief. At best this gives the parties occasion to reflect upon and discuss their own cultural traditions and identities, and those of others. At worst, however, it leads to incidents of unrest, violence, and feelings of insecurity and animosity. Such cultural confrontations can result in various kinds of religio-political repression on the part of the majority – which may ultimately turn out to reinforce the very religious and cultural manifestations that the majority was trying to repress in the first place. This can lead to the development of an unfortunate and exaggerated religious fanaticism in members of the minority, and an equally unfortunate and exaggerated sense of nationalism and/or religious zeal in the majority. Examples from Antiquity include the Roman persecution of Christians, and the Christians' own pursuit of martyrdom. Examples today include the rigid radicalization of certain Muslim groups in Europe, as well as certain European countries' rigid reactions to meeting other cultures, resulting for instance in a feeling of nationalist supremacy, impulsive generalizations, suspicions arising from a lack of knowledge about the other camp, derogatory statements, ridicule, and humiliation of the minority or its members.

Neither the Romanization processes of Antiquity nor today's globalization processes diminish the importance of religion. On the contrary, we can observe how all of the involved camps sharpen their focus on religion in order to (re)construct and assert their own identity. One reason for this is that ancient Romanization and modern globalization alike imply cultural and religious pluralism, unavoidably raising questions about the undermining of cultural and religious continuity. Consequently, there are certain striking and contradictory trends in religious Romanization that we can, to some extent, compare with observations from contemporary globalization: the tendencies to encompass both "global flow" and "cultural closure". Possessing the desire and the power to navigate in the "global flow" seems to trigger a search for fixed orientation points and frames of reference, as well as an effort to affirm old boundaries and construct new ones. These trends, which I have referred to as "flux" and "fix", seem to be linked to the insecurity and fear that arise in the face of foreign religions and cultures, and in the face of one's own unstable identity constructions. Ancient religious Romanization and modern cultural globalization exhibit, in various ways, the tension-filled dynamics between cultural flow and closure; between flux and fix. The different issues examined in this book illustrate how these cultural and religio-political tensions are manifested as images of religious enemies, and how they are (and have been) acted out in Europe, past and present. The constant feelings of political, religious, and socio-psychological flux in globalization/Romanization seem(ed) to increase the need to fix, or fixate on, identity – to demarcate, define, and differentiate identity, and to consolidate power in a multicultural world where national and regional borders are more or less permeable and porous. In the Ancient world and in contemporary Europe, this was and is accompanied by a growing need to differentiate oneself in relation to others; to delineate the boundaries between "the others" and "us" by constructing religious enemies.

Some of today's complex globalization processes lead to new sorts of religious and social dynamism and tensions, and also to intensified religio-political dialogue, interaction, and infighting between and amongst a variety of social, religious, political, and ethnic groups. As we recognize this situation, we must also seek ways to come to terms with it. I believe this realization is one of the strongest arguments that speak for revising or completely replacing the existing secularization paradigm, which has failed, and which we have already been labouring under for too long. Acknowledging religion as a social fact – which means: as an unavoidable and dynamic variable in public life – is a decisive precondition for establishing a new paradigm for academically exploring religion and identity in our globalized, postmodern world.

The array of cases and questions studied in this book show that in Antiquity, one of the deepest gaps and most serious conflicts in acculturation was caused by Christianity's linking of religion to morals; two areas that had been far more independent of one another up until that point. In the pre-Christian world religion and morals had different roots and constituted separate, albeit interconnected, spheres. Unlike the God of the Christians, the traditional gods and cults did not dictate specific moral rules for human norms and behaviour. And unlike Roman cult, the very fabric of Christianity consisted of the intimately interwoven fibres of religion and morals: in one direction ran the dark threads of sin, guilt, fear, and repentance, and in the other ran the bright, hope-filled strands of divine forgiveness, salvation, and eternal bliss in the world beyond. The Christian polarity between "redemption" and "damnation" served as an excluding factor in traditional religious terms, making the religious enemy images woven into the lengthening tapestry of the new religion stand out even more clearly.

Among all of the cults in the Ancient world, the cult of Christ was the only one that consistently regarded all others as rivals. This led to a hitherto unseen stringency in the religious and social dividing of groups into "us" and "them". This division would permeate and define not only the way the Christians perceived themselves, but also the way non-Christians perceived the Christian community. The Christian religious polarity was instrumental in shaping the demand that people make choices based on religiously defined morals; a demand that was completely new in a *religious* context. Hence, as a matter of principle, the Christian merging of religion and moral (philosophy) made religious pluralism, doubt, and neutrality impossible. From a conventional Roman point of view, Christianity – despite its apparent naivety – was not only an expression of intellectual mediocrity, but also an expression of the fanatic's all-devouring, unyielding opposition towards other ways of thinking and living. Christian attitudes and practices were regarded as being both narrow-minded and shamelessly conceited in relation to the Roman state, and indeed in relation to the rest of humanity: to the Roman traditionalist, it seemed clear that the Christians set themselves above all of it.

The close link between the assumptions that Christianity was the only true doctrine and that a Christian life represented the peak of moral integrity was a ubiquitous feature in the Christian literature. Therefore the issue of religious and moral superiority also became a thematic undercurrent in the religious conflict and the ongoing discussions about acculturation. The relationship between moral superiority and the (re)construction of non-Christian and Christian identity, respectively, became a significant element during the early period of religious conflict between the Roman majority and the Christian minority. On the one hand, because their everyday lives unfolded in the same physical world, the parties in the conflict were operating on the basis of a general referential framework that they shared. On the other hand, on certain important religious and cultural issues the two camps perceived one another as enemies. The Romans had an enemy image of Christians depicting them as stubborn fanatics who were going against the traditional Roman state, its social order, and its imperial authority, and this made them a threat against the foundation and the future of the Empire itself. The Christians had an enemy image of the Romans portraying them as heathens and non-believers who were obstructing the True Faith and the universal idea of God's Regimen on Earth. In short, Christianity's new and non-negotiable religious norms and values, the entrenched religious authority, the fear of damnation, and the hope of eternal life came to stand out as the indisputable alternative to the non-dogmatic, multicultural Roman Empire and its diversity of religions and philosophical schools of thought.

From the earliest beginnings of this ancient acculturation process, the construction of the Christians' identity was typified by endeavours to build, legitimize, and defend their new religious and social norms, as these were strongly opposed to Roman traditions. Also, while buttressing their own positions, the Christians fortified their arguments with harsh condemnations and attacks on Roman culture. And the sources reveal another, and important, aspect in this religious clash, which lies in the variable uses of the flexible terms *religio* and *superstitio*. The Christian interpretation and rhetorical application of these concepts completely changed their content: In the Christian vocabulary *religio* grew to be synonymous with Christianity, even while the new usage branded traditional Roman religion as *superstitio*.

So in the new, radical questions and quarrels that were related to cult and culture, and which arose out of the meeting of two very different cultures, the terms *religio* and *superstitio* formed part of the rhetorical strategies and the religious enemies being constructed in both camps. The Romans used the terms to define and at times legitimize the persecution of Christians as proponents of socially detrimental ideas that were undermining traditional Roman *religio*. In Christian parlance the roles were inverted, with Christianity being defined as the one and only true *religio*, and Roman religion being denounced as dangerous *superstitio*. The links we find in the sources between the construction of religious enemies and the plasticity of the *religio*-versus-*superstitio* terminology – and its effectiveness as a rhetorical device – reflect not only the fault lines, conflicts, and enmities in the ancient

acculturation processes. These links also reflect how identities in societies, and religious perceptions, are held together by the use of internalized, normative vocabularies. What is more, the links also reflect that if vocabularies are used in new and different ways, in many cases they can play a role in shifts and reassessments in the way things are perceived in a given society. A norm or action once regarded as laudable can come to be seen as disgraceful, and vice versa. This sort of strategic rhetorical shifts in the meanings of key terms – in the past and in the present – can turn society's religious, social, and moral views upside down. And as it will have become clear throughout the preceding chapters, this mechanism plays an all-important role in the construction of religious enemies.

***

This study has analysed fragments that can help us to understand how the systematic construction of religious enemy images emerged in what was probably the most crucial acculturation process in European history. Taking the prudent course, however, it has made no attempt to answer the impossible question of why, of all the many contending religions, it was Christianity that ultimately held sway. What is beyond doubt is that a whole range of historical, religio-historical, sociological, and financial aspects came into play as the contest unfolded.

What this book has done is to take a sociological approach and focus diachronically and synchronically on two select topics: acculturation, and the construction of religious enemy images. In this perspective, fear and the ability to construct such images, combined with the hope and the promise of salvation and eternal life, are important ingredients in the particular socio-religious Christian cocktail that would eventually subdue even the powerful cult of Sol Invictus – The Invincible Sun – on Roman soil. In the brimstone phraseology of the revered church father Tertullian: "Where there is no fear, in like manner there is no amendment [and] repentance is vain."[315] Or as the ancient writer Lucian similarly pointed out, though from a very different and definitely non-Christian angle: the two greatest tyrants

---

315 Tertullian, *De Paenitentia* 2.

in Man's life are fear and hope.³¹⁶ The contemporary French political thinker Dominique Moïsi also reaches a similar conclusion on today's cultural and religious conflicts and identity constructions. His recommendation is that Europe should place hope, not fear, at the forefront, and that the continent's aspirations for the future ought to be accompanied by a historically rooted self-knowledge and open-mindedness towards cultural differences and changes, though without relinquishing fundamental European values.³¹⁷

Tertullian's aspirations for the future could hardly be more different. The church father joyously anticipates Judgement Day, promising his Christian readers that if they forswear pagan festivals and earthly pleasures, they can look forward to spectacles that are much grander by far: watching their heathen enemies be tormented in the unquenchable fires of Hell.³¹⁸ Looking back on Europe's cultural history, such ardent recommendations did not go unheeded. But as we now look forwards, the many questions and problems relating to Europe's future deserve to be pondered with temperance, preferably combined with a fair measure of historical and sociological rumination upon past and present links between religion, identity, and the makings of religious enemies.

---

316 Lukian, *Alexander* 8.
317 Moïsi (2009) pp. 154-159.
318 Tertullian, *De Spectaculis* 29-30.

References

Al-Azmeh A. & Fokas E. (eds) (2007) *Islam in Europe: Diversity, Identity and Influence*, Cambridge.

Asad T. (2006) "Trying to Understand French Secularism" in de Vries H. & Sullivan L.E. (eds) (2006) *Political Theologies. Public Religions in a Post-Secular World*, New York NY, pp. 494-526.

Ash T.G. (2004) *Free World: America, Europe and the surprising future of the West*, New York NY.

Assmann J. (2006) *Monotheismus und die Sprache der Gewalt*, Vienna.

Assmann J. (2010) *The Price of Monotheism*, Stanford, transl. R. Savage from *Die Mosaische Unterscheidung oder der Preis des Monotheismus* (2003).

Athanassiadi P. & Frede M. (eds) (1999) *Pagan Monotheism in Late Antiquity*, Oxford.

Banchoff T. (ed.) (2007) *Democracy and the New Religious Pluralism*, Oxford.

Banchoff T. (ed.) (2008) *Religious Pluralism, Globalization and World Politics*, Oxford.

Barnes T.D. (1971) *Tertullian. A Historical and Literary Study*, Oxford.

Barnes T.D. (1973) "Porphyry Against the Christians: Date and Attribution of Fragments", *JTS* 24, 1973, pp. 424-442.

Barnes T.D. (1981) *Constantine and Eusebius*, Cambridge.

Barnes T.D. (1998) "Constantine, Athanasius and the Christian Church" in Lieu S.N.C. & Montserrat D. (1998) *Constantine. History, Historiography and Legend*, London, pp. 7-20.

Barnes T.D. (2011) *Constantine: Dynasty, Religion and Power in the Later Roman Empire*, Cambridge.

Bauman Z. (2001) "The Great War of Recognition", *Theory, Culture & Society*, 18 (2-3; 2001), pp. 137-150.

Bauman Z. (2004) *Europe. An Unfinished Adventure*, Cambridge.

Baynes N.H. (1972) *Constantine and the Christian Church*, 2nd ed., London.

Beard M., North J. & Price S. (1998) *Religions of Rome*, vols I–II, Cambridge.

Beck U. & Beck-Gernsheim E. (2002) *Individualization. Institutionalized Individualism and its Social and Political Consequences*, London.

Becker A. H. & Reed A.Y. (eds) (2003) *The Ways that Never Parted: Jews and Christians in Late Antiquity and the Early Middle Ages*, Tübingen.

Becker C. (1954) *Tertullians Apologeticum. Werden und Leistung*, Munich.

Beckford J.A. (2003) *Social Theory & Religion*, Cambridge.

Beckford J.A. (2008) "Religious Interaction in a Global Context" in Geertz A.W. & Warburg M. (2008) *New Religions and Globalization. Empirical, Theoretical and Methodological Perspectives*, Aarhus, pp. 23-42.

Bendlin A. (2011) "On the Uses and Disadvatages of Divination. Oracles and their Literary Representations in the Time of the Second Sophistic" in North J. & Price S. (eds) (2011) *The Religious History of the Roman Empire. Pagans, Jews and Christians*, Oxford, pp. 226-241.

Berger P. (1963) *An Invitation to Sociology. A Humanistic Approach*, New York NY.

Berger P. (1983) "On the Obsolescence of the Concept of Honour" in Hauerwas S. & MacIntyre A. (eds) (1993) *Revisions: Changing Perspectives in Moral Philosophy*, Notre Dame IN, pp. 172-181.

Berger P. & Luckmann T. (1966) *The Social Construction of Reality. A Treatise in the Sociology of Knowledge*, New York NY.

Berger P. (ed) (1999) *The Desecularizarion of the World*, Washington DC.

Berger P., Davie G. & Fokas E. (2008) *Religious America, Secular Europe?*, Farnham UK.

Berger P. (ed.) (2010) *Between Relativism and Fundamentalism. Religious Resources for a Middle Position*, Cambridge.

Berner U. (2008) "Early Christianity as a Global Religion" in Geertz & Warburg (2008) pp. 145-161.

Beyer P. (1994) *Religion and Globalization*, London.

Birley A. (1987) *Marcus Aurelius. A Biography*, 2nd revised ed., London (1st ed. 1966).

Botermann H. (1996) *Das Judenedikt des Kaisers Claudius. Hermes*, vol. 71.

Bowersock G.W. (1975) "Herodian and Elagabalus", *Yale Class. Stud.* 24 (1975), pp. 229-236.

Bowersock G.W. (2002) *Martyrdom & Rome*, Cambridge (1st edition. 1995).

Brennecke H.C. (1995) "Der Absolutheitsanspruch des Christentums und die religiösen Angebote der Alten Welt" in Mehlhausen J. (ed.) (1995) *Pluralismus und Identität*, pp. 380-397.

Brown W. (2006) "Subjects of Tolerance: Why We Are Civilized and They Are the Barbarians" in de Vries & Sullivan (2006) pp. 298-317.

Burr V. (1995) *Social Constructionism*, London.

Bush G.W. (2002) "State of the Union Address," U.S. Department of State, 29 January 2002, available at www.state.gov.g/wi/.

Byrnes T. & Katzenstein P. (2006) *Religion in an Expanding Europe*, Cambridge.

Cameron A. (2011a) "Early Christianity and the Discourse of Female Desire" in North & Price (2011) pp. 505-530.

Cameron A. (2011b) *The Last Pagans of Rome*, Oxford.

Casanova J. (1994) *Public Religions in the Modern World*, Chicago IL.

Casanova J. (2009) "Immigration and the new religious pluralism: a European Union–United States comparison" in Levey G.B. & Modood T. (eds) (2009) *Secularism, Religion and Multicultural Citizenship*, Cambridge, pp. 139-163.

Castelli E. (2004) *Martyrdom and Memory. Early Christian Culture Making*, Columbia.

Cesari J. & McLoughlin S. (eds) (2005) *European Muslims and the Secular State*, Aldershot.

Chausson F. (1995) "Vel Iovi vel Soli: Quatre études autour de la Vigna Barberini (191-354)" MEFRA (1995) 107, pp. 661-765.

Clark G. (2004) *Christianity and Roman Society*, Cambridge.

Clarke G.W. (1996) "The origin and spread of Christianity" in *The Cambridge Ancient History*, 2nd ed. vol. X, pp. 848-872, Cambridge.

Council of Europe, "Living together: Combining diversity and freedom in 21st-century Europe". Report of the Group of Eminent Persons of the Council of Europe, published May 2011. Members of the Group: J. Fischer, E. Bonino, T.G. Ash, M. Hirsch, D. Hübner, A. Kadioglu, S. Licht, V. Lukin and J. Solana.

Davie G. (1994) *Religion in Britain since 1945: Believing without Belonging*, Oxford.

Davie G. (1999) "Europe: The Exception That Proves the Rule?" in Berger (1999) pp. 65-83.

Davie G. (2000) *Religion in Modern Europe: A Memory Mutates*, Oxford.

Davie G. (2002) *Europe: The Exceptional Case. Parameters of Faith in the Modern World*, London.

Davie G. (2010) "An English Example: Exploring the Via Media in the Twenty-First Century" in Berger (2010) pp. 35-55.

Derrida J. (2003) *Philosophy in a time of terror. Dialogues with Jürgen Habermas and Jacques Derrida*, Chicago IL.

de Vries H. & Sullivan L.E. (eds) (2006) *Political Theologies. Public Religions in a Post-Secular World*, New York NY.

Drake H.A. (2000) *Constantine and the Bishops. The Politics of Intolerance*, Baltimore MD.

Drobner H.R. (2007) *The Fathers of the Church*, Peabody MA, transl. S.S. Schatzmann from *Lehrbuch der Patrologie* (1994).

Droge A.J. & Tabor J.D. (1992) *A Noble Death: Suicide and Martyrdom Among Christians and Jews in Antiquity*, San Francisco CA.

Dunn J.D.G. (1999) (ed.) *Jews and Christians. The Parting of the Ways A.D. 70 to 135*, Cambridge.

Edwards M., Goodman M. & Price S. (eds) (1999) *Apologetics in the Roman Empire*, Oxford.

Elliott J.K. (1993) *The Apocryphal New Testament. A Collection of Apocryphal Christian Literature in an English Translation based on M.R. James*, Oxford.

Farquharson A.L.S. (1944) *The Meditations of the Emperor Marcus Antoninus I–II*, Oxford.

Fiedrowicz M. (2000) *Apologie im frühen Christentum. Die Kontroverse um den christlichen Wahrheitsanspruch in den ersten Jahrhunderten*, Paderborn.

Fox R.L. (1986) *Pagans and Christians*, London.

Fraser N. & Honneth A. (eds) (2003) *Umverteilung oder Anerkennung? Eine politisch-philosophische Kontroverse*, Frankfurt am Main.

Frede M. (1999) "Eusebius' Apologetic Writings" in Edwards, Goodman & Price (1999).

Frend W.H.C. (1965) *Martyrdom and Persecution in the Early Church*, Oxford.

Frey M. (1989) *Untersuchungen zur Religion und zur Religionspolitik des Kaisers Elagabal* (*Historia* Supp. 62), Stuttgart.

Friedrich-Ebert-Stiftung, http://library.fes.de/pdf-files/do/08338.pdf.

Gasparro G.S. (2011) "Mysteries and Oriental Cults: A Problem in the History of Religions" in North & Price (2011) pp. 276-324.

Geertz A.W. & Warburg M. (2008) *New Religions and Globalization. Empirical, Theoretical and Methodological Perspectives*, Aarhus.

Gergen K.J. (1991) *The Saturated Self. Dilemmas of Identity in Contemporary Life*, New York NY.

Gergen K.J. (2001) *Social Construction in Context*, London.

Gilhus I.S. (2008) "*Orbis terrarum Romanorum est*: Globalization Processes in the Roman Empire" in Geertz & Warburg (2008) pp. 131-144.

Gleason P. (1983) "Identifying Identity. A Semantic History", *The Journal of American History* (69; 1983), pp. 910-931.

Goar R.J. (1972) *Cicero and the State Religion*, Amsterdam.

Goodman M. (1997) *The Roman World. 44 BC – AD 180*, London.

Goodman M. (2007) *Rome & Jerusalem. The Clash of Ancient Civilizations*, London.

Goodman M. (2011) "Josephus and Variety in First-Century Judaism" in North & Price (2011) pp. 419-434.

Gordon R. (2011) "The Roman Imperial Cult and the Question of Power" in North & Price (2011) pp. 37-70.

Gradel I. (2002) *Emperor Worship and Roman Religion*, Oxford.
Greeley A.M. (1995) "The persistence of religion", *Cross Currents* 1995:45, pp. 24-41.
Greeley A.M. (2003) *Religion in Europe at the End of the Second Millennium: A Sociological Profile*, New Brunswick NJ.
Gruen E. (2002) *Diaspora. Jews amidst Greeks and Romans*, London.
Gutmann A. (ed.) (1994) *Multiculturalism: Examining the Politics of Recognition*, Princeton NJ.
Habermas J. (2001) *Glauben und Wissen*, Frankfurt am Main.
Habermas J. & Derrida J. (2003) *Philosophy in a time of terror. Dialogues with Jürgen Habermas and Jacques Derrida*, Chicago IL.
Habermas J. (2009) *Europe. The Faltering Project*, Cambridge.
Habermas J. (2012) *The Crisis of the European Union. A Response* (German version 2011), Cambridge.
Hadaway K., Marler P.L. & Chaves M. (1993) "What the polls don't show: a closer look at US church attendance", *American Sociological Review* 1993:58, pp. 741-752.
Hadaway K., Marler P.L. & Chaves M. (1998) "A Symposium on Church Attendance", *American Sociological Review* 1998:63, pp. 111-145.
Hall A.S. (1973) "New Light on the Capture of Isaura Vetus by P. Servilius Vatia", *Akten des VI Int. Kongresses für Griechische und Lateinische Epigraphik* (*Vestigia* 17), Munich, pp. 568-571.
Hall S.G. (1991) *Doctrine and Practice in the Early Church*, London.
Hall S. & du Gay P. (1996) *Questions of Cultural Identity*, London.
Hammer O. (2008) "Purity and Mixture – Religious Plurality and the Domestication of Alterity" in Geertz & Warburg (2008) pp. 61-93.
Hansen M.H. (2010) *Demokrati som styreform og som ideologi* ["Democracy as a form of government and an ideology", in Danish], Copenhagen.
Harland P.A. (2009) *Dynamics of Identity in the World of the Early Christians: Associations, Judeans, and Cultural Minorities*, London.
Harland P.A. (2011) "Acculturation and Identity in the Diaspora. A Jewish Family and 'Pagan' Guilds at Hierapolis" in North & Price (2011) pp. 385-418.
Harnack A. von (1908) *The Mission and Expansion of Christianity in the First Three Centuries*, London, I, p. 505.
Hauerwas S. & MacIntyre A. (eds) (1993) *Revisions: Changing Perspectives in Moral Philosophy*, Notre Dame IN.
Heibges U. (1969) "Religion and Rhetoric in Cicero's Speeches", *Latomus* 28 (1969), p. 846.
Held D. (2006) *Models of Democracy* (3rd ed.), Cambridge.

Hervieu-Léger D. (2004) "Religion und Sozialer Zusammenhalt", *Transit: Europäische Review* (2004) 26, pp. 101-119.

Himmelfarb G. (2004) *The Roads to Modernity: The British, French and American Enlightenments*, New York NY.

Hoffmann R.J. (1994) *Porphyry's Against the Christians. The Literary Remains.* Edited and translated by R.J. Hoffmann, Amherst NY.

Honneth A. (2003) "Die Pointe der Anerkennung: Eine Entgegnung auf die Entgegnung" in Fraser & Honneth (2003).

Honneth A. (2004) "Recognition and Justice: Outline of a Plural Theory of Justice", *Acta Sociologica* 47 (4; 2004), pp. 351-364.

Honneth A. (2011) *Das Recht der Freiheit. Grundriss einer demokratischen Sittlichkeit*, Berlin.

Humphries M. (2006) *Early Christianity*, London.

Huntington S.P. (2002) *The Clash of Civilizations and the Remaking of the World Order* (1st ed. 1996), London.

Jacobson J. (1997) "Religion and ethnicity: dual alternative sources of identity among young British Pakistanis" in *Ethnic and Racial Studies* 20; 2, pp. 238-256.

Jacobson J. (1998) *Islam in Transition: Religion and Identity among British Pakistani Youth*, London.

James W. (1956) *The Will to Believe: And Other Essays in Popular Philosophy*, New York NY.

Jelen T. & Wilcox C. (eds) (2002) *Religion and Politics in Comparative Perspective: the One, the Few and the Many*, Cambridge.

Jenkins R. (1996) *Social Identity*, London.

Jensen B.E. (1999) "History and the Politics of Identity. Reflections on a Contested and Intricate Issue", *Historiedidaktikk i Norden 7. Bruk og misbruk af historien*, Trondheim, pp. 43-67.

Joas H. (2012) *Glaube als Option. Zukunftsmöglichkeiten des Christentums*, Freiburg.

Just R. & Schor G.R. (eds) (2011) *Vorboten der Barbarei. Zum Massaker von Utøya*, Hamburg.

Jørgensen C.R. (2008) *Identitet. Psykologiske og kulturanalytiske perspektiver*, Copenhagen.

Kee H.C. (1983) *Miracle in the Early Christian World*, London.

Khosrokhavar F. (1997) *L'Islam des Jeunes*, Paris.

Klausen J. (2005) *The Islamic Challenge: Politics and Religion in Western Europe*, Oxford.

Klein R. (1968) *Tertullian und das römische Reich*, Heidelberg.

Krauss F.B. (1930) *An Interpretation of the Omens, Portents, and Prodigies Recorded by Livy, Tacitus, and Suetonius*, Philadelphia PA.

Lampe P. (2003) *From Paul to Valentinus: Christians at Rome in the First Two Centuries*, Minneapolis MN.

Laurence J. & Vaisse J. (2006) *Integrating Islam: Political and Religious Challenges in Contemporary France*, Washington DC.

Le Gall J. (1976) "Evocatio", *Mélanges J Heurgon* I, Rome, pp. 519-524.

Levey G.B. & Modood T. (eds) (2009) *Secularism, Religion and Multicultural Citizenship*, Cambridge.

Lieu S.N.C. & Montserrat D. (1998) *Constantine. History, Historiography and Legend*, London.

Lieu J., North J. & Rajak T. (eds) (1992) *The Jews among Pagans and Christians in the Roman Empire*, London.

Lieu J. (1996) *Image and Reality. The Jews in the World of the Christians in the Second Century*, Edinburgh.

Lieu J. (2004) *Christian Identity in the Jewish and Graeco-Roman World*, Oxford.

Lieu J. (2011) "Forging of Christian Identity and the *Letter to Diognetus*" in North & Price (2011) pp. 435-459.

Lincoln B. (2003) *Holy Terrors*, London.

Madelay J. & Enyedi Z. (eds) (2003) *Church and State in Contemporary Europe*, London.

Mead G.H. (1934) *Mind, Self, and Society*, Chicago IL.

Mendieta E. & Van Antwerpen J. (eds) (2011) *The Power of Religion in the Public Sphere*, New York NY.

Meyer B. & Geschiere P. (1999) *Globalization and Identity: Dialectics of Flow and Closure*, Oxford.

Millar G.B. (1992) "The Jews of the Graeco-Roman Diaspora between Paganism and Christianity, AD 312-438" in Lieu, North & Rajak pp. 97-123.

Mirowski P. (2009) "Postface: Defining Neoliberalism" in Mirowski P. & Plehwe D. (eds) (2009) *The Road from Mont Pelerin. The Making of the Neoliberal Thought Collective*, Cambridge, pp. 417-456.

Mirowski P. & Plehwe D. (eds) (2009) *The Road from Mont Pelerin. The Making of the Neoliberal Thought Collective*, Cambridge.

Moïsi D. (2009) *The Geopolitics of Emotion. How Cultures of Fear, Humiliation and Hope are Reshaping the World*, London.

Müller J.-W. (2010) *Verfassungspatriotismus*, Berlin.

Müller J.-W. (2011) *Contesting Democracy. Political Ideas in Twentieth-Century Europe*, London.

Nielsen J. (2004) *Muslims in Western Europe*, Edinburgh.

North J. (2008) "Action and Ritual in Roman Historians; or how Horatius held the door-post" in Rasmussen A.H. & Rasmussen S.W. (2008) pp. 23-36.

North J. (2011) "Pagans, Polytheists, and the Pendulum" in North & Price (2011) pp. 479-502.

North J. & Price S. (eds) (2011) *The Religious History of the Roman Empire. Pagans, Jews and Christians*, Oxford.

Noy D. (2000) *Foreigners at Rome: Citizens and Strangers*, London.

Nussbaum M.C. (2012) *The New Religious Intolerance. Overcoming the Politics of Fear in an Anxious Age*, London.

Obama B.H. (2009), Speech given in Ankara on 6 April 2009, available at www.Whitehouse.gov/the_press_office/Remarks-By-President-Obama-To-The-Turkish-Parliament

O'Meara J. (1959) *Porphyry's Philosophy from Oracles in Augustine*, Paris.

Pedersen N.A. (1996) *Studies in the Sermon on the Great War. Investigations on a Manichaean-Coptic Text from the 4th Century*, Aarhus.

Pedersen O.K. (2011) *Konkurrencestaten* ["The competitive state", in Danish], Copenhagen.

Podemann Sørensen J. (2008) "A Theory of Ritual" in Rasmussen A.H. & Rasmussen S.W. (2008) pp. 13-22.

Porter R. (2000) *Enlightenment: Britain and the Creation of the Modern World*, London.

Price S. (2011) "Homogeneity and Diversity in the Religions of Rome" in North & Price (2011) pp. 253-275.

Ramadan T. (1999) *To be a European Muslim*, Leicester.

Rasmussen S.W. (2003) *Public Portents in Republican Rome*, *ARID* supplementum XXXIV, Rome.

Rasmussen S.W. (2008a) "Priests, Politics and Problems in Identity Construction in Ancient Rome" in Rasmussen A.H. & Rasmussen S.W. (2008) *Religion and Society. Rituals, Resources and Identity in the Ancient Graeco-Roman World*, *ARID* supplementum XL, Rome, pp. 259-265.

Rasmussen S.W. (2008b) "Ritual and Identity: a Sociological perspective on the Expiation of Public Portents in Ancient Rome" in Rasmussen & Rasmussen (2008) pp. 37-42.

Rasmussen A.H. & Rasmussen S.W. (2008) *Religion and Society. Rituals, Resources and Identity in the Ancient Graeco-Roman World*, *ARID* supplementum XL, Rome.

Rives J.B. (1999) "The Decree of Decius and the Religion of Empire", *JRS* 89 (1999).

Rives J.B. (2007) *Religion in the Roman Empire*, Oxford.

Robertson R. (1992) *Globalization. Social Theory and Global Culture*, London.

Rosenberger V. (1998) *Gezähmte Götter. Das Prodigienwesen der römischen Republik*, Stuttgart.

Roy O. (2004) *Globalized Islam. The Search for a New Ummah*, New York NY.

Roy O. (2007) *Secularism Confronts Islam*, New York NY.

Rutgers L.V. (1995) *The Jews in Late Antique Rome*, Leiden.

Rutherford R.B. (1989) *The Meditations of Marcus Aurelius. A Study*, Oxford.

Saeed A. (2009) "Muslims in the West and their attitudes to full participation in western societies: some reflections" in Levey & Modood (2009) pp. 200-215.

Scullard H.H. (1951) *Roman Politics 220-150 B.C.*, Oxford.

Skinner Q. (1998) *Liberty before Liberalism*, Cambridge.

Slingerland H.D. (1997) *Claudian Policymaking and the Early Imperial Repression of Judaism at Rome*, Atlanta GA.

Smallwood E.M. (1981) *The Jews under Roman Rule from Pompey to Diocletian*, Leiden.

Solin H. (1983) "Juden und Syrer im westlichen Teil der römischen Welt. Eine ethnisch-demographische Studie mit besonderer Berücksichtigung der sprachlichen Zustände", *ANRW* II.29.2, pp. 587-789.

Stern M. (1984) *Greek and Latin Authors on Jews and Judaism*, 3 vols 1974-1984, Jerusalem.

Stroumsa G.G. (2011) "Purification and its Discontents. Mani's Rejection of Baptism" in North & Price (2011) pp. 460-478.

Stryker S. & Burke P.J. (2000) "The Past, Present, and Future of an Identity Theory", *Social Psychology Quarterly* (vol. 63; 2000), pp. 284-297.

Taylor C. (1994) "The Politics of Recognition" in Gutmann (1994).

Taylor C. (2004) *Modern Social Imaginaries*, London.

Taylor C. (2007) *A Secular Age*, London.

Taylor C. (2009) "What is Secularism?" in Levey & Modood (2009) pp. xi–xxii.

Taylor C. (2011) *Dilemmas and Connections*, London.

Taylor L.R. (1975) *Party Politics in the Age of Caesar*, Berkeley CA.

Turcan, R. (1985) *Héliogabale et le sacré du soleil*, Paris.

Van Dam R. (2007) *The Roman Revolution of Constantine*, Cambridge.

Warburg M. (2008) "Religion and Globalisation, or Globalisation and Religion?" in Geertz & Warburg (2008) pp. 43-59.

Weber M. (1904) "Die 'Objektivität' sozialwissenschaftlicher und sozialpolitischer Erkenntnis", *Archiv für Sozialwissenschaft und Sozialpolitik*, XIX. Band, 1 Heft, pp. 22-87, Tübingen.

Weber M. (1905/1992) *Die protestantische Ethik und der Geist des Kapitalismus*, *Archiv für Sozialwissenschaft und Sozialpolitik* XXI. Band, Tübingen.

Weber M. (1920) *Die Wirtschaftsethik der Weltreligionen. Vergleichende religionssoziologische Versuche. Gesammelte Aufsätze zur Religionssoziologie*, Bd. I, Tübingen 1920, pp. 237-275.

Weber M. (1992) *Max Weber Gesamtausgabe: Wissenschaft als Beruf. Politik als Beruf*, W.J. Mommsen &W. Schluchter (eds), Tübingen, vol. 17, pp. 86-87.

M. Weber (2011) *Max Weber Gesamtausgabe: Abriss der universalen Sozial- und Wirtschaftsgeschichte*, W. Schluchter & J. Schröder (eds), Tübingen, vol. 6, pp. 380-396.

Weber M. (2012) *Max Weber. Collected methodological writings*, H.H. Bruun & S. Whimster (eds), translated by H.H. Bruun, London.

White L.M. (1990) *Building God's House in the Roman World. Architectural Adaptation among Pagans, Jews and Christians*, London.

Wilamowitz-Moellendorf U. von (1900) "Ein Bruchstück aus der Schrift des Porphyrius gegen die Christen" in ZNW 1, 1900, p. 101ff.

Wilken R.L. (2003) *The Christians as the Romans Saw Them*, New Haven NJ (2nd rev. ed.).

Williams S. (1985) *Diocletian and the Roman Recovery*, New York NY.

Wissowa G. (1971) *Religion und Kultus der Römer*, Munich (1st ed. 1912).

Østergård U. (1998) *Europa. Identitet og identitetspolitik* ["Identity and identity politics", in Danish], Copenhagen.

The vast majority of translated passages from classical works are based on the Loeb Classical Library and on a variety of translated sources, many of which are available today on the Internet. Although it is impossible to name them all individually, I gratefully take this opportunity to thank the many people who have contributed to making these and other valuable resources available in the public domain.

Interesting internet sources include, but are not limited to: www.newadvent.org; www.tertullian.org; penelope.uchicago.edu; www.kingjamesbibleonline.org; www.lexundria.com; www.classics.mit.edu; www.papers.ssrn.com; www.augustinus.it; and www.theoi.com.

Sources

Apocrypha (Apocryphal and non-canonical texts)
Corpus Inscriptionem Latinarum (Berlin, 1863-)

Inscriptiones Latinae Selectae (1892-1916) edited by H. Dessau, Berlin.
L'année épigraphique (Paris, 1888-)
Augustus, *Achievements*
Augustine, *Confessiones* (*Confessions*)
Augustine, *De Civitate Dei contra Paganos* (*The City of God against the Pagans*)
Augustine, *De Vera Religione* (*On True Religion*)
Augustine, *Epistulae* (*Letters*)
Augustine, *Retractationes* (*The Retractions*)
Augustine, *Sermones* (*Sermons*)
Bible (King James Version)
Cassius Dio, *Historia Romana* (*Roman History*)
Celsus, *On the True Doctrine. A Discourse Against the Christians*. Transl. from *Adversus Christianos* with a general introduction by R.J. Hoffmann (1987), Oxford.
Cicero, *De Divinatione* (*On Divination*)
Cicero, *De Natura Deorum* (*On the Nature of the Gods*)
Cicero, *De Officiis* (*On Duties*)
Cicero, *De Finibus Bonorum et Malorum* (*About the Ends of Goods and Evils*)
Cicero, *De Republica* (*On the State*)
Cicero, *De Legibus* (*On the Laws*)
Cicero, *Pro Flacco* (*In Defense of Flaccus*)
Cyprian, *Epistulae* (*Letters*)
Justinian, *Digesta* (*Digest*)
Epictetus, *Discourses*
Eusebius, *Historia Ecclesiastica* (*Ecclesiastical History*) Transl. from A.C. McGiffert (1890) *Nicene and Post-Nicene Fathers*, Second Series, Vol. 1, Schaff P. & Wace H (1890), Buffalo NY. Revised and edited for New Advent by Kevin Knight 2009.
Eusebius, *Praeparatio Evangelica* (*Preparation for the Gospel*)
Eusebius, *Vita Constantini* (*Life of Constantine*)
Herodian, *History*
Historia Augusta (Augustan History), *Life of Elagabalus*
Iulius Obsequens
Josephus, *Antiquitates Judaicae* (*Jewish Antiquities*)
Josephus, *Bellum Judaicum* (*The Jewish War*)
Juvenal, *Saturae* (*Satires*)
Lactantius, *De Mortibus Persecutorum* (*On the Deaths of the Persecutors*)
Livy, *History*
Lucian, *Alexander of Abonouteichos*

Marcus Aurelius, *Meditations*

Origen, *Contra Celsum* (*Against Celsus*)

Origen, *Origen: Contra Celsum*. Transl. into English with an introduction and notes by H. Chadwick (1980), Cambridge (3). [kap 1, note 31]

Origen Werke, published by P. Koetschau (1899), *Die Griechischen Christlichen Schriftsteller der ersten drei Jahrhunderte*, Leipzig.

Petronius, frg. 37, cf. *Satyricon*

Plato, *Phaedo*

Plato, *The Apology of Socrates*

Plautus, *Aulularia* (*The Pot of Gold*)

Pliny the Elder, *Naturalis Historia* (*Natural History*)

Pliny the Younger, *Epistulae* (*Letters*)

Plutarch, *Parallel Lives, Coriolanus*

Porphyry, *Against the Christians*; "Gegen die Christen". 15 Bücher. Zeugnisse, Fragmente und Referate, published by A. von Harnack (1916), Berlin.

Porphyry, *Philosophy from Oracles*

Seneca the Younger, *Ad Helviam* (*To Helvia*)

Seneca, *De Providentia* (*On Providence*)

Seneca, *Epistulae* (*Letters*)

Seneca, *De Superstitione* (*On Superstition*)

Suetonius, *Claudius*

Suetonius, *Divus Julius*

Suetonius, *Divus Vespasianus*

Suetonius, *Nero*

Suetonius, *Tiberius*

Tacitus, *Annales* (*Annals*)

Tacitus, *Historiae* (*Histories*)

Tertullian, *Ad Scapulam* (*To Scapula*)

Tertullian, *Apologeticum* (*Apology*)

Tertullian, *Ad Uxorem* (*To My Wife*)

Tertullian, *De Cultu Feminarum* (*On the Apparel of Women*)

Tertullian, *De Paenitentia* (*On Repentence*)

Tertullian, *De Praescriptione Haereticorum* (*On the "Prescription" of Heretics*)

Tertullian, *De Spectaculis* (*On the Shows*)

Valerius Maximus

Virgil, *Aeneid* (*The Aeneid*)

Illustrations

Fig. 1.   Mosaic, Musée de L'Arles Antique. Photo: Christian Sørensen.
Fig. 2.   Relief, Palazzo Altemps, Rome. POLFOTO.
Fig. 3.   Detail from relief, Palazzo Altemps, Rome. POLFOTO.
Fig. 4.   Relief, Roman Art Collection at the Louvre.
Fig. 5.   Wall fresco, the Dura-Europos Collection at the Yale University Gallery of Fine Art.
Fig. 6.   Arch of Titus, Rome. POLFOTO.
Fig. 7.   Pont du Gard. Photo: Christian Sørensen
Fig. 8.   Temple in Nîmes. Photo: Christian Sørensen
Fig. 9.   Relief, Ara Pacis, Rome. Photo: Christian Sørensen
Fig. 10. Relief, Ara Pacis, Rome. Photo: Christian Sørensen
Fig. 11. Head of Constantine, Palazzo dei Conservatori, Musei Capitolini, Rome. POLFOTO.
Fig. 12. Mosaic from the necropolis under Saint Peter's Basilica, Rome.
Fig. 13. Temple of Saturn, Forum Romanum, Rome. Photo: Christian Sørensen.
Fig. 14. Roman coin. Photo: A. Tkalec AG.
Fig. 15. Priests, Martin Bigum. Photo: Martin Bigum.
Fig. 16. Flag of the European Union. POLFOTO.
Fig. 17. Detail from the Forum Romanum, Rome. Photo: Christian Sørensen.

Index

A

acculturation 12, 15, 29, 46, 52, 83, 88, 95, 100, 105, 113, 125, 128, 138-139, 143, 146, 152, 167-168, 193, 215-218
Aeneas 133, 161-163
Alaric 159
Alexander of Abonoteichus 59-60
al-Qaeda 196-197
Ambrosius 158
Ara Pacis 133-135
Artemis 77-78
assimilation 18, 168, 191, 211
Augustine 15, 45-48, 51-53, 93-97, 155-166, 168-170
Augustus 68, 131-133, 136-137, 142, 146, 148
Aurelian 138, 143-144

B

Berger, P. 10, 21, 175, 180, 188, 193-194, 206
Bible 43, 73, 75, 85, 156
bin Laden, O. 195-196
Breivik, A. 186-188
Bush, G.W. 195

C

Caracalla 126, 138
Cartoon controversy 174, 200-201
Casanova, J. 175, 179, 181, 190, 194
Celsus 40-46, 48, 56

church fathers 32-33, 38, 47, 66, 153, 155, 168, 202
Cicero 25-26, 53, 61-62, 66, 88-89, 95, 104, 121, 156
clash of civilizations 83, 167, 196, 199
Claudius 68, 91, 93
Constantine the Great 15, 84, 113, 145, 147
conversion 37, 53, 58-59, 73, 75, 81, 145-146, 158, 166
cosmos 121-123, 205-207, 209
cultus deorum 25, 38

D

Davie, G. 10, 175, 180, 188, 193-194, 206
democracy 18, 181, 186, 193, 198-199, 202-203, 205, 207
Derrida, J. 23, 183, 195-196
Diocletian 52, 102, 126-127, 145, 154
disenchantment 207-210
divination 26, 59-63, 66, 69-70, 151

E

Elagabal, emperor 138-142
Elagabal, god 138, 140-141
emperor worship 29, 55, 105-106, 131, 135-137
Epictetus 123, 213
EU 15, 181-183, 192, 202

European secularism 188, 190-191, 193-194, 206
Eusebius 46, 49-50, 84, 112-117, 119-120, 129, 145-146, 148-149
evocatio 27-28

F

fix 16, 25, 65, 88, 99, 105-106, 108, 130, 171, 173-174, 176-177, 190, 196, 215
flux 16, 25, 88, 95, 99, 105, 108, 121, 130, 171, 173, 176, 179-181, 196, 211, 215
Freedom of religion 15, 18, 146, 149, 181, 191, 198
fundamentalism 175, 180, 194

G

Galerius 127
Gelasius 149, 153
globalization 9, 12, 16, 24, 88, 108, 148, 171-176, 181, 183, 192, 196-197, 200, 203-204, 206, 210, 214-215

H

Habermas, J. 23, 183, 191, 195-196, 203-204
Hansen, M.H. 7, 181, 186, 191-192, 203
Herodian 139-141
Hervieu-Léger, D. 180
Huntington, S. 155, 167-170, 198

I

immigration 18, 22, 178-179, 181-183, 185, 190
integration 15, 18, 179, 184, 191-192, 198, 201-202

J

Jerusalem 40, 73-74, 83, 97, 100-104
Julius Caesar 89, 131-133, 137
Juno Regina 28
Jupiter Capitolinus 103
Juvenal 86, 90

L

Lactantius 146, 148
Licinius 148
Livy 26-28, 64, 66-67
logos 120
Lucian 59-60, 218
Lupercalia 149, 153

M

magic 80, 207-210
Manichaeism 155-156, 158, 166
Marcus Aurelius 114, 120-123, 138
Mars Ultor 132-133
Martyrdom 14-15, 29, 52, 81-82, 108, 112, 115-119, 124, 128-129, 145, 211, 214
Martyrs of Lyons 112, 119
migration 12, 88, 172, 178, 202, 206
miracle rivalry 14, 61, 73, 76-77, 80-81
miracles 14, 43, 61, 69-75, 77, 80-81, 208
Moïsi, D. 24, 183-185, 197, 219
monotheism 29-30, 49, 54, 57-58, 95, 153
mos maiorum 27, 38
Müller, J.-W. 181, 183, 191-192, 207

N

Neo-Platonism 51, 53
Nero 98-99
New Testament 47, 73, 76, 79, 81

O
Obama, B. 196
Old Testament 47, 85, 158
Origin 25, 73, 98, 184, 189

P
pax deorum 64
Pedersen, O.K. 157, 192, 204-205
persecution of Christians 14, 52, 82, 98, 109-110, 112, 117-119, 124, 126-128, 130, 144-145, 149, 214, 217
philosophers 38-41, 46, 48, 50, 57-58, 87, 163-164
Plato 42-43, 49, 109, 163-164
Pliny the Elder 64, 67
Pliny the Younger 109-111, 117
Plotinus 46-47, 53
Plutarch 30-31
polytheism 30, 54, 163-164
Pompey 101-102
Porphyry 40-41, 45-54, 56, 164
portents 14, 26, 61-69, 74, 76, 86, 152

R
radicalization 211, 214
religio 15, 25-27, 31, 55, 66, 75, 80, 88, 93, 99, 107, 148-149, 152, 161, 166, 173-174, 189, 202, 209, 217
religious pluralism 16, 29, 50, 54-58, 139, 146, 152, 170-173, 179, 181, 188, 192-193, 198, 201, 210, 213-214, 216
res publica 27
Roman authorities 28-29, 32-33, 87, 89, 106-107, 110, 114-115, 119, 125, 127-128, 149, 211

Romanization 14, 16, 28-29, 88, 99, 105-108, 130, 214-215
ruminatio 17

S
secularization paradigm 9-10, 212, 215
Seneca 37, 53, 93-97, 123
Skinner, Q. 190-191
Socrates 42-43, 108-109
Sol Invictus 15, 138, 142-144, 150-151, 218
Stoicism 53, 120, 123
Suetonius 66, 68-69, 87-89, 91, 98
superstitio 15, 25-27, 53, 55, 66, 75, 80, 87-89, 93-96, 98-100, 106-107, 110, 126, 129, 148-149, 151-152, 166-167, 173-174, 189, 202, 209, 217
supplicatio 111-112

T
Tacitus 66, 85-87, 89-90, 98-99
Taylor, C. 21, 66, 175, 188, 201, 206, 209
Tertullian 13, 33-40, 59, 124-126, 189, 211, 218-219
Theodosius 46, 152
Tiberius 39, 68, 87-88, 98, 102
Titus 102-104
Trajan 63, 109-112, 117, 119

V
Virgil 161-162

W
Weber, M. 11, 55, 115, 117, 206-210